MORMONS AND JEWS

MORMONS AND JEWS

Early Mormon Theologies of Israel

STEVEN EPPERSON

Signature Books • Salt Lake City • 1992

Cover design: Brian Bean

Cover painting: ***The Mount of Olives and the Garden of Gethsemane as Seen from the East Wall of Jerusalem,*** **Gary E. Smith, oil on canvas, 1982.**

The paper used in this publication meets the minimum requirements for Information Sciences—Permanence of Paper for Printed Library Materials, ANSI Z39.48-1984.

Composed and printed in the United States of America.

Library of Congress Cataloging-in-Publication Data

Epperson, Steven

Mormons and Jews : early Mormon theologies of Israel / Steven Epperson.

p. cm.

Includes bibliographical references and index.

ISBN 1-56085-006-X

1. Mormon Church—Relations—Judaism. 2. Judaism—Relations—Mormon Church. 3. Mormon Church—Doctrines. 4. Jews—Restoration. 5. Smith, Joseph, 1805-1844. 6. Hyde, Orson, 1805-1878. I. Title.

BX8643.J84E67 1992

289.3—dc20 92-4952

CIP

Contents

Introduction

> In the early part of March last 1840, I retired to my bed . . . and while contemplating and inquiring out, in my mind, the field of my ministerial labours . . . the vision of the Lord, like clouds of light, burst upon my view. The cities of London, Amsterdam, Constantinople, and Jerusalem all appeared in succession before me; and the Spirit said unto me, "Here are many of the children of Abraham whom I will gather to the land that I gave to their fathers, and here also is the field of your labours. . . . Speak comfortably to Jerusalem, and cry unto her that her warfare is accomplished—that her iniquity is pardoned."
>
> —Orson Hyde, *A Voice from Jerusalem* . . . (Liverpool: Parley P. Pratt, 184?), iii

In April 1840 a small Christian denomination sent a missionary to the Holy Land who did not proselytize or teach against Jewish learning and worship. Rather, Orson Hyde was sent from the Nauvoo, Illinois, conference of the Church of Jesus Christ of Latter-day Saints (Mormon) to "converse with the priests, rulers and elders of the Jews and obtain from them . . . the present views and movements of the Jewish people" (ibid., iv); to convey words of comfort, forgiveness, and blessing from the Lord; and to call them to gather to the Holy Land of

Promise because of a "great desolation" which placed European Jewry in peril. On the morning of 24 October 1841, Hyde climbed the Mount of Olives overlooking the city of Jerusalem and blessed the land of Israel for the gathering of "Judah's scattered remnants," for the rebuilding of Jerusalem and its Temple, and for the restoration of a distinct, independent Jewish nation and government with Jerusalem as its capital (ibid., 29-32).

The intense interest of nineteenth-century Mormons in the Jewish people, Hebrew Scriptures, and the Holy Land was shared by other Christians. However, Mormon belief and practice differed from typical Christian interpretations and performances. This book presents American and British attitudes about Jews and Judaism during the early to mid-nineteenth century and then contrasts Joseph Smith's theology of covenant Israel. It discusses how the Book of Mormon and sections of the Doctrine and Covenants articulated this theology. It demonstrates how Joseph Smith interpreted Hebrew Scriptures (the "Old" Testament) and Apostolic Writings (the "New" Testament) to support the gathering of the Jewish people to Palestine and the restoration of its national commonwealth. It also examines Smith as student of Hebrew and publicist of the Jewish/Mormon encounter. The sum of Smith's contribution was the creation of an independent Christian theology of Israel which affirmed the autonomy, integrity, and continuity of covenant Israel—embodied in the life and witness of the Jewish people. Furthermore, Smith bore record, in his writings, sermons, and actions, to the ongoing importance and reality of Israel's witness to the church.

Smith's vision was not shared by all of his co-workers. Some of his closest associates propounded a different version of the relationship of Mormons to Jews. This other position bears a stronger resemblance to traditional Christian understanding which viewed Jews and Judaism in negative terms. The "extraordinary mission" of Mormon leader Orson Hyde to Europe and Palestine in 1840-42 was the most important early expression of Smith's vision and manifested solidarity with restorationist aspirations of the Jewish diaspora. Brigham Young, Smith's disciple and successor, continued Smith's views. His independence from classic sources of Christian theology and eschatology (teachings about "last things," "the end of the world," "life after death," etc.)—largely through ignorance of their existence—made possible a more positive view than scholarly familiarity with these traditional sources might have yielded.

I wish to express my thanks and respect to Paul van Buren. It took an Anglican/Episcopalian theologian engaging in the contemporary dialogue between Christians and Jews to show me the unique and constructive contribution of my own Mormon community to this important theological issue. Franklin Littell, Norbert Samuelson, and Richard Bushman also helped through their careful reading and criticism.

I wish to thank also the archive staffs at the Beinecke Library at Yale University, the Marriott Library at the University of Utah, and the Historical Department of the Church of Jesus Christ of Latter-day Saints for their assistance. Particularly I appreciate the staff at the Salt Lake City Public Library, where the bulk of this book was written. They provided valuable resources as well as a sanctuary of sorts for me (along with many of the city's homeless).

I thank the late Iris Epperson for her support and my children for their love and patience.

But above all everything here belongs to Diana. Only she knows how much.

CHAPTER ONE

Through Gentile Eyes: Judaism in Early Nineteenth-century America and England

Mormon positions on social and religious issues were both congruent with and distinct from those of other contemporary religious groups. The challenge is determining how, when, and why Mormons diverged from traditional Christian views of Jewish covenant and destiny.

To begin to understand this, it is necessary to examine popular attitudes and religious beliefs held by Christians toward Jews and Judaism at the time of the emergence of the Mormon church. Only then can we begin to understand the independence of Smith's vision.

Carlos Baker has written that the Bible provided European colonizers and settlers with such a compelling parallel that they saw themselves in the image of the "Chosen People." Not only did they call America the promised land but "grew to regard themselves as so like the Jews that every anecdote of [Jewish] tribal history seemed like a part of their own recollection."[1] If gentile Americans came to look upon themselves as a "Chosen People," how did they express themselves about the living sons and daughters of Abraham in America?

Historians of the 1950s and early 1960s depicted American gentile-Jewish relations in the early nineteenth century as more positive than those which blighted the European historical record.[2] Indeed one American minister proudly claimed that the United States was "the only Christian nation which has never persecuted the descendants of Israel."[3] Thomas Jefferson worked to eliminate discrimination against Jews along with other religious minorities. George Washington's "Address to the Hebrew Congregation in Newport, Rhode Island," delivered in 1790, demonstrated support for a Jewish presence in the fledgling nation.[4] Certainly attitudes between gentiles and Jews were not always favorable. Still historians suggested that good relations predominated from colonization well into the 1870s.

A contrasting picture of widespread anti-Jewish expressions in public media has been brought into focus by more recent historical scholarship.[5] Michael Dobkowski faults earlier historians for "de-emphasizing the importance of literary and social stereotyping as indices of prejudice. This is unfortunate, for, conceivably, ideology drove a wedge between Jews and gentiles simply by sharpening negative stereotypes."[6] European immigrants brought impressions derived from anti-Jewish theology, Christian passion pageants, legends of Wandering Jews and Shylocks, and anti-Jewish legislation.

Louis Harap has shown that American playwrights followed the conventions of the British stage. "Without exception," he writes, Jewish characters are Shylocks: "none of the Jewish characters has a wife or a mother. Their milieu is not human but strictly financial."[7] John J. Appel points to the caricatures of Jews in American editorial cartoons, which began appearing as early as 1834: "the caricaturist's vocabulary, invented in an unsympathetic or hostile Christian European milieu, had already endowed the long nosed Jew of American humor with features that easily were turned to anti-Semitic uses. . . . His 'evocative image' relied on several centuries of Christian, European images, motifs and symbols, all unsympathetic or hostile to the Jew as outsider, Christ killer, or representative of the new, capitalist order."[8] A reporter for the *New York German Correspondent* in 1820 noted to readers that "'Jew' is an epithet which is frequently uttered in a tone bordering on contempt. Say what you will, prejudices against the Jews exist here, and subject them to inconveniences from which other citizens of the United States are exempt."[9]

Isaac Meyer Wise began publishing the *American Israelite* in 1854 in part to counteract the abuse to which Jews were subject in antebellum America. "A rascally Jew figures in every cheap novel," wrote Wise; "every newspaper printed some stale jokes about Jews to fill up space, and every backwoodsman had a few jokes on hand to use in public addresses; [and] all this called forth not one word of protest from any source."[10]

Historians who have made Puritans into "benevolent Hebraists" and the founding fathers into "magniloquent philosemites" tend to overlook the degree to which Christians from the seventeenth through the nineteenth centuries—Jeffersonian rationalists, liberals, and transcendentalists included—were variously committed to a theology which represented the Jew "as a villain in the drama and mystery of salvation,"[11] as a "rebel against God's purpose,"[12] and as a practitioner of a retrograde, depraved religion. In this prevailing view, Jews and their religion were "artifacts, unwilling witnesses to a divine purpose which had raised up Christianity and Christians in their stead as the Lord's precious possession," his covenant people and "new Israel." The fate reserved for Jewish people was conversion and integration within the body of Christ. Sermons, diary entries, private correspondence, biblical commentaries, theologies, and ecclesiastical histories composed in America during these centuries are virtually univocal in their articulation of the basic anti-Jewish prejudice which informs so much Christian theology and culture.[13]

Even Ezra Stiles (1727-95), Congregationalist minister, hebraist, president of Yale, and one of the least prejudiced Christians of his time, wrote in his diary, "How melancholy to behold an Assembly of Worshippers of Jehovah, open and professed enemies to a crucified Jesus."[14] Later he would press for a constitution for the new republic which would openly own Christianity as the religion of the land.[15] Stiles's successor at Yale, Timothy Dwight (1752-1817), in a sermon before the American Board of Commissioners for Foreign Missions at its fourth annual meeting on 16 September 1813 singled out the refusal of the Jewish people to submit to the Christian gospel as an obstacle to God's kingdom: "'Crucify him. . . . His blood be upon us and on our children.' To this day, the same spirit is retained by their descendants. . . . The very curse, which their ancestors invoke, appears still to rest upon them. . . . 'If ye believe not . . . ye shall die in your sins.' It cannot be doubted, that this declaration extends its terrible efficacy, with equal certainty, to every subsequent generation [of Jews]."[16]

Congregationalist presidents of Yale were not alone in their appraisal of Jewish people. Liberal Protestant and transcendentalist theologians and historians bent on rediscovering the essentials of the Christian faith criticized "judaizing" tendencies and teachings as a plague on the church.[17] Theodore Parker (1810-60) wrote in May 1841: "The theological doctrines derived from our fathers seem to have come from Judaism, Heathenism and the caprice of philosophers, far more than they have come from the principles and sentiments of Christianity. Many tenets that pass current in our theology seem to be the refuse of idol temples and off-scourings of Jewish and heathen cities." "Forsaken Israel, wandering alone," had at one time served its purpose, but lacking the essentials for it to be "a complete religion," it has been replaced by the "religion of Jesus."[18]

The treatment of Judaism in the works of other prominent American religious figures, including James Freeman Clarke, Lyman Abbott, and Crawford Toy, is cut essentially from the same cloth. Christian universality is contrasted with Jewish particularism. The "new" Israel of grace had replaced the "old" Israel of ritual and law. The redemptive role of the Jewish people and its covenant ended with the coming of Jesus.

The "Ecclesiastical Histories" of John Mosheim (1790), Joseph Milner (1827), John Marsh (1827), and Philip Schaff (1858) underscored the conclusions of liberal Protestant theologians and their more conservative peers. Mosheim, writing of first-century Jews, concluded, "They were . . . sunk in the most deplorable ignorance of God, and of divine things and had no notion of any other way of rendering themselves acceptable to the Supreme Being, than by sacrifices."[19]

Milner proposed an oft-repeated charge that the provisionally-correct worship of "the true God" instituted during the period of the Mosaic economy had been thoroughly "obscured and corrupted with Pharisaic traditions and Sadducean profaneness." As a result the religious state of a "destitute" Jewish nation was essentially no "better than the rest of the world." Indeed "scarcely in any age had ignorance and wickedness a more general prevalence."[20] Although Philip Schaff conceded as Milner would not that "their morals were outwardly far better than those of the heathen," still "underneath the garb of strict obedience to their law, they concealed great corruption. They are pictured in the New Testament as a stiff necked, ungrateful, and impenitent race, the seed of the serpent, a generation of vipers."[21]

Yet Schaff describes a living, struggling Jewish community which he encounters in Jerusalem with genuine sympathy and human understanding. Such passages about the Jewish people in *Through Bible Lands: Notes of Travel in Egypt, the Desert and Palestine* highlight the ambivalence in gentile attitudes towards Jews and Judaism and make clear the recurring dissonance between inherited and perceived impressions of religious and ethnic difference. As long as "the Jew" as an abstraction or the Judaism of "the Mosaic economy" was the subject of inquiry, the theologian, historian, preacher, or journalist repeated familiar antitheses—old/new, law/grace, carnal/spiritual, tribal/universal, ritualistic/ethical and so on—by which Christianity's superiority was contrasted with Israel's abjectness and superfluity. Thus when passages from Schaff's *Creeds of Christendom, Encyclopedia,* or *History of the Christian Church* are considered, the unguarded passages encountered in *Through Bible Lands* sound the chance, dissonant note which escaped the composer's drive to harmony.

The high regard of American Puritan divines for Hebrew scriptures and the lengths to which they went to identify themselves with the covenant people have been cited by historians as manifesting the basic compatibility between Jew and Christian in the United States. A so-called identity of Jewish and Christian interests was a frequent theme of Christian theology and biblical exegesis—but one which could issue in negative appraisals.[22] The figure of the Jewish nation or of Jewish parties such as the Pharisees when deployed to criticize sectarianism, laxness, or apostasy within the church reinforced distortions about Judaism. Doctrinal anti-Judaism frequently filtered down to the masses from the pulpit as preachers relentlessly sketched the Jew as the archetypical reprobate.[23]

Of all religious categories employed by American and British Christians to structure their relationship to the Jewish people, none was more important in the first half of the nineteenth century than the prophetic, with its interest in events leading to and inaugurating the Millennium, the thousand-year reign of Christ on earth. Numerous historians have established that the study of biblical prophecy was a ubiquitous and respectable pursuit of both intellect and faith flourishing in the seventeenth century through the 1850s.[24] When expressing prophetic and millennialist ideas during this period, biblical exegetes, preachers, prophets, Anglicans, Baptists, and radicals "employed the same body of religious ideas, spoke the same religious language, pondered the same set of biblical images."[25]

The early nineteenth-century religionists lay on the far side of the historical-critical upheavals which irrevocably changed biblical scholarship and theology in the second half of the nineteenth century.[26] According to the earlier reading, the Bible provided literal program notes and inspired propositions about the relationship between humanity and God in the divinely-patterned drama of history. The scriptures established the basic interpretive frame for Christians: creation, incarnation, and eschaton, along with signs for determining the end of one act and the beginning of another.[27] However, the confusion resulting from multiple prophetic chronologies enabled exegetes as diverse as Joachim of Fiore, Michael Sattler, and Joseph Smith to look in fresh ways at social and political events and argue differently for God's faithfulness, providence, and promises.

Christian exegetes confronted with the text of Hebrew Scriptures have been hard pressed to reconcile prophecies about the restoration of national Israel with confident expectations of the universal, millennial triumph of the Christian church. Traditionally church apologists denied that these prophecies had anything to do with "old" Israel, "A peculiar people that might have claimed the right hand of primogeniture of mankind."[28]

In effect, Christianity appropriated Israel's patrimony and taught that gentile converts to Christianity constituted the new Israel. This teaching was so deeply entrenched in the Christian consciousness that even a Quaker dissenter would say to "the Jew," "Now we the seed of Abraham, of the true Jew inwardly . . . we are the redeemed of the Lord, through the purchase of the blood of Immanuel." And he excoriates "Jews and the scattered tribes of Israel" bitterly, "Oh why do ye yet in your hearts seek murther? Why say and contend ye for more blood?"[29]

Traditional theologians also discouraged any notion of the revival of a national Israel by denying a material, future, messianic reign. These doctors of the church insisted instead on St. Augustine's idea of a "realized millennium" swallowing up "the whole history and life span of the Church militant on earth."[30] The teaching of a literal, future millennium was suppressed through the sixteenth century by the Roman church, and Luther and Calvin continued the Augustinian position. Indeed the Second Helvetic Confession of 1566 condemned "Jewish dreams that there will be a golden age on earth before the Day of Judgment."[31]

More literalistic Christian views of the Millennium were encouraged by the influential Geneva Bible and the idea that the Bible was "inspired directly and verbally by the Holy Spirit."[32] Many Christians were then led to anticipate that the last days were imminent and that they would live to witness the inauguration of the millennial reign of Christ with his saints. Linked to these beliefs was the conviction that restoring the Jewish people to a nation in the Holy Land and converting them en masse to Christianity were necessary precursor events to the Millennium. In the words of Thomas Draxe in *The Worlds Resurrection: Or the General Calling of the Jews. . .* (1608), the "Jews shall towards the end of the world, be temporally restored into their own Country, rebuild Jerusalem, and have a most reformed, and flourishing church and commonwealth."[33] Thomas Brightman's *A Revelation of the Revelation,* which strongly influenced Puritan thinking, contended that John's Apocalypse, a "sure survey of historie" from Jesus Christ to the end of the world, not only accurately projected the trials through which the church would pass but delineated how the "Jewish nation now Christian" would, after their conversion, be miraculously delivered from the Turks and restored to Jerusalem, which would become the "world centre of true religion."[34] It was up to scholars of prophecy such as John Napier in *A Plaine Discovery of the Whole of the Revelation of St. John* (1593) and Joseph Mede in *Clavis Apocalyptica* (1627) to work out "scientific" methodologies for interpreting the complex chronologies and stratagems leading up to divine history's parousia.[35]

Virtually all Christian scholars and commentators thus believed that conversion of Jews was a necessary precursor to final Christian victory. Jewish conversion would direct pious attention to the "signs of the time" leading up to the millennial new age.[36] English divines, New England Puritans, new Divinity men, and interdenominational missionaries anxiously believed that gathering Jews "into one fold together with the Gentiles . . . shall be life from the dead to the Gentiles," that a general Jewish conversion "would stimulate the conversion of the nations bringing on the millennium."[37] Conversion and restoration would thus validate "prophetic" Christianity and induce non-believers and members of nominal Christian churches to become truly converted.

However, until the end of the eighteenth century, missionary activity aimed at Jewish communities in England and America was almost unheard of.[38] Christ's representatives preferred to read the oracles and attend prodigious historical events and miraculous infusions of grace. In the decades of the 1790s and early 1800s, these elements seemed to conjoin. A revolution in France threatened to topple the Roman church and heralded the end of "the Beast."[39] French troops marched toward the Levant, surely pointing, it was reasoned, to the pouring out of the "sixth vial" of the Apocalypse which would encompass "the end of the Turkish woe and the conversion of the Jews."[40] The wrenching away of the imperial crown from a pope's hand by Napoleon seemed a sign of the ascent of the Antichrist and served to stoke the ardent fires of England's "millennial nationalism."[41] British prophetic diviners not so secretly yearned to identify their nation, which after the naval battle at Trafalgar rode almost unchallenged upon the seas, with that maritime nation obscurely sketched in Isaiah 18, which would be God's chosen vessel to bring about Israel's renascence.

The ascent of prophecy's popularity in the decades between 1790 and 1840 received further stimulus from evangelical "awakenings" in England and America. The fires of the revivals illuminated both urban and rural populations. Pre- and post-millennialists, apocalyptics and meliorists, were all quickened by heightened prophetic expectations. By 1828 W. H. Oliver spoke of "the vogue for prophecy" attaining "new heights."[42] Millennial interest began to focus on Jewish conversion. Beginning in 1809 with the London Society for Promoting Christianity Among the Jews (London Society)[43] and then in 1816 and 1820 with the American Society for Evangelizing the Jews and the American Society for Meliorating the Conditions of the Jews (ASMJC),[44] missionary work was vigorously prosecuted and widely published.[45]

Levi Parsons, a missionary called along with Pliny Fisk in 1818 by the American Board of Commissioners for Foreign Missions (ABCFM) to undertake a mission to Palestine, spoke for the sentiments of most American Christians in a sermon delivered at the Park Street

Church in Boston on 31 October 1819. Just prior to his departure on a mission to Palestine he affirmed that "The blessed Gospel has commenced its gradual, yet irresistible progress. . . . Encouraged by these events (mounting interest in Jewish restoration, 'Jewish children . . . receiving a Christian education,' etc.) the Christian world are awakening from their long and criminal slumbers, and are inquiring . . . 'Lord, what wilt thou have us to do.'" Parsons continued in response to this inquiry: "let the Jews be subjects of your prayers. . . . The Jews have special claims upon our charity. . . . The millions of Jews must be furnished with the word of God, and with the instructions of Missionaries. . . . Conversions to Christianity are rapidly increasing. A general movement is taking place. Every eye is fixed on Jerusalem."[46]

During the nineteenth century hundreds of societies were formed and labored all over the world to convert the children of Abraham.[47] By 1824 in America alone, Joseph Frey's ASMCJ was established in nearly two hundred local groups.[48] *Israel's Advocate,* the official publication of the ASMCJ, was reportedly sent to more than two thousand homes in the United States.[49] Chronicles of conversions began to appear in the religious press, including Joseph Wolff's journal accounts of bringing "the light to the Jews of Palestine."[50] The various governing boards of the ASMCJ included such notables as Elias Boudinot, past member of the House of Representatives and director of Jew Jersey-Princeton; John Livingston, president of Queens College-Rutgers; Jeremiah Day, president of Yale; and U.S. presidents James Monroe and John Q. Adams.[51]

Boudinot delivered the inaugural address of the ASMCJ on 12 May 1820 and later willed four thousand acres in Pennsylvania to the society to assist in its project of establishing a colony for European Jewish converts to Christianity.[52] Later a farm of four hundred acres in

Harrison, Westchester County, much closer to New York City and Jewish settlements, was leased for seven years. An agent representing the society was selected to work in Europe "to collect the dispersed of Israel."[53] Though the colony scheme was never fully realized and the society's domestic conversion activity was a relative failure, interest in the ASMCJ and allied societies was sustained at a high level of interest and support for decades.[54] Enthusiasm for reform societies, missionary work, and prophetic-millennial theology combined with an increase in Jewish immigration to keep interest in Jewish conversion on America's evangelical agenda.[55]

In general American Jews perceived such attempts by Christians as a threat.[56] They attempted to counter this attack on Jewish identity and values with their own forums. Solomon Jackson's *The Jew* (March 1823 to March 1825) was the first American Jewish newspaper. It was inaugurated expressly as a "defensive instrument against the missionaries."[57] It included among its articles a running attack on the ASMCJ's *Israel's Advocate* and on the society's motives and methods. It occasionally fired polemical broadsides, attacking the authenticity of the New Testament and various Christian beliefs.

S. J. Kohn has shown how Mordecai Manuel Noah's "Ararat" project to establish a Jewish settlement on Grand Island, New York, as a means of preparing for national restoration in Palestine, was mounted in large measure to counter "the tremendous propaganda to convert Jews to Christianity by the new Evangelical movement." A colorful political figure in municipal, state, and national politics, Noah was also an observant Jew who "dreamed of, prayed for the restoration of israel in the Holy Land."[58] He saw Ararat as a testing ground for new Jewish political-national ideas and as a partial answer to problems of persecution and assimilation in Europe and the United States.[59] The pomp of the 2 September 1825 dedication of the Ararat project obscures the seriousness of the Jewish perception of a threat. They believed that an evangelical nation striving for a Christian culture posed a serious challenge to Jewish identity and religious autonomy. But for many millennialist Christians, it was plain that the "1,260 days" exile of the woman in Revelation 12 was coming to an end. She approached the time with maternal jealousy and would claim all her children—both gentile and Jew—as her own.

NOTES

1. Carlos Baker, "The Place of the Bible in American Fiction," in *Religious Perspectives in American Culture,* ed. James Ward Smith and A. Leland Jamison (Princeton, NJ: Princeton University Press, 1961), 245.

2. John Higham writes that "throughout the ante-bellum period, Jews continued to enjoy almost complete social acceptance and freedom." See "Social Discrimination Against Jews in America, 1830-1930," *Publications of the American Jewish Historical Society* 42 (Sept. 1957): 3. Bertram Korn remarks that "anti-Jewish feelings did not pervade the American scene, nor was it fostered by government sanction or the traditions of the aristocracy. . . . American society possessed no traditional history of anti-Semitism." See "Factors Bearing Upon the Survival of Judaism in the Ante-Bellum Period," *American Jewish Historical Quarterly* 53 (June 1964): 346. Oscar Handlin notes that the traditional lexicon of Jewish caricature still had not surfaced in the American press in the mid-nineteenth century. In John J. Appel, "Jews in American Caricature: 1820-1914," *American Jewish History* 81 (Sept. 1981): 108, 109. And Kenneth Scott Latourette points out that "relatively little effort was made by either Roman Catholics or Protestants to win this vast body of non-Christians. . . . they paid singularly little attention to the Jews." See *The Great Century: A.D. 1800-A. D. 1914: Europe and the United States of America. A History of the Expansion of Christianity,* vol. 4 (New York: Harper and Brothers, 1941), 293.

3. Quoted in Robert Healey, "From Conversion to Dialogue: Protestant American Mission to the Jews in the 19th and 20th Centuries," *Journal of Ecumenical Studies* 18 (Summer 1981): 382.

4. Reprinted in Charles Stember et al., *Jews in the Mind of America* (New York: Basic Books, 1966), v.

5. Jonathan Sarna, "Anti-Semitism and American History," *Commentary* 71 (Mar. 1981): 42.

6. Michael Dobkowski, *The Tarnished Dream: The Basis of American Anti-Semitism,* Contributions in American History, No. 81 (Westport, CT: Greenwood Press, 1979), 3.

7. Louis Harap, *The Image of the Jews in American Literature* (Philadelphia: Jewish Publication Society, 1974), 257.

8. Appel, "Jews in American Caricature," 107.

9. Sarna, "Anti-Semitism and American History," 43. Sarna also cites *New York Herald* editor James Gordon Bennett and his "particular vehemence" in the denunciation of Jews.

10. Isaac Mayer Wise, *Reminiscences* (Cincinnati: L. Wise & Co., 1901), 272. Anti-Jewish caricatures and stereotypes had been deeply etched in the public discourse of colonial America. See Jacob R. Marcus, *The Colonial American Jew: 1492-1776,* vol. 3 (Detroit: Wayne State Press, 1970); also Stanley F. Chyet, "The Political Rights of the Jews in the United States: 1776-1840," *American Jewish Archives* 10 (1958). Various studies have revealed the extent to which Jews in colonial America were subject to persecution and denied basic political rights. Stanley Chyet writes that "there was no fraudulent historical record; it proclaimed a capricious, vicious god; it fostered a depraved chauvinistic morality; its worship was meaningless mummery; and it practically ignored the existence of an afterlife." Jefferson couched his criticism more delicately than James Rivington. Still the recognition of "the mark of their reprobation," no matter how recondite in Jefferson's case, is akin to Rivington's crassness. Both men's views were thoroughly informed by an inherited Christian, ideological prejudice. See Robert M. Healey, "Jefferson on Judaism and Jews," *American Jewish History* 73 (June 1984): 363.

11. Marcus, *The Colonial American Jew,* 1119.

12. John Higham, "Social Discrimination Against Jews," 4.

13. Though Jewish inhabitants in early New England Puritan settlements were entirely absent, still Increase Mather felt compelled in 1669 to preach, "The guilt of the bloud of the Lord of Heaven and earth lyeth upon that nation" who are perpetrators of "the most prodigious murther that ever the sun beheld. . . . the guilt thereof lyeth upon the Jewish nation to this day"; see Robert M. Healey, "The Jew in 17th Century Protestant Thought," *Church History* 46 (Mar. 1977): 74. William Penn in *Advice to His Children* (1726) cites the Jews as an example of reprobation and one not to be imitated; quoted in David Max Eichhorn, *Evangelizing the American Jews* (Middle Village, NY: Jonathan David Publishers, 1978), 8. Cotton Mather in *The Faith of the Fathers* (1669) found grim satisfaction as witness to the truth of Christianity in the "obstinate Aversion" of Jews "to that Holy Religion." Yet he could also "from the dust, where I lay prostrate" pray that he would live to see the day wherein he would be the instrument in baptizing a single Jew as a crowning act to his ministry; quoted in Marcus, *The Colonial American Jew,* 1119.

14. Eichhorn, *Evangelizing the American Jews,* 17. On Stiles, see Arthur A. Chiel, "Ezra Stiles and the Jews: A Study in Ambivalence," in *A Bicentennial Festschrift for Jacob Marcus* (New York: American Jewish Historical Society and KTAV, 1976).

15. Marcus, *Colonial American Jews,* 1120.

16. Quoted in Bill J. Leonard, ed., *Early American Christianity, Christian Classics* (Nashville: Broadman Press, 1983), 315.

17. Robert Andrew Everett, "Judaism in 19th Century American Transcendentalist and Liberal Protestant Thought," *Journal of Ecumenical Studies* 20 (Summer 1983): 398.

18. Ibid., 400.

19. John Lawerence Mosheim, *An Ecclesiastical History, Ancient and Modern, from the Birth of Christ, to the Beginnings of the Present Century. . . in Six Volumes* (London: T. Cadell, 1790), 47.

20. Joseph Milner, *The History of the Church of Christ, Volume The First: Containing the Three First Centuries* (London: T. Cadell, 1827), 1-2.

21. Philip Schaff, *History of the Christian Church: Vol. 1, Apostolic Christianity A.D. 1-100* (1858; Grand Rapids, MI: Wm. B. Eerdmans Publishing Co., 1960), 63-64. See also John Marsh, *An Epitome of General Ecclesiastical History from the Earliest Period: with a Condensed Account of the Jews Since the Destruction of Jerusalem 16th ed.* (1827; New York: A. S. Barnes & Co., 1867), 163-64.

22. See Healey, "From Conversion to Dialogue," 378-79.

23. Healey, "The Jew in 17th Century Protestant Thought," 73.

24. Compare W. H. Oliver, *Puritans, The Millennium and the Future of Israel: Puritan Eschatology, 1600-1660* (Cambridge: James Clarke & Co., 1970), 19-31; James West Davidson, *The Logic of Millennial Thought: Eighteenth Century New England* (New Haven: Yale University Press, 1977), 43-47; Ernest Sandeen, *The Roots of Fundamentalism: British and American Millenarianism, 1800-1930* (Chicago: University of Chicago Press, 1970), 4-13.

25. Oliver, *Puritans,* 17.

26. Davidson, *Logic of Millennial Thought,* 12. At least with regard to millennialism, Davidson concluded, "Eighteenth century New England is closer to the first century than to the twentieth."

27. See Frank E. Manuel, *Shapes of Philosophical History,* (Stanford: Stanford University Press, 1965), 13-23. According to Manuel, those periods were triadic, Danielic, sabbatical, or meliorist.

28. R. Burton, *Journey to Jerusalem, Containing the Travels of 14 Englishmen in 1667 to the Holy Land and Other Places Noted in Scripture. . . .* (Hartford: J. Babcock, 1796), n.p.

29. John Perrot, *Immanuel the Salvation of Israel: The Word of the Lord Concerning the Jews and the Scattered Tribes of Israel. . . .* (London: Thomas Simmons, 1660), 4, 7.

30. Peter Toon, *Puritans, the Millennium and the Future of Israel* (N.p.: J. Clarke, 1970), 17.

31. Ibid., 9.

32. Ibid., 24.

33. Cited in Carl F. Ehle, Jr., "Prologomena to Christian Zionism in America: The Views of Increase Mather and Wil-

liam Blackstone Concerning the Doctrine of the Restoration of Israel," Ph.D. diss., New York University, 1977, 49.

34. Toon, 30.

35. Compare Ehle, "Prologomena to Christian Zionism," 52-65; Oliver, *Puritans*, 34-36.

36. See Healey, "The Jew in 17th Century Protestant Thought," 76; Mel Scult, *Millennial Expectations and Jewish Liberties: A Study of the Efforts to Convert the Jews in Britain, up to the Middle Nineteenth Century: Studies in Judaism in Modern Times* (Leiden: E. J. Brill, 1978), ix-xii; Davidson, *Logic of Millennial Thought*, 66; Oliver, *Puritans*, 90.

37. Jonathan Edwards, quoted in Ehle, "Prologomena to Christian Zionism," 196.

38. R. H. Martin, "United Conversionist Activities Among the Jews in Great Britain, 1795-1815: Pre-Evangelism and the London Society for Promoting Christianity among the Jews," *Church History* 46 (December 1977): 440. Zvi Sobel cites the exception in "Jews and Christian Evangelism: The Anglo-American Approach," *American Jewish Historical Quarterly* 48 (Dec. 1968). In 1728 the Callenburg Institutio Judaicaum was established at the University of Halle for the training of missionaries and the preparation and printing of Jewish tracts. From the institute many students "went out on itinerant missions in Europe, America, and North Africa" (245).

39. Ernest Sandeen called the French Revolution a prophetic Rosetta Stone, the key to interpreting biblical chronologies during prophecy's hay days, 1790-1850.

40. Davidson, *Logic of Millennial Thought*, 66.

41. Oliver, *Puritans*, 64-65, 134-36.

42. Ibid., 64.

43. R. H. Martin, "United Conversionist Activities, 437-38, 440.

44. George L. Berlin, "Solomon Jackson's The Jew: An Early American Jewish Response to the Missionaries," *American Jewish History* 71 (Sept. 1981): 11.

45. Lorman Ratner, "Conversion of the Jews and Pre-Civil War Reform," *American Quarterly* 13 (Spring 1961): 50.

46. Quoted in Robert T. Handy, ed., *The Holy Land in American Protestant Life, 1800-1918: A Documentary History* (New York: Arno Press, 1981), 80-82.

47. Eichorn, *Evangelizing the American Jews,* 4.

48. Berlin, "Solomon Jackson's The Jew," 11.

49. S. Joshua Kohn, "Mordecai Manual Noah's Ararat Project and the Missionaries," *American Jewish Historical Quarterly* 55 (Dec. 1965): 184.

50. Kohn, "Mordecai Manual Noah," 184-85.

51. Eichhorn, *Evangelizing the American Jews,* 50-51.

52. Ratner, "Conversion of the Jews," 45.

53. Kohn, "Mordecai Manual Noah, 180.

54. Ratner, "Conversion of the Jews," 43.

55. Baptists and Episcopal bodies began their own organizations in the 1840s.

56. Berlin, "Solomon Jackson's The Jew," 14.

57. Ibid.

58. Kohn, "Mordecai Manual Noah," 166.

59. The Ararat speech of Noah at the dedication ceremony is reprinted in *Publications of the American Jewish Historical Society* 21 (1913): 230-52. For an account of the Ararat project, see Jonathan D. Sarna, *Jacksonian Jew: The Two Worlds of Mordecai Noah* (New York: Homes and Meier, 1981), chap. 4.

CHAPTER TWO

Jewish Identity and Destiny in the Book of Mormon

Joseph Smith was called "an apostle of Jesus Christ," "first elder" of the Mormon church, "a seer, a translator, a prophet," and "brother." The doctrinal and institutional development of his thought, worked out through his revelations, sermons, teachings, and occasional writing, established his preeminence and galvanized his followers. It also divided the loyalties and bonds of friends and families and drove away bewildered or embittered men and women unable to adjust to his restless vision. But it was Smith, Mormons believe, who laid the foundation of the earthly kingdom of God and tragically paid for his efforts through martyrdom in an obscure town in western Illinois at the age of thirty-eight.[1]

Though principal author of the LDS religious community, Joseph Smith left, as one scholar described it, only "scattered pieces of Mormon doctrine when he died in 1844. He had left a relatively complete theology, but it was available only in scattered talks, revelations, journal entries, editorials and in the personal records of his colleagues."[2] In these widely dispersed sources spanning his adult years, Smith's understanding of Israel and Jewish people is disclosed. From the outset he manifests a persistent attention to Israel's covenant and election, its gathering and restoration. But this attention to Israel and the Jewish people has been persistently misread and overlooked for a number of reasons.

Smith's preoccupation with the descendants of Abraham, Isaac, and Jacob was not an anomaly in the 1820s through the 1840s, an era of widespread millennial expectation.[3] As understood in evangelical circles, converting the Jewish people to Christianity would irresistibly lead to the summation of mortal history and the triumph of Christ's kingdom.[4]

An alternate view found in the most popular millennialist movement until 1844, led by William Miller, sidestepped the problem of converting Jews through a "figurative" reading of the scriptures.[5] Miller and his followers understood "the church" and its members as constituting a "new" Israel. Miller's "spiritual" or figurative exegesis rested on his realistic appraisal of Jewish resistance to Christianity. The coming Lord could not wait upon this "recalcitrant" people and their conversion to make his appearance. As one scholar has noted, when Miller encountered the Christian reading of scripture which insisted "that the Jews convert to Christianity and return to Israel before the Second Advent, he was able to provide an interpretation that complemented his predicted year. When the prophets used the word Jew, they were actually talking about Christians, since 'the putting on of Christ constitut[es] them Abraham's seed, and heirs according to the promise.' All who accepted Christ, then, would be considered converted 'Jews,' and all the Saints [Christians] together at the Last Day would constitute the Kingdom of Israel."[6] Jewish people dropped out altogether from Miller's picture and were to suffer the common fate of the ungodly in the coming cataclysm.

Miller's anti-Jewish adventism, the attention given to Jewish missions by "prophetic" evangelical circles, and Christendom's traditional claim as sole heir to Abraham's heritage were at odds with the position Joseph Smith formulated during his life. Smith was certainly not immune to his cultural environment, but revelatory events and the requirement of forging a new religious community compelled him to develop a singular theology. Most significantly, the Book of Mormon, a new book of scripture published by Smith in 1830, reconfirmed Israel's covenant. However, the habits of reading and thinking which Christians brought to the Book of Mormon, even those who had converted to Mormonism, along with the complex structure of this book, long obscured this distinctive theology.

An 1823 revelation received by Joseph Smith set into motion events leading to publication of the Book of Mormon and demonstrated Smith's enduring interest in the Jewish people and a restored Israel. The message of this revelation turned upon a reading of the eleventh chapter of Isaiah, which deals with the coming of a messianic kingdom of righteousness and peace, the gathering of the dispersed of Israel, and the ending of enmity between Judah and Ephraim.[7] This revelation provided Smith and his church with the core terms and blueprint for their restoration movement.[8] Covenant, election, restoration, gathering, and reconciliation between hostile families within the household of Israel and between gentiles and Jews figured prominently in the text of the Book of Mormon and were, hereafter, to be fixed preoccupations of Smith.

The Book of Mormon featured narrative and doctrinal elaboration of these themes. However, the status of the book itself has often obscured attention to such themes. The Book of Mormon presents itself as an ancient priestly record, a sacred annal written and preserved by a succession of pious sectaries first transplanted to the western hemisphere from Jerusalem around 600 B.C. Joseph Smith "translated" this record, engraved on golden plates, through the power of God.

The nature of this translation has been an issue of perennial dispute among students, apologists, and detractors. To the untroubled core of the faithful, the Book of Mormon is a literal history of ancient Americans. To guardians of evangelical and biblicist assumptions, it is a work of blasphemy, a religious imposture foisted upon an unwary public. Pundits have termed it "chloroform in print" (Mark Twain) and the "*Book of Pukei* . . . attributed to that spindle shanked ignoramous Jo Smith" (Abner Cole).[9] Historians and social scientists seeking naturalist explanations for its appearance in the spring of 1830 have speculated on cerebral bicamerality, trance writing, shamanistic possession, religious "genius," childhood trauma, and adult neurosis. Archaeologists, philologists, juris doctorae, Egyptologists, and ecclesiastics have all added theories explaining its genesis. What is certain is that Joseph Smith confidently announced his proprietorship over the 5,000 copies of the Book of Mormon turned out by E. B. Grandin's press in March 1830 and in the editions which followed during Smith's lifetime. He asserted his commitment to the text and was in turn throughout his life claimed by its narratives and doctrines.

Unfortunately, the dispute over authorship obscures attention to what one scholar has called "the fascinating question of the content and meaning."[10] Whatever a reader believes about the origin of the Book of Mormon, the text itself can be considered as a self-contained literary unit, as a world in its own right.

The book presents a complicated frame for its contents, which is the first obstacle for attention to the book's emphasis on Israel. The book claims to be a highly abridged redaction of a host of source materials. The task of editing secular and holy records from a thousand years of history is said to have depended primarily on two men, Mormon and his son and successor Moroni, who winnowed and distilled the contents of the source collections inherited from their predecessors. These they grouped into a final edition by book and author. The literary forms of the text range from historical narratives to private spiritual meditations, from prophetic to apocalyptic declamation. The many styles and voices which make up the book reflect the concerns of a religious, priestly/prophetic elite who wrote and maintained the records.

Fidelity to context in interpretation means considering the Book of Mormon's consistent focus on Jesus Christ. Mormon and Moroni portray themselves as disciples of the risen Jesus Christ, who is said to have ministered in the Western Hemisphere after his resurrection. As editor of the book, Mormon has abundantly marbled into the text, both in its ante- and post-Christian chapters, veins of his own post-resurrection belief. The purpose of his redaction is to witness to the remnants of his people in future eras that the risen Lord, of whom he is a disciple, is the "messenger of covenant" and the "Holy One of Israel." The unwary reader may be jarred by resulting anachronisms, including placing explicitly christological details and formulations in pre-Christian settings. Like the pseudepigraphical writings with which it shares certain similarities, the Book of Mormon contains, according to one scholar, "lengthy sections that look very Jewish and others that look peculiarly Christian. The Pseudepigrapha and the Book of Mormon preserve some passages that prophecy the future coming of an ambiguously described messiah, and others that describe his advent in a singularly descriptive and particularistic way."[11]

Mormon is untroubled by anachronism and never disguises his literary and theological purposes. Narratives are arranged and earlier texts emended according to his doctrinal aim. Bruce Jorgensen, a professor of English at Brigham Young University, in a study on the typological unity of the Book of Mormon has pointed out the systematic structure and "unity of purpose" of the text.[12] Mormon, Jorgensen suggests, has deftly created a narrative whole aiming at spiritual and corporate transformation by weaving the evocative imagery of apocalyptic visions into indigenous accounts of the post-resurrection ministry of the glorified Christ.

The explicit messianism of the text, the stated time frame of its production, and its intended, distant audience are obviously crucial elements of the Book of Mormon. Jesus' post-resurrectional activity is portrayed similarly to apocryphal renditions of the "Evangelium Quadraginta Dierum" (the forty-day period of the resurrected Christ's ministry to his disciples in Palestine [cf. Acts 1:3]).[13] Sorting out the world of the text thus requires first considering the stories of earlier generations included in the Book of Mormon and then considering the explicitly Christian commitments of the books' editors which frame them. The Book of Mormon initially presents itself as the product of devout sectaries who fled from Jerusalem into the wilderness prior to its destruction in 588 B.C. Their order as a community and the principal hermeneutical criteria of their devotion were provided by anticipating the coming of an eschatological prophet, "even a Messiah," "their Lord and their Redeemer." This figure, the leaders, prophets, and priests steadfastly affirm, will help realize Israel's redemption by presiding over and acting through the terms of covenantal promise made by God with Abraham (1 Ne. 22:9-10, 12, 14; 3 Ne. 20). The messiah would vouchsafe Israel's territorial inheritance and affirm that through Abraham's seed all the "kindreds of the earth" would indeed be blessed.

A decidedly apocalyptic thrust emerges in the visions and prophecies of these sectaries who come to be known as Nephites.[14] Their first patriarch Lehi responds to the unsettling proclamations of eleventh-hour prophets in Jerusalem by joining in preaching repentance, announcing the imminent destruction of the city, and emphasizing his faith in the coming messiah who will judge and redeem. The Book of Jeremiah and the contemporary Lachish Letters confirm how ill-received such prophets were.[15] Lehi's criticism of the Jerusalemites was vehemently rejected, and certain parties sought his life. This persecution and rejection precipitated Lehi's flight into the wilderness and his search for a new inheritance.

This initial story of opposition, estrangement, and coerced flight establishes an important theme in the Book of Mormon. Preserving this story fostered a sense of identity and mission. Eventually the Nephites weighed the Jerusalemites from whom they had "broken off" and found them wanting. Themselves passing through trials, humiliation, and rejection and finally being delivered and bestowed with a new home, they elaborated their own belief in a "Holy Messiah" as "suffering servant" of the Lord: scorned, driven off, yet ultimately exalted.[16]

The trials, martyrdom, and vindication of their "Holy One" in Jerusalem made intelligible and acceptable the Nephites' exile as "a lonesome and a solemn people . . . born in tribulation, in a wilderness" (Jac. 7:26). Just as they were rejected in Jerusalem, so too would their Holy One be rejected, and his life taken (2 Ne. 6:9-11; 10:3; 25:9-18; Moro. 3:12). When Jerusalem repudiated prophets sent to her in perilous times, the Lord revisited them in judgment and exiled them from their covenant house and home (2 Ne. 25:14-15). This affirmed the Lord's promise that he "shall make bare his arm in the eyes of the nations" (1 Ne. 22:10). But they were assured they would be redeemed in and through a "Holy Messiah" (2 Ne. 2:6; 1 Ne. 22:12).

Anticipation of this redeemer became the crux of belief and the focus of preaching and practice among the Nephites (2 Ne. 25:23-26, 28-29; 30:2). Their belief in the coming prophet was at once the constitutive core of their community and the major cause for their provisional estrangement from those left behind in Jerusalem. This explicit messianism of the Nephites conspicuously affected their attitude toward the institutions of temple and law and their beliefs about the covenant. Once physically removed to the New World, they took great pains to build a temple "after the manner of the temple of Solomon" (2 Ne. 5:16).[17] An order of priests and an office of high priest were associated with this temple. The temple became the frequent site for public instruction (Jac. 1:17; 2:2, 11; Al. 16:13; 3 Ne. 11:1) and the structural symbol legitimizing the leaders of the community (Mos. 1:18). Still this temple plays a shadowy and rather inconsequential role in the Book of Mormon narrative. Members of the priesthood teach the law of Moses (Jar. 1:11) and administer the affairs of the religious community (Mos. 23:16-18; 26-28; Al. 4:18-19). The cultic function of the temple is mentioned just once in passing (Mos. 2:3). As house of the Lord, it figures only symbolically in prophetic indictments against the sins of the people: "the Lord dwells not in unholy temples" (Mos. 2:37).

It is the eschatological temple to be built in Jerusalem with the advent of a restored Israel which figures prominently in the Book of Mormon. After the mountains are made low and the valleys exalted, the "mountain of the Lord's house" would be established "in the top of the mountains . . . exalted above the hills" to which "all nations shall flow" (2 Ne. 12:2; compare Is. 2:2). There the "purified" sons of Levi, purged "as gold and silver," shall "offer unto the Lord an offering in righteousness" (3 Ne. 23:3; compare Mal. 3:1). To it "the Lord whom ye seek . . . even the messenger of covenant, whom ye delight in . . . shall suddenly come" (3 Ne. 24:1; compare Mal. 3:1). In contrast the provisional, incomplete nature of the sectaries' fugitive temple is made clear in the text both by silence regarding its structure and cultus and by stress on its contingent relation to the prophetic office filled by Nephite religious leaders.

The status of the law of Moses is similarly affected by the messianism of the Nephites. Its eminence in the life of the community is frequently underlined. Both prophet and priest admonish the people to remember the law, to keep its commandments and performances. It was given to Moses from heavenly hands (3 Ne. 15:5). It was bestowed because of the faith of heaven, the patriarch Moses, and of Israel assembled at Sinai (Eth. 12:11). A measure of Nephite esteem for the law can be gauged by the extreme measure employed to obtain a copy of the "record of the Jews" and its "genealogy of [their] forefathers" (1 Ne. 3:3; 1 Ne. 4). The leaders and prophets of the Nephite people acknowledge its essential role in preserving their language, institutions, religious belief, and practice (Om. 1:17; Mos. 12:25-29). Its "performances and ordinances . . . keep them in remembrance of God and their duty towards him" (Mos. 13:30). As they affirm: "salvation did come by the law of Moses" (Mos. 12:31-33).

However, the Nephites' fervent expectation of a new "deuteronomic" prophet (2 Ne. 22:20-21; 3 Ne. 20:23) and the messianic kingdom which would be inaugurated with his coming always qualified their allegiance to Mosaic legislation (2 Ne. 11:4, 25:25-30; Al. 24:15, 34:4). Though instructed to keep the law "because of the commandments" (2 Ne. 25:25), they maintained that one day it would be replaced with a messianic Torah (Al. 34:13, 14; 3 Ne. 1:25).[18] Antinomian enthusiasts, claiming that the Law was null and void, occasionally arose from and plagued the Nephite religious community attempting to keep law and messiah in balance (Al. 1:3-4; 30:14-28; 3 Ne. 1:24-25). Such premature and unsanctioned efforts to loose ties of loyalty to Mosaic law were universally condemned by Nephite prophets and leaders. Yet the established apocalypticism of the community dictated the anticipated completion and perfection of Mosaic legislation.[19]

At the same time, the Nephites continued to remember their rejection at Jerusalem. They engraved on their metal plates, the imperishable medium of their scripture, an angry backward glance at those who refused their apocalyptic messianism. Certainly this messianism heightened their ambivalence toward cultus and law, but the Nephite authors also expressed in their writings a fervent faith in God's covenant with Abraham and the restoration of Jacob's whole house—a message which nineteenth-century Mormons could not mistake.[20]

So great was the Nephite reverence for this covenant that they affirmed that the very Jews who had rejected them were still the Lord's "covenant people" (2 Ne. 29:4-5). It is the Jews who kept a record of the "covenants of the Lord, which he hath made with Israel," a genealogy of their forebearers (1 Ne. 1:3, 12), and "many of the prophecies of the holy prophets" (1 Ne. 13:23). This stewardship over the sacred text of covenant would result in its "proceeding forth from the mouth of a Jew" in "fulness" and "purity" unto the nations of the world and would be the means of "bringing forth salvation unto the Gentiles" (2 Ne. 29:4). The sacred text's insistence upon accountability by all under the covenant would preserve a nation from "dwindl[ing] and perish[ing] in unbelief" (1 Ne. 4:13) and would furnish it with a vocabulary of creation and redemption if it would respond in faith and fidelity to its covenants with the Lord.

The Nephites were not only concerned about the Lord's covenant with Israel and the Jews but also the gentiles' relation to this covenant. Nephi, Lehi's son, turns to those gentiles who would be endowed with knowledge of Israel's covenant and pointedly asks:

"What do the Gentiles mean? Do they remember the travails, and the labors, and the pains of the Jews, and their diligence unto me . . .? O ye Gentiles, have ye remembered the Jews, mine ancient covenant people? Nay; but ye have cursed them, and have hated them. . . . But behold, I will return all these things upon your own heads; for I the Lord have not forgotten my people . . ." (2 Ne. 29:4-50). Fulfilling the terms of the covenant made with Abraham that "In thy seed shall all the kindreds of the earth be blessed" (1 Ne. 15:18) is the recurring theme of the Book of Mormon. Israel had been scattered abroad, "broken off and . . . driven out because of the wickedness of the pastors of my people" (1 Ne. 21:1), as well as smitten by gentiles who in their arrogance should esteem the remnants of Jacob "as naught among them." Still the Lord affirms, in contrast to the anti-Jewish, displacement theologies of historical Christianity, in a passage from Isaiah quoted prominently by Nephi, "Thou art my servant, O Israel, in whom I will be glorified" (1 Ne. 21:3).

The Lord would be glorified first, these pious sectaries believed, when they added their writings to those of their predecessors "unto the confounding of false doctrines" and the bringing of their posterity "to the knowledge of the fathers" (2 Ne. 3:12). Also gentiles would come to a knowledge of the Lord and the terms of his covenant with those who call themselves Israel, thus making Abraham the "father of many nations." It was the Nephites' belief that God who made covenant with Abraham would not "suffer that the Gentiles shall forever remain in that awful state of blindness" (1 Ne. 13:32).

Paradoxically, light unto the gentiles and further glory unto the Lord of covenant were contingent on transgression by Jerusalemites and Nephites. The latter entertained no illusions about the outcome of their religious experiment in the wilderness. Strewn throughout the text are poignant and bitter predictions of the demise of their society and of their failure to maintain a life of covenant before the Lord. Similarly they predict the rejection of their Holy One and Redeemer by Jerusalem. In a maneuver reminiscent of their rather unconventional interpretation of the transgression of the first parents, Book of Mormon authors see this "transgression" as a means for blessings to be extended to the gentiles.[21]

It was expected that the gentiles would fare poorly in their stewardship—"They shall sin against my gospel . . . and shall be lifted up in the pride of their hearts above all nations" (3 Ne. 16:10). But a remnant among them, "who have care for the house of Israel, that realize and know from whence their blessings come" (Mor. 5:10), would assist the "remnant of Jacob" to gather to the "land [of] their inheritance" (3 Ne. 21:23; 1 Ne. 22:6). The Lord would be glorified through his servant Israel in this act of gathering, in which the gentiles would play an assisting role.

In the penultimate days leading to the messianic kingdom, two great gatherings of scattered Israel were to occur. First, the "remnants" or "seed" of the families of the Nephites would gather to Zion, the "New Jerusalem," to be reared in the Americas. Then Judah along with those of Israel long since scattered in the "north countries" (Eth. 13:11) would again be established and restored in Israel with Jerusalem as their capital. The Book of Mormon repeatedly asserts that Israel's restoration depends on realizing the *territorial* terms of the covenant not in its conversion to, or identity with, the church.

With this emphasis on what early Saints called the restoration of Israel,[22] the Book of Mormon, published in 1830, amounted in effect to an elaborate recapitulation of Joseph Smith's 1823 vision. The text from Isaiah 11 and Malachi 3 quoted to Smith in this early revelation reappeared in crucial sections of the Book of Mormon. Indeed the book's authors emphasize their thematic preoccupation and doctrinal intent by quoting sixteen chapters from Isaiah in the early chapters of the book (1 Ne. 20, 21/ Is. 48, 49; 2 Ne. 7, 8/ Is. 50, 52; 2 Ne. 12-24/ Is. 2-14). These chapters from Isaiah, which include editorial glosses inserted by Nephi, affirm Israel's covenant (1 Ne. 20:1, 9-11; 21:5; 2 Ne. 8:6). Though scattered for the sake of transgressions (1 Ne. 20:1; 2 Ne. 8:17-22; 2 Ne. 13; 15:7, 13; 19:8-21), Israel yet would be gathered and restored to the Lord's favor (2 Ne. 8:11; 2 Ne. 14). Meanwhile judgment would befall Israel's oppressors. A holy messiah would arise to establish justice and peace and reign from his Zion, his Jerusalem (2 Ne. 21:1-4).

Significantly for those gentiles who were to read these passages attesting to the authority of Isaiah's prophecies, Israel would be a "light to the Gentiles, that thou [Israel] mayst be my salvation unto the ends of the earth" (1 Ne. 20:6). Gentile nations would "flow unto" the "mountain of the Lord's house" to be taught the law and the word of the Lord (2 Ne. 12:2, 3); they would aid in Israel's gathering (1 Ne. 21:22-23). And finally because of their faithfulness, they would join with and "cleave to the house of Jacob" (2 Ne. 24:1).

The beliefs and overriding concerns of the Nephites arose from the context of Israel's covenant with the Lord of Abraham, Isaac, and Jacob. This is clearly underlined by the book's affirmation of Israel's life of covenant and its confident hope in Israel's vindication and restoration. In the Book of Mormon, gentiles are enjoined to "cleave" to Israel not to convert Israel. It is the gentiles who are being brought into and made beneficiaries of Israel's covenantal household not the other way around.

According to the records received and edited by Mormon and Moroni, Christ confirmed the covenantal faith and aspirations of the early writers when he visited the Americas. Thus the final editors reaffirmed this inherited messianic tradition and devotion to covenant and wed it textually to the words and deeds of the exalted Lord. They record that their Holy One promises an end to Israel's exile and bondage. The Messiah affirms Israel's future gathering to territorial patrimonies (3 Ne. 20:22, 29). Restored to lands of inheritance set aside by divine covenant, Israel's whole house would enjoy the fruits of liberation, peace, knowledge, and security from "oppression . . . and from terror" (3 Ne. 22:3-17). The terms of Abraham's covenant would be acknowledged "in the eyes of all nations." Israel had been and remained the peculiar vessel of covenant. The record of Israel's witness would be presented to the gentiles by the extraordinary restoration of these scriptures.

Specifically the gentiles would receive the blessings of Israel's God through the work and witness of Israel's deuteronomic prophet. Though sent first to his own people to turn "everyone of you from his iniquities" (3 Ne. 20:26), his call to repentance and fidelity to the Lord God of Israel would go out unto all nations. In the events of gathering, restoration, and in the extension of covenantal responsibility to the righteous among the nations, the "Father shall bare his holy arm . . . and the earth shall see the salvation of the Father" (3 Ne. 20:30-31, 35, 39).

The climax is one of reconciliation. Israel will see through its gathering and restoration the fidelity and mercy of the Lord. Gentiles will assist and cleave unto the house of Jacob rather than be its scourge (3 Ne. 21:23). Reconciled to Israel's God through repentance and solidarity with his people, the righteous among the nations will be accounted Abraham's seed and find "glorious rest."

Finally it was the fervent faith of the Book of Mormon writers that with Israel's salvation manifested through these momentous events, Israel would see that the cause of their God and of his messianic prophet, this son of Israel, had always been the same: "and all the ends of the earth shall see the salvation of the Father; and [that] the Father and I are one" (3 Ne. 20:35). Thus in Abraham's seed all the people of the earth would be blessed (3 Ne. 20:25, 27).

Such were the views on Israel, its covenant and future, as expressed in a book coming off a modest printing press in a small Erie Canal town in the spring of 1830. At first reading there is no mistaking the intense christocentrism of the Book of Mormon.[23] Given this emphasis on Christ in the structuring of the Book of Mormon, it is not so surprising that gentiles reading the book since 1830 generally missed its distinctive theology of Israel and Judaism. Christian readers bring other expectations to the book which obscure important distinctions. First, they bring to the text the bitter split between "synagogue" and "church" which dates back to the "New" Testament or Apostolic Writings. Gentile readers bring and have brought to Israel's scripture the impress of Christian triumphalism, anti-Judaic theology, and all of the rhetoric and reality of historically polarized religious traditions and communities. This agenda licenses a habit of christologizing Israel's prophetic literary corpus. In the case of traditional Christian apologetics, the Hebrew Scriptures, for example, became a vast storehouse of prooftexts not only for Christian claims about Jesus of Nazareth but also the rationale for Israel's displacement in the covenantal scheme of salvation by a gentile church intent upon claiming exclusive rights to Israel's heritage.

Thus when gentiles read the debate between factions of Israel's contentious families on the pages of the Book of Mormon, further doctrinal justification is mistakenly provided to the long conceptual assault on the election and integrity of Israel. Nephite criticism of cultus and law and of the Jerusalemites from whom they parted has been interpreted as rejecting Jewish election, Torah, and cult altogether. The agenda of Christendom and its mission was misunderstood as a complete replacement for all that is criticized on the pages of the Nephite record.

However, the consciously orchestrated text of the Book of Mormon is for all its christocentrism peculiarly pitched toward the realization of God's covenant with Israel. Israel's covenant dominates the text the way a "main theme" presides through the exposition, development, and recapitulation of a sonata. The introduction of secondary themes, modulations among one or several keys and "architectural" divisions into movements, serve to develop and underline rather than emasculate the central idea introduced in the design's exposition. God's covenant with Israel as it is worked out through the text of the Book of Mormon is an ever valid, living reality between Israel's God and Israel's whole family. The authenticity of this covenant will be manifest to all nations when Israel gathers to its territorial patrimonies, is restored as a people and nation, and thus will become a light unto the gentiles. The publication of the text of the Book of Mormon in 1830 also was understood by its readers as heralding the imminent end of the "fulness of the gentiles." In Smith's eyes it was important that gentile readers heed its call to repent and gather to a refuge designated by the Lord.

Judged by the written evidence which Joseph Smith left behind, such was the Book of Mormon's principal message to the Latter-day Saints.[24] Four years after the book was published, he emphatically underlined the centrality of his visions and of the Book of Mormon in providing the agenda and the goal for the work of the Latter-day Saints: "Take away the Book of Mormon and the revelations, and where is our religion? We have none; for without Zion, and the place of deliverance, we must fall. . . . For God will gather out his Saints from the

Gentiles, and then comes desolation and destruction, and none can escape save the pure in heart who are gathered."[25]

The Book of Mormon designated the geographical sites for this great gathering of Israel (1 Ne. 22:6) and indicated to whom exactly the land would be "deeded" by the Lord (Eth. 13:1-12).[26] In a country poised at the edge of a decade of intense nationalism and possessed with a grandiose vision of America's "manifest destiny," Joseph Smith published a book in which rights to the land being settled by men and women of European descent were granted by a solemn covenant of the Almighty to "our western tribes of Indians."[27] It is only through complying "with the requisitions of the new covenant," Smith wrote, that gentiles have any hope at all to claim this "promised land" as their heritage as well. But clearly Smith understood that the land's rightful inhabitants were the Israelite remnants of the people of the Book of Mormon of whom Smith believed the American Indians to be a part.[28] And in the Book of Mormon, a harrowing fate is promised to those who usurp this right and fight against the Lord's covenant people: "He that shall breathe out wrath and strifes . . . against the covenant people of the Lord who are of the house of Israel, and shall say: We will destroy the work of the Lord, and the Lord will not remember his covenant which he hath made unto the house of Israel—the same is in danger to be hewn down and cast into the fire; For the eternal purposes of the Lord shall roll on, until all his promises shall be fulfilled" (Morm. 8:21-23).

Nevertheless in the months preceding and following the publication of the Book of Mormon, Smith's immediate understanding of the document over which he claimed proprietorship was captivated by its theme of transformation, of repentance and conversion. Two of Smith's revelations from the same year attest to this particular reading of the text. In one, dated March 1830, a description of the document was given to Martin Harris, one of Smith's earliest disciples and a financial backer of the book's first edition. He was told that the Book of Mormon was the Lord's word "to the Gentiles, that soon it may go to the Jews, of whom the Lamanites [American Indians] are a remnant."

A month later in a revelation coinciding with the organization of the "Church of Christ" in New York, Smith underlined that the "editorial intent" affixed to the Book of Mormon's title page included imparting the gospel "to the Gentiles and the Jews also." Such statements indicated one of the ways in which the text of the Book of Mormon can be and has been read. However, statements by leading figures in the first decades of the LDS church explicitly linking Book of Mormon passages to calls for the evangelizing and converting of Jews are scarce. Jewish missions were explicitly rejected by most leaders of the LDS church and were never part of the church's program in the nineteenth century.

The repudiation of missions on the one hand or the feeble and scattered advocacy of conversion on the other can be seen as a product of the Book of Mormon itself. The conversion of the Jewish people to the church is never mentioned nor advocated in the Book of Mormon. Indeed according to the Book of Mormon, it is the Gentiles who are to convert "through [the] preaching of Jews" (3 Ne. 15:22). At the same time the book's editors hoped that events would transpire in such a way as to show Jesus as "one with the Father" in Israel's salvation. But nowhere is this hope then linked to conversion to the gentile church.

After 1830 Joseph Smith no longer interpreted or preached that the Book of Mormon was an elaborate proselyting tract for "Gentiles and Jews alike." Instead themes connected with God's covenant to Israel and the complex of events which confirmed and would yet authenticate that covenant predominated Smith's exegesis of the text. It is remarkable that a church at once as sectarian-minded and mission-oriented as was Smith's was so reticent to carry out a Jewish mission. The absence of a Mormon mission to the Jewish people, when combined with Smith's contempt for Christian missions to Jews, is a striking deviation from the nearly universal enthusiasm accorded Jewish missions in the first half of the nineteenth century. Indeed when Mormons finally commissioned one of the church's twelve apostles to take a mission to Jews in western Europe and the "Holy Land," he was sent with a manifestly non-evangelistic, non-proselyting commission and agenda.

As interpreted by Joseph Smith and his associates, the immediate and abiding worth of the Book of Mormon lay elsewhere. While it is true that the April 1830 "Revelation on Church Organization and Government" referred to the Book of Mormon as a gospel "to the Gentiles and the Jews also," the revelation also affirmed the sacred text in ways which eclipse "conversionist" interpretations. "The Book of Mormon," it was grandly announced, "was given by inspiration, and . . . confirmed to others by the ministering of angels." The document issuing from Grandin's press was both timely and timeless in its import, "Proving to the world that holy scriptures are true, and that God does inspire men and call them to his holy work in this age and generation . . . Thereby showing that he is the same God yesterday, today and forever. Amen" (D&C 20:10-12).

All of "God's promises would be fulfilled." That was the book's testimony to the earnest seekers for light and knowledge who expectantly took up the texts of the book's first edition. Foremost among the Lord's promises were his covenants with Israel. To this the words of Mormon attest: "Ye need not any longer hiss, nor spurn, nor make game of the Jews, nor any of the remnant of the house of Israel; for behold, the Lord remembereth his covenant unto them, and he will do unto them according to that which he hath sworn" (3 Ne. 29:8).

NOTES

1. For the best treatment of Joseph Smith, see Richard Bushman, *Joseph Smith and the Beginnings of Mormonism* (Urbana: University of Illinois Press, 1984). See also Donna Hill, *Joseph Smith: The First Mormon* (Garden City, New York: Doubleday, 1977); Fawn Brodie, *No Man Knows My History: The Life of Joseph Smith*, 2d ed., rev. and enlarged (New York City: Alfred A. Knopf, 1971); and Smith's narrative history written with the help of scribes and church historians, Joseph Smith et al., *History of the Church of Jesus Christ of Latter-day Saints*, ed. B. H. Roberts, 7 vols. (Salt Lake City: Church of Jesus Christ of Latter-day Saints, 1927-32); hereafter cited as HC.

2. David J. Whittaker, "Early Mormon Pamphleteering," Ph.D. diss., Brigham Young University, 1982, 86.

3. David L. Rowe, *Thunder and Trumpets: Millerites and Dissenting Religion in Upstate New York, 1800-1850*, American Academy of Religion, Studies in Religion (Chico, CA: Scholars Press, 1985). In this excellent study of the Millerite movement, Rowe pointed out that "any religious journal of the day included commentaries on the prophesies from one theological position or another as part of their regular fare" (54).

4. See chaps. 1 and 2 of Rowe, *Thunder and Trumpets*.

5. See Ernest R. Sandeen, in *The Rise of Adventism: Religion and Society in Mid-Nineteenth Century America*, ed. Edwin S. Gaustad (New York: Harper and Row, 1974), 113.

6. Rowe, *Thunder and Trumpets*, 98.

7. HC 1:33-44.

8. See Leonard J. Arrington and Davis Bitton, *The Mormon Experience: A History of the Latter-day Saints* (New York: Alfred A. Knopf, 1979), 127-29; Laurel B. Andrew, *The Early Temples of the Mormons: The Architecture of the Millennial Kingdom in the American West* (Albany: State University of New York Press, 1978), 8-9; Andrew F. Ehat and Lyndon W. Cook, eds., *The Words of Joseph Smith: The Contemporary Accounts of the Nauvoo Discourses of the Prophet Joseph*, Religious Studies Monograph Series, vol. 6 (Provo, UT: Religious Studies Center, Brigham

Young University, 1980), 48n4; Gordon Irving, "The Mormons and the Bible in the 1830s," *Brigham Young University Studies* 13 (Summer 1973): 284-87.

9. Cited in Bushman, *Joseph Smith and the Beginnings,* 120.

10. Lawrence Foster, *Religion and Sexuality: Three American Community Experiments of the Nineteenth Century* (New York: Oxford University Press, 1981), 297.

11. James H. Charlesworth, "Messianism in the Pseudepigrapha and the Book of Mormon," in *Reflections on Mormonism: Judeo-Christian Parallels,* ed. Truman G. Madsen, The Religious Studies Monograph Series, vol. 4 (Provo, UT: Religious Studies Center, Brigham Young University, 1978), 124.

12. Bruce W. Jorgensen, "The Dark Way of the Tree: Typological Unity of the Book of Mormon," in *Literature of Belief: Sacred Scripture and Religious Experience,* ed. Neal E. Lambert, Religious Studies Monograph Series, vol. 5 (Provo, UT: Religious Studies Center, Brigham Young University, 1981), 219-20.

13. See Hugh Nibley, "Evangelium Quadraginta Dierum," *Vigilae Chrisianae* 20 (1966): 1-24.

14. According to the Book of Mormon text, what we know of the ministry and life of Lehi comes to us second-hand through writings of his son Nephi. For an article on Lehi and the character of his record as redacted by his son, see S. Kent Brown, "Lehi's Personal Record: Quest for a Missing Source," *Brigham Young University Studies* 24 (Winter 1984): 19-42.

15. See Jeremiah 38:4. Hugh Nibley, "The Lachish Letters," in *The Prophetic Book of Mormon* (Salt Lake City: Deseret Book/Foundation for Ancient Research and Mormon Studies, 1989), 380-406.

16. Compare Gershom Scholam, *Sabbatai Sevi: The Mystical Messiah, 1626-1676,* Bolingen Series XCIII (Princeton, NJ: Princeton University Press, 1973), 55-57, 795-96, 804-805. See also Scholem's *The Messianic Idea in Judaism: And Other Essays on Jewish Spirituality* (New York: Schocken Books, 1971), 32-33, 50-52.

17. Another community of Israelites established far from the precincts of the Holy City, the Jewish military colony at Elephantine on the Nile, with whom Lehi and his descendants were contemporaries, also reared a temple in exile as a center for faith and worship. The Elephantine garrison "saw nothing

wrong in having their own temple even though a temple to the God of Israel existed in Jerusalem." See Abraham Schalit, "Elephantine," in *Encyclopedia Judaica*, vol. 6 (Jerusalem: Macmillan Co., 1971), 608.

18. Ambivalence toward the law and its ultimate authority was not unique to this particular group of Israelites. This very Deuteronomic tradition (Deut. 18:15-22) was employed by the Qumran sectaries to validate their "restatement of scriptural rules." See Bernard Jackson, "Law," in *Harper's Bible Dictionary*, ed. Paul Achtemeier (San Francisco: Harper and Row, 1985), 550.

Gershom Scholem has pointed out the "anarchic element in the very nature of Messianic utopianism: the dissolution of old ties which lose their meaning in the new context of Messianic freedom." *The Messianic Idea in Judaism*, 19. On the antinomian component to messianic movements of David Alroy in Kurdistan, the Yemeni "Messiah," and Sabbatal Sevi, see 22, 50-52.

19. Scholem's language seems to apply quite aptly to the Nephites. Their messianic prophet would come and "perfect what cannot yet find expression in . . . the law of the unredeemed world." Ibid., 19.

20. Grant Underwood, "Book of Mormon Usage in Early LDS Theology," *Dialogue: A Journal of Mormon Thought* 17 (Autumn 1984): 39.

21. In Lehi's view of the garden story, Adam and Eve transgress in order for a much greater good to be realized: first, the knowledge of good and evil necessary for experiencing joy in this world (which he claims is the whole intent of the divine creation of humanity); and second, the knowledge which makes possible "even the family of all the earth." "Behold," Lehi reasons, "all things have been done in the wisdom of him who knoweth all things." See 2 Ne. 2.

22. Underwood, "Book of Mormon Usage," 39.

23. Further impetus in ascribing messianic titles to the risen Lord can be found in the narratives describing the community set up by Christ in ancient America and the near two-hundred-year period of peace, equity, and justice sustained by his disciples. Compare 4 Ne. 1-22.

24. Underwood, "Book of Mormon Usage," 52, 56, 59.

25. Remarks made at a conference of elders, 21 April 1834. In *Teachings of the Prophet Joseph Smith,* ed. Joseph Fielding Smith (Salt Lake City: Deseret Book Co., 1977), 71.

26. Ibid., 84-86.

27. Letter to N. E. Saxton, 4 Jan. 1833, in *The Personal Writings of Joseph Smith,* ed. Dean C. Jessee (Salt Lake City: Deseret Book, 1984), 273.

28. Ibid.

CHAPTER THREE

Joseph Smith's Encounter with Biblical Israel

Joseph Smith's interest in God's Israel was not exhausted with publication of the Book of Mormon. In the fourteen years until his death, he returned repeatedly to questions of Israel's covenant and election, its gathering and restoration, the reconciliation of its estranged families, and the place of its "adopted" sons and daughters in the Lord's scheme of salvation.

Diaries, journals, and pamphlets produced by early Mormons reveal the prominent place of the Bible in their culture. It was the great motherlode of prooftexts for their polemical and apologetic works, the source and pattern for their strident sectarianism, their pre-millennialism, their corporate organization, their ethics and behavior. This text was read in a literal fashion; that is, Mormon readers understood the characters, events, and settings of Israel's scriptures to possess historical and material integrity in the same manner that readers understood the referents of "secular" histories. "Prophecies and doctrine, the covenants and promises contained in them," wrote George J. Adams in 1841, "have a literal application."[1] At the same time a certain tension was embedded in the Mormon approach to the Bible. For unlike most orthodox Christians of the middle decades of the 1800s, Mormons believed that the Bible was an imperfectly composed text. This meant that although Mormons read the text in a literal way, they were willing through the inspiration of their prophet to add to or emend its canon. Still it was only by means of the Bible that Joseph Smith and his followers encountered the Jewish people during the early years of the church. It was in the sum of these occasionally contradictory strategies for encountering the biblical text that Smith's distinctive view of the Jewish people and Mormonism's relation to them was forged.

For Mormons the Bible's historical accounts were in the main understood as accurate and factual renditions of signal events in Israel's story—its prophetic passages predicting events already or soon to be fulfilled. Mormon exegetes were contemptuously opposed to what they deemed to be wayward or overwrought interpretive methods and conclusions. Allegorical, mystical, or spiritual readings of holy writ were particularly singled out for attack. However, their sparring, carried out both on the scruffy, contested turf of the sects and in well appointed denominational arenas, entailed more than a naked love for combat and controversy. They believed in nothing less than the integrity of God. His promises to covenant peoples, the rightful inheritance of those people, and Mormon "cartography" of the religious landscape were at stake. In Latter-day Saint eyes any assault on the literal referent and context of covenants was warfare on the Maker of covenant, the Israel of God, and the righteous among the gentiles—the Latter-day Saints.

In the "last days" Israel's sovereign had decreed through prophets ancient and modern the restoration and gathering of his scattered house. That gathering included gentiles being called out of "mystic Babylon" by emissaries of Latter-day restoration. They were to congregate in a designated place of refuge in order to escape "the wrath to come." To "universalize" or "spiritualize" away the concrete terms and the specific agenda laid out for Israel[2] in those penultimate days only demonstrated to those who could rightly read the signs, times, and seasons the willful ignorance of the divines of a "fallen" church. This "gentile" hermeneutical strategy was aligned with the misappropriation by the gentile churches of the responsibilities and blessings of Israel's covenant with its Lord. A misbegotten monarch—what Mormons called "apostate" Christianity—still paraded about bearing the laurels rightly belonging to the Lord's "precious possession," arrogating to itself the titles of "the true Israel of God" or "converted Jews" or "universal Church."[3]

Upon this alloyed crown, Mormon pamphleteers and preachers began to hammer away. "Why deny the literal gathering of the Jews to the land God gave their fathers?" Mormon missionary William Appleby demanded of the Millerites.[4] George Adams, in a Mormon tract directed at English detractors of his young church, stated, "We believe that the Scriptures of the Old and New Testament are true . . . and that all mystical and private interpretations of them ought to be done away."[5] Underlining the literal application of the covenants and promises recorded in scripture, Moses Martin singled out the beneficiaries as "the literal seed of Abraham . . . together with all those who are grafted in. . . . These are all to be saved, without any ifs or ands about it."[6]

However, Mormons consistently qualified this faith in the scriptures. Taking cues from the text of the Book of Mormon, Joseph Smith stated, "From sundry revelations which have been received, it was apparent that many important points touching the salvation of men, had been taken from the Bible, or lost before it was compiled."[7] The Book of Mormon laid the blame for this impoverishment of the text at the door of the gentile church: "Thou hast beheld that the book proceeded forth from the mouth of a Jew. . . . these things go forth from the Jews in purity unto the Gentiles, according to the truth which is in God. And after they go forth . . . from the Jews unto the Gentiles, thou seest . . . they have taken away . . . many parts which are plain and precious; and also many covenants of the Lord have they taken away" (1 Ne. 13:23-29). Hence George Adams, while claiming faith in the truth of the scriptures, further noted that "the scriptures now extant do not contain all the sacred writings which God ever gave to man."[8]

These differing views on the Bible affected the tenor of relations between Mormons and non-Mormons. The Religious Tract Society of London realized that belief in the errancy of scripture and in an open scriptural canon, represented by the Book of Mormon and the Doctrine and Covenants, was an assault on the dearly-held belief in the sufficiency of the Bible. In a series of hard-hitting pamphlets aimed at stemming the growth of Mormonism in England, an essential item in the society's denunciation of the new religion was the statement of faith that the "Bible . . . does not lead us to expect any other book, or writings or messages inspired by God. . . . We may here know all that needs to be known."[9] But the unreliability of such a profession of faith had long before been driven home to Smith and hosts of religious seekers like himself in the opening decades of the nineteenth century. Troubled and perplexed by the religious excitement generated by camp meetings and revivals, Smith in retrospect observed: "How to act I did not know, and unless I could get more wisdom than I then had, I would never know; for the teachers of religion of the different sects understood the same passages of scripture so differently as to destroy all confidence in settling the question by an appeal to the Bible."[10] The production of the Book of Mormon provided a supplemental authoritative scriptural text. Latter-day Saints believed that the "seeker for truth" could make an appeal with confidence to an augmented canon of scriptures "untainted" by the agenda of the gentile "apostate" church.

However, an independent work of scripture containing "the covenants of the Lord which he hath made unto the house of Israel; and . . . the prophecies of the holy prophets" (1 Ne. 13:23) was not enough for Smith. Haunted by the Book of Mormon's vision of a flawed biblical text and confidant of his powers displayed in the production of the Book of Mormon, Smith set out three months after the book's publication to "revise" the text of the Authorized or King James Version of the Bible and supply those "plain and precious" aspects of the text which had been excised or neglected. An examination of what is known among Latter-day Saints as Smith's "Inspired Version of the Bible" (or JST) provides further insights into Smith's understanding of God's Israel.[11]

From June 1830 through July 1833, Smith periodically labored upon his "plainer translation." Reading the King James Bible, he would mark problematic or highly suggestive passages for correction, emendation, or the insertion of extended narratives. Subsequently these revisions would be dictated to a scribe. At his death the work stood uncompleted. Due to the draft-like nature of extant proofs and to the unusual nature of this "translation" which ultimately eludes classification,[12] it has yet to supplant the Authorized Version as the text officially sanctioned for use in LDS meetings and literature.

However, these qualifications do not diminish the importance of the Inspired Version a textual source for understanding the early development of Mormon thought and practice. Robert J. Matthews in his detailed studies of the Inspired Version has pointed out the chronological and doctrinal congruence between Smith's work on the Bible and doctrinal revelations he received which were quickly accorded authoritative status and worked into the Doctrine and Covenants,

Mormonism's third canonical text. Calling the revelations "consequences" and not merely coincidences of the revision, Matthews has written that "The Prophet's work of translation of the Bible . . . was the means and process . . . for the reception of many revelations of the doctrines of the gospel in the very early days of this dispensation."[13] These doctrines were various: the antemortal existence of Jesus Christ and the human family, the nature and duration of matter, the economic order of the church, the nature and composition of the church's various lay priesthood quorums, ethics in time of conflict, and interpretation of beasts and sealed books in the Apocalypse of John (D&C 76, 84, 93, 104, 107, 132).

In addition to these revelations and writings spun off from the work of translating, the textual revisions themselves disclose many of Smith's principal concerns in the church's early years. His agenda included more than creating a sect or denomination. Restoration would mean as well building a holy city of refuge for a nation and a people of priests upon a territory sanctified by covenant. There the fruits and obligations of covenants and priesthood and the knowledge of heaven and earth from all ages past and present would be enjoyed in a society without caste and want. Only the grand configurations of an extraordinary template could harmonize multifarious Mormon converts into a passionately hopeful and intricately articulated whole.

Joseph Smith's revisions of the Bible underlined that the narratives of gathering and covenant as related in Hebrew Scriptures provided a prototype and warrant for Latter-day Saints. The Book of Mormon had provided some answers about the nature of the relationship which would exist between the Latter-day Saints and the rest of covenant Israel. But the revision of the Bible also elaborated the connection between Israel and the Saints. Smith introduced several crucial narrative expansions into otherwise terse biblical accounts from the lives of Israel's patriarchs. These included fully wrought apocalypses attributed to Enoch, Abraham, and Moses as well as generous portraitures of Adam, Enoch, and the enigmatic cultic priest/king Melchisedek.[14] These additions consistently emphasized a parallel between ancient Israel and the restored church and gospel of the Saints.

Enoch, who figures either as a cipher in genealogical tables or as a mysterious, transfigured mortal in the accepted scriptural canon, becomes in Smith's account the father of all gatherings and prototypical high priest. He is the exemplar of all those who enter into covenant with the Lord (JST Gen. 13:13; 14:24). It is Enoch who lays the foundations and builds the first city of Zion, where the righteous of his generation gather. Smith's text takes pains to underscore the literal, spatial nature of this original gathering under Enoch's tutelage and leadership (JST Gen. 6:22-7:78).[15] In Latter-day Saint eschatology, the city of Enoch and the Mormon Zion will "wed" on the eve of the Millennium (Eth. 13:2-6, Moses 7:62-64; Rev. 21:9-10).

Abraham's call out of Haran and his pilgrimage toward and through the patrimony of his covenant is elaborated upon as another case in the extended tale of gathering. For Smith it is the gathering of covenant people which constitutes the essential skeletal frame upon which the flesh of Israel's narrative is hung. These ancient struggles with and devotion to God's covenantal purposes pointed to the continuing relevance of such practices for contemporary Mormons. In Enoch's initial reticence to shoulder his prophetic task and in the opposition which his work generated, in Abraham's wanderings and sacrifices, each Latter-day Saint could find striking scriptural parallels to the perils through which he or she had to pass.

A significant textual variant is introduced in the account of the bestowal of patriarchal blessings by Jacob on his sons which similarly emphasizes such parallels. Jacob rehearses for his son Joseph the blessings and promises of covenant pronounced on the former by the Lord in Canaan. Ephraim and Manasseh are adopted as sons and accorded an equal status among Israel's other male progeny (JST Gen. 48:5-7). The role of Joseph in the deliverance of Jacob's family is extolled with the promise given him that the "God of thy fathers shall bless thee, and the fruit of thy loins, that they shall be blessed above thy brethren, and thy father's house. . . . Thy brethren shall bow down to thee . . . [for] thou shalt be a light unto my people, to deliver them in the days of their captivity from bondage" (JST Gen. 48:9-11). The importance of this passage for Joseph Smith and his followers is disclosed in Genesis 50, where a lengthy variation is inserted into the established text. This chapter deals with Jacob's favorite, Joseph. It is his filial piety, his magnanimity toward errant brothers, his memory which are praised. But a nineteenth-century namesake would make that chapter bear a profounder burden.

Beginning in the twenty-fourth verse in Smith's version, the dying Joseph delivers a series of prophetic statements and predictions bearing an uncanny resemblance, first, to major events and figures in Israel's bondage to and exodus from Egypt (JST Gen. 50:24, 29, 34-35) and, second, to a much later and far distant religious landscape strikingly similar to that staked out by Mormons (JST Gen. 50:26-28, 30-33, 36).

Of particular note is the way in which two separate histories, one for the "fruit of the loins of Judah" (v. 31) and one for the "fruit of my [Joseph's] loins" (v. 24), are plotted out in two distinctly separate narrative lines and in two separate territories. Joseph first assures his brethren that "the God of my father Jacob [will] be with you to deliver you out of affliction in the days of your bondage" (v. 24). A seer and prophet would be raised from Israel's midst to liberate them from servitude, and the

Lord would protect Israel's seed forever (v. 34). "The fruit of the loins of Judah shall write" (v. 31) narratives and doctrine which would protect Israel's identity by keeping it in remembrance of its covenants which called it into being.

But the patriarch also speaks of a "branch" of the house of Israel, which "shall be broken off and . . . carried into a far country" (v. 25). This branch comes from among Joseph's offspring, and although separated from their brethren, "they shall be remembered in the covenants of the Lord" (v. 25). To this scattered group in the "latter days" would the Lord bring a "choice seer," who plays a crucial role in re-establishing among Joseph's issue a "knowledge of the covenants which I have made with thy father" (vv. 27-28, 30). At that day the writings of this distant band and their choice seer would be joined with those of the "loins of Judah." Together their records "shall grow together unto the confounding of false doctrines, and the laying down of contentions, and establish peace among the fruit of thy loins, bringing them to a knowledge of their fathers in the latter days; and also . . . of my covenants, saith the Lord" (v. 31). That choice seer's name incidentally would be "Joseph, and it shall be after the name of his father" (v. 33).

Through the introduction of such independent material into the biblical text, Joseph Smith, Jr., sought to produce that warrant which would establish the consanguinity of Hebrew scriptures, Book of Mormon, and the Latter-day Saint undertaking. In that "branch . . . carried into a far country," Mormons could detect reference to Nephites and sense their own distinctive contribution.

Mormons claimed that the writings of the Nephites had been carefully preserved and cached away like the copper and parchment scrolls of the Qumran community. Once unearthed these records would be a catalyst for righteousness and renewal. To distant offspring and to the righteous among the gentiles, that record would be carried through the work of the "choice seer" of Joseph's loins, his latter-day namesake and alter ego. His work and writings would come together with the work and writings of an ascendant Judah in the last days before the messianic era. At the same time, but in two distinct territories, covenant peoples would establish anticipatory kingdoms for the whole household of Israel's sons and daughters (JST Gen. 50:31).

Thus Smith turned to the Hebrew scriptures for the framework, the terms and institutions, of his life's work. Mormon historian Gordon Irving points out that "it was largely the Old Testament patriarchs who were chosen to personify gospel principles . . . including the gathering of the elect, . . . [and] the importance of the covenantal relationship of God with Israel."[16] Smith was drawn to Israel's saga of gathering, its commitment to a consecrated territorial inheritance, its witness to election and covenant, and its belief in a personal God who enters into agreements as one of the contractual parties. Israel's traditional insistence on the corporal unity of body and spirit, its institutions of temple and priesthood, and the historical, corporate, public nature of its covenantal life inspired Smith.

Indeed it was the "judaizing"—Smith's and his most ardent disciples' this-worldliness, their attention to finite, concrete tasks of kingdom building—which brought upon them an avalanche of gentile outrage and which precipitated scores of defections out of Mormon ranks by disoriented primitivists.[17] At the same time that Smith spoke unfailingly of the integrity of God's covenant with Israel, he routinely ridiculed Christian proselyting societies and their efforts to convert Jewish people. Smith was profoundly alienated from institutional Christianity. The estrangement of the Mormon community from Christendom was apparent to "gentile" Christians. Charles Wordsworth, archdeacon of Westminster Abbey, summed up the opposition of churchmen to Mormonism and its emphasis on a this-worldly Zion in a sermon delivered in that great abbey. His remarks were leveled at Smith's successors and disciples in the Great Basin, but similar criticism was directed at Smith in the earliest years of the church. "It was," he intoned, "the duty of Christ's ministers to dispel the dreams of self-idolizing delusions." The fields and orchards of Mormon settlements "do indeed gratify the eye." And as the result of human industry, "they indeed have their uses, manifold and great. But: let us not be dazzled by them, they cannot regenerate the world; they do not constitute the true grandeur and genuine strength of a nation; that is of the heart, of the soul, and of the spirit; it is not of the earth, earthy; but of heaven, heavenly; it is not of man, but of God; it is not of Time, but Eternity."[18]

For their part, early Latter-day Saints did little to bridge the barriers which separated them from such mainstream Christian values and expectations. Instead they self-consciously cultivated their estrangement from the gentile Christian world.[19] In Mormon eyes that landscape was barren, incapable of sustaining the vigorous shoot of restoration. Mormon writers riposted gentile charges of fostering a "social Gomorrah"[20] and "sensual voluptuousness" by ridiculing the "absurdities of immaterialism"[21] in traditional Christian metaphysics and by preaching the essential continuum of sacred and secular spheres. As if to underscore their philosophical disagreement with the metaphysicians, Mormon apostles ritually hewed, carried, and placed the first log of their city at the heart of the Zion they were commanded to establish.[22]

Smith's "translation" of the Bible text "restored" statements by Jesus to his disciples which supported Mormon commitments. Variants are introduced to the Sermon on the Mount which strengthen the Mormon doctrinal commitment to a this-worldly messianic kingdom. It is not enough to "seek ye first the kingdom of God" (KJV Matt. 6:33). Rather "seek not the things of this world but seek ye first to build up the kingdom of God and to establish his righteousness." Similarly the King James version of Luke's statement "the kingdom of God is within you" is altered in Smith's revision to "the Kingdom of God has already come unto you" (JST Luke 17:21). Smith's revised text consistently renders in concrete terms passages in which the nature of God's kingdom is hedged with ambiguity or interiorizing.

Mormons believed that the kingdom's boundaries as limned by the doctrines of the gentile church had been outrageously gerrymandered: aimless, vaguely universal, a matter of the heart alone, partaking of a realm beyond time, toil, and tears. The messianic/millennial kingdom had been killed by a thousand qualifications. Accordingly Smith reworded the "parable of the vineyard" in Matthew 21 to include the precipitous downfall of a second set of stewards, "And when the Lord therefore of the vineyard cometh [a second time], he will destroy those . . . wicked men, and will let again his vineyard unto other husbandmen, even in the last days, who shall render him the fruits in their season." He added this scriptural gloss: "And then understood they the parable which he spoke unto them, that the *Gentiles* should be destroyed."[23]

Despite such reservations about Christianity, early Mormon perceptions of Jewish people and Judaism were mediated by the canon of Christian scripture and filtered through the common opinion of Smith's contemporaries informed over the centuries by anti-Judaic theologies and anti-Jewish prejudice. Smith believed that the Jews were the Lord's "ancient covenant people." That description in Smith's hands, however, did not mean outdated or supplanted. Still, it is clear that Smith was ignorant of the history of Jewish life and thought since 70 C.E. His knowledge of Israel before the rise of

Christianity was filtered through the Hebrew scriptures, as read through the Apostolic writings, and finally through his own agenda for the Latter-day Saints. It would be the mid-1830s before Smith and associates began to confront the reality of a contemporary Jewish people unmediated by the veil of scripture. Thus the Christian reading of the controversy between the early church and Rabbinic Judaism can be seen as the interpretive frame for a number of Smith's revisions of the Bible focusing on the covenant with ancient Israel.

As early as Genesis 17, Smith's version manifests its particular concern with covenant. Abraham had been singled out for his righteousness and enjoined to "walk uprightly before [the Lord], and be perfect" (JST Gen. 17:1). He is established by covenant and endowed with land, progeny, and paternity. Yet according to Smith's variant reading, the Lord speaks darkly of other individuals and people having "gone astray from my precepts . . . and not kept mine ordinances, which I gave unto their fathers" (v. 4).

Covenants of accountability, as distinguished from the unilateral and unconditional covenant extended to Noah, as recorded in Genesis 9, extend in Smith's Inspired Version back through the beginnings of the "patriarchy" and are established between willing parties, one divine and one mortal (JST Gen. 9:15, 21). Abraham is given to know that for him and his descendants, the physical mark of the intimacy and exclusivity of this divine-human contract (circumsion) would be required to denote assent. Other families of covenant preceeding Abraham have "turned from the commandments" (JST Gen. 17:6) and have thus forfeited their claims. All those who claim Abraham as father are warned that realizing the terms of the covenant is contingent on covenantal fidelity.

In Smith's revision, the terms of Israel's election in such passages as Deuteronomy 4:5, 6 and 7:6-9 and also

Leviticus 11:44-45 stood without emendation or correction. Israel had been chosen by a "faithful God" to be his "precious possession . . . to a thousand generations." However, Israel's people must love, serve, and keep the commandments of the God who had elected them and given them a homeland. If it failed, Israel would be cursed and scattered among the nations (Deut. 4:25-28; 29:10-28).

Confronting these biblical passages and the reality of Israel's exile among the nations in the early nineteenth century compelled Smith to assign Israel's scattered condition to its transgression of covenant. His translation burrowed into the sources of Israel's commitment to covenant, so honestly assessed by the writers and prophets of the Hebrew scriptures. According to Smith's textual variant of Exodus 34 and Deuteronomy 10:1, 2, Israel's practice of idolatry in Moses' absence altered the terms upon which the Lord had intended their relationship to be established. The Lord had called all Israel to be "a kingdom of priests, and an holy nation" (Ex. 19:6). Moses bore with him the tables of that hieratic constitution whereby all Israel would have been inducted into the holy priesthood. Thereafter all of Israel's worthy sons and daughters would have entered into the Lord's presence along with Moses.

Unlike the reading given this event in the Midrash Rabbah on Exodus, the breaking of the tables and the production of another pair meant less for Israel in Joseph Smith's variant rather than more.[24] Because of transgression, the "democratization" of the priesthood initially envisaged was amended. The priesthood was taken away "out of their midst" (JST Gen. 34:1-2), and the Lord swore in his "wrath that they shall not enter into my presence." The "law as at the first" was instead renewed and the priesthood severely restricted to a limited order of officiates of the cult.

In the Smith variant covenant, law, and priesthood are without doubt divine gifts. The sectaries of the Book of Mormon, claiming descent from this assembly at Sinai, wrote of their reverence and esteem for what was bestowed upon Israel. But there is an unmistakable sense of diminishment in what was finally bestowed according to Smith's revision. That sense of diminishment is accompanied by the conviction in the narratives which follow Israel's camp through the wilderness into Canaan and through the period of tribal confederacy, monarchy, and gentile occupation that no small measure of Israel's misfortune can be laid to its failure to enter the sanctuary as a people.

Given such emphasis on the law and covenant, it is ironic that when Smith came to "revise" the Apostolic Writings, or "New" Testament, the controversy between Jesus and the Pharisees is heightened rather than muted. The pharisaic party, which championed the learning and observance of the law as a means of forging a "nation of priests" and to which Jesus was in fact quite close, is cast as deviant from Torah. According to Smith's revision, if the Pharisees had really understood the Torah, they would have recognized in Jesus of Nazareth the goal of Torah. "We have Moses and the prophets," they say. To this Jesus replies, "Ye know not Moses, neither the prophets; for if ye had known them, ye would have believed on me; for to this intent they were written. For I am sent that ye might have life" (JST Luke 14:36). Elsewhere Pharisees are lumped indiscriminately with scribes, priests, and levites, who "teach in their synagogues, but do not observe the law, nor observe the commandments; and all have gone out of the way, and are under sin" (JST Matt. 7:4; see also JST Matt. 9:16).

In a letter dated 4 January 1833 written to the editor of a newspaper, Smith implies that Jesus' fellow Jews faced another Sinai in the person and "ministry" of the

Nazarene. A covenant was offered, "but they rejected him and his proposals and in consequence thereof they were broken off and no covenant was made with them at that time." However, Smith holds out the hope that the "time has at last arrived when the God of Abraham of Isaac and of Jacob has set his hand again the second time to recover the remnants of his people . . . with them to bring in the fulness of the Gentiles and establish that covenant with them which was promised when their sins should be taken away. See Romans 11:25, 26 & 27 and also Jeremiah 31:31, 32 & 33."[25]

In this early formulation Smith locates himself within the ranks of Christian millennialists of the early decades of the nineteenth century: the hopes of a gathering of scattered Israel, the culmination of the "times of gentiles," the eschatological covenant of Jeremiah and its reiteration in Romans 11 were all common citations from the generous stock of millennialist assumptions.

That such a reading implicitly located Smith and the Mormons within the Christian context even as he emphasizes the Mormon connection to ancient Israel helps to explain their distance from Judaism as well as Christianity. Although the Mormon sense of kinship with God's Israel was profound, the route of conversion to Judaism was never an option for most Mormons. Smith and his disciples did not follow ex-Quaker, ex-Mormon Warder Cresson's example and convert to Judaism.[26] Such a course was precluded by lingering ties to various Christian traditions and communities, by selective appropriation of both "testaments" of the Bible, and by the explicit Christocentrism of the Book of Mormon. The risen, living Christ was experienced as the source of most of Smith's revelations. Further, Mormons felt no need to convert to Judaism because they identified themselves as among the "seed" of Israel's patriarchs. Beginning with Smith, Mormons were informed they were of "the children of Israel, and of the seed of Abraham" (D&C 84:34, 103:17, 132:31).[27] They were among the "heirs" of the Abrahamic covenant either "according to the flesh" (D&C 86:9) or by "adoption." Either way they were enjoined to "Go ye, therefore, and do the works of Abraham." In joining the infant Latter-day Saint church, converts saw themselves as crossing into the house of Israel.[28]

But for all of Smith's sense of kinship with the Lord's scattered Israel, he did not conceive his fraternal role as one of deference. This stance he shared with his namesake, Jacob's favorite. Smith's claims as prophet and seer had been legitimated by a sheaf of revelations and inspired scriptural revisions. He had produced a book attributed to Hebraic sectaries in the New World (the Book of Mormon), apocalypses ascribed to Enoch and Moses (Pearl of Great Price), and a textual revision of the Bible.

For Latter-day Saints, this work confirmed the authority of their prophet and the independence of their religious movement within the crowded religious field of antebellum America. The reasons for Smith distancing himself and his movement from both Christianity and Judaism becomes clear. He was attempting to create a separate religious community, at once profoundly Christian and related to biblical Israel but independent from both. Smith and his associates were drawing up a new map of faith and practice by means of an alternative sighting of bodies celestial, earthly, and textual. Revelatory instructions from heavenly emissaries; the physical gathering of an elect people to a designated covenantal inheritance to be won through exodus and city building; the creation of new scripture, textual variants of received texts, and dissident readings of holy writ—all came together to enfranchise previously marginalized religious seekers.

From the beginning of his revelatory experiences, Smith was enjoined to remain apart from "all the sects . . . for they all were wrong . . . [and] all their creeds were an abomination."[29] However, withdrawing fellowship was not enough. The Saints were commanded to "go ye out of Babylon . . . out from among the nations" and to "gather ye together, O ye people of my church, upon the land of Zion" (D&C 133:4-7). In other words the Mormons set out to recapitulate ancient Israel's biblical saga. Israel's record—its tale of a promised land, its judges, kings, prophets, exodus, temple building, and priesthood—provided both textual warrant and proper forms for the Saints establishing their own kingdom.

During this period Smith had also penned a number of revelations tied to specific occasions. Some are connected to his work on the Bible revision. Of these, a small number of significant passages further disclose Smith's understanding of the Jewish people and the nature of the configuration of Latter-day Saints and covenant Israel. These revelations confirm the impulse demonstrated by Smith's revisions—towards a new tradition which comes out of a Christian context but emphasizes its literal connection to the Lord's covenant with Israel and to concrete events which will realize the terms of that covenant.

Many of Smith's closest associates had had intimate ties with the then fashionable preoccupation with the book of Revelation ascribed to John the Apostle, and to the events of the last days. Smith inherited certain exegetical assumptions about "prophetic" passages of scripture which ostensibly dealt with the destiny of the Jewish people. For example, his use of passages from Zechariah 12 and 13 as translated in the Authorized Version and from the book of Revelation confirm standard readings of these passages and their awesome events. According to the standard Christian reading, a stunning succession of eschatological events would culminate with the spectacle of the returning Risen Christ in the "time of his power," who would deliver Jerusalem and the gathered Jewish inhabitants from an arrayed host of enemies. His triumph would be crowned through his acclamation by his now willing kinsfolk as Messiah, son of David.[30]

During his career, as one scholar of Mormonism has written, "interest in the millennium reached a high point among British and American Christians. . . . conferences, sermons, books, plans, and reforms of every sort were oriented around the biblical prophecies of a reign of righteousness."[31] Turning to the Apocalypse of John as a way to gauge and interpret the times was a ubiquitous reflex among almost all Christians of Smith's era. In an anonymous compilation of millennialist prophecies and commentaries from Great Britain and the continent reprinted in Philadelphia and sold out in a week, the editor sounded a commonly accepted tenet of belief: "The Revelation of St. John, or rather of *Jesus Christ* to him, contains the most full and important series of prophecies ever bestowed on mankind; extending from the close of the first century of Christianity . . . to the end of time."[32]

In March 1832 Smith penned a revelation in the form of a completed questionnaire dealing with some of the enigmas embedded in this "most full and important series of prophecies" (D&C 77). For those among the Saints agitated by the thunder and trumpets of the approaching apocalypse and by the obscure runes strewn through John's text, Smith's contribution would probably have been disappointing. Absent in this interpretation is the rapt attention to temporal details which was the bread and butter of annotators and expositors of the Bible. Smith makes no attempt to synchronize events of the past, present, and future with the elusive figures of John's apocalyptic vision. Rather the hermeneutical principle directing the matter-of-fact cadences of Joseph's revelation was not *temporality* but *gathering*.[33] Smith consistently emphasizes *space* rather than *time*. Whereas other diviners of Revelation invariably identified its seraphic messengers as heralds of a new spiritual order of the universal church, Joseph stubbornly insisted on the independence and literal nature of two messianic centers established in the latter days.

Thus the angel "ascending from the east" in Revelation 7:2, "if you will receive it . . . is Elias which was to come to gather together the tribes of Israel and restore all things" (v. 15). The book eaten by John in the "10th chapter of Revelation" is the "mission" and "ordinance" of Elias to gather and restore Israel (v. 14). Until that holy ordinance is performed, the four eschatological heralds "sent forth from God, to whom [are] given power over the four parts of the earth, to save and destroy" are held in check by "Elias" who abjures them to "Hurt not the earth neither the seas, nor the trees." Thus the prerogatives of the gathering of Israel take precedence over the advancing season of millennial harvest (vv. 8, 9).

Some medieval apocalyptics saw in the "oriental" angel of Revelation 7:2 a "new leader . . . ascend[ing] from Babylon, namely a universal pontiff of the New Jerusalem, that is, of Holy Mother the Church."[34] Nineteenth-century prophetic expositors divined such heavenly messengers as either the Lord's millennial night watchmen tolling the last moments before the eschaton or as symbols of the new, evangelical spirit "inspiring the contemporary European and American Missionary and Bible societies . . . having the everlasting gospel to preach to all the world . . . until the world is won to Christ."[35] In contrast Smith understood such agents as heralds of the end of Israel's bitter exile and of its gathering to its covenantal patrimonies.

References in the prophetic writing to Jerusalem and Israel were taken literally by Smith and made him reluctant to give the text a "spiritual" reading. By common practice the well-nigh universal reading of Revelation 11 by Christians had transformed the specificity of the theater of operations of the text from Jerusalem to some troubled nation within the sphere of Christendom. Hence the "holy city," site of the martyrdom of the two "witnesses," becomes in turn revolutionary France, apostate western Christianity, or the site of a "worldwide suppression of religious freedom and human rights." As to the witnesses themselves, they are variously "faithful Christian ministers," the Old and New Testaments, protestants in general, the "Words and Ordinances of the Lord," "the fugitive church in exile for 1260 days," "witnesses against Rome," "the true church," "the faithful of all ages," or "unknown and figurative."[36]

Here Smith could have safely entered the ranks of Christian commentators by abstracting and universalizing Jerusalem and the latter-day witnesses or by appending to them explicitly nineteenth-century Christian attributes and evangelical zeal. Such a move would have reassured readers habituated to traditional exegesis. In addition it surely would have gratified the many students of the apocalyptic preoccupied with the detailed temporal analysis so fashionable in prophetic circles. But Smith demurs. In the streets of the city of Jerusalem would walk "two witnesses," not ministers or books or persecuted Christian sects or the faithful in all ages, but "two prophets that are to be raised up to the Jewish nation in the last days, at the time of the restoration, [who] prophecy to the Jews after they are gathered and have built the city of Jerusalem in the land of their fathers" (D&C 77:15). Smith never recommends enlightening benighted Jews by favoring them with the "gospel in its fulness," the way his associate and counselor Oliver Cowdery would have it.

Revelations and letters written at that time by Smith also stress the geographical specificity of the gathering.

In November 1831 he had warned, "Let them, therefore, who are among the Gentiles flee unto Zion. And let them who be of Judah flee unto Jerusalem, unto the mountains of the Lord's house" (D&C 133:12, 13). "In this day of calamity," he wrote to *Evening and Morning Star* editor W. W. Phelps, the need of Israel and its adopted kinsfolk for a "place of refuge and of safety" had been provided by their Lord.[37] To N. C. Saxton on 4 January 1833, Joseph mined the Hebrew scriptures for prooftexts pointing to two great independent locations for gathering: "The City of Zion, spoken of by David in the 102 Psalm will be built upon the land of America and the ransomed of the Lord shall return and come to it with songs and everlasting joy upon their heads. . . . But the tribe of Judah will return to old Jerusalem . . . [and] shall obtain deliverance at Jerusalem. See Joel 2:32, Isaiah 26:20, 21, Jer. 31:12, Psalm 50:5, Ezekiel 34:11, 12, 13. These are testimonies that the good Shepherd will lead them out from all nations where they have been scattered in a cloudy and dark day, to Zion and to Jerusalem."[38]

Hence just over a year after his excursus in John's apocalyptic text Joseph Smith was made to understand by way of revelation that it was incumbent that the hearts of Israel be animated by the faith and promises of their prophets and that the eschatological vision of Israel's prophets be realized in a gathered and restored Israel, "lest [the Lord] come and smite the whole earth with a curse" (D&C 98:17). The "mission and ordinance of Elias" were to be performed by latter-day messengers "raised up to the Jewish nation" and to the righteous among the gentiles, similarly bidden to gather. Separately, independently, these peoples were to establish cities and lands of covenantal sanctuary wherein the "tabernacle of God" would dwell and thus hold the curse in check.

In a later return to Revelation, Smith again read the text to support his vision. His open letter "To the Elders of the Church of the Latter-day Saints" in September 1835 employs John's vision of the New Jerusalem (Rev. 21:2, 3) to confirm his doctrine, "Behold the tabernacle of God is with men, the elect must be gathered from the four quarters of the earth."[39] He then elicits prooftexts from Deuteronomy 30:1-4, 7 and the Book of Mormon[40] to support his case for the gathering, its literal fulfillment, and its double location.

Gathering was thus the pressing issue in Smith's life.[41] The task of the Saints was to gather the scattered members of the Lord's gentile vessel. The fruit of their labors would be a city, the New Jerusalem raised by human hands, established on "this continent by way of distinction to the ones to be rebuilt on the eastern continent."[42] The Saints were not to obstruct the independent reassembly of Israel's scattered vessel. Smith also understood that his church and its priesthood could assist in Israel's physical ingathering through the prayers of the righteous and their own acts of gathering and temple building.

For many Christians the logical step following from such emphasis on restoration and gathering in the last days would be emphasis on conversion. As one scholar of the period has written, "the reorganization of the Society to Promote Christianity Among the Jews brought the concept of the restoration and conversion of the Jews sharply to the forefront, and for a time its warmest advocates were the premillennialists of Britain and the Continent—including such men as Way, Marsh, M'Neile, Pym and Noel. In fact, this was one of the most prominent characteristics of the entire group of British expositors." The "molding influence" of these commentators in America was considerable.[43]

Some of Joseph Smith's closest associates came to the same focus on conversion. In the early 1830s Oliver

Cowdery was "associate" president of the church with Smith. He wrote that the restoration of Israel would be according to the "new covenant" of Jeremiah: having "forsaken the Lord . . . worshipping other gods, which were no gods," they would yet "know the voice of the Shepherd . . . [and] be favored with the gospel in its fulness."[44] Sidney Rigdon, once an influential minister in the Campbellite movement, was converted to Mormonism and called to be "a spokesman unto my Servant Joseph." Rigdon wrote in January 1834 about Israel's restoration. It would, he believed, be wrought "not by virtue of any previous covenant with the house of Israel but by one which was to be made with the house of Israel and the house of Judah in the last days. . . . The house of Israel in the last days, was to be taught by a people of stammering lips and another tongue. . . . In former days they had enlightened the Gentiles: in latter days the Gentiles were to enlighten them."[45]

For Cowdery and Rigdon, as well as most contemporary prophetical expositors and evangelists, the necessary corollary of the gathering of the Jewish people was their conversion to "the gospel in its fulness." Though Joseph Smith was in these early years eclipsed by the learning and polish of his second elder, Cowdery, and of his counselor, Rigdon, he was reluctant to draw their confident conclusions.

Instead Smith reread the Apocalypse of John in such a way as to re-interpret the triumph of the church. By focusing on the restoration of sacred, covenantal space and on "the elect" to inhabit two sanctuaries an ocean and continents apart, he contributed to an understanding of the Lord as the good shepherd of both Christians and Jews. This was perhaps the figure most felicitously appropriate to embody Smith's concern with and belief in the necessity of gathering Jews and righteous gentiles. Where some of his closest allies would turn this image into a conventional conversionist representation, no doubt to gratify and legitimate what they considered to be the task of the Church of the Latter-day Saints, Smith's use of the good shepherd of the parable remained more humble, more realistic, and perhaps more akin to its source. It was not the church but the Lord who would reign.

NOTES

1. George J. Adams, *A Few Plain Facts, Showing the Folly, Wickedness, and Imposition of the Rev. Timothy R. Matthews, Also a Short Sketch of the Rise, Faith and Doctrine of the Church of Jesus Christ of Latter-day Saints* (Bedford, Eng.: C. B. Merry, 1841), 13.

2. A strategy which Moses Martin derisively characterized as "so fashionable in this generation." Moses Martin, *A Treatise on the Fulness of the Everlasting Gospel, Setting Forth its First Principles, Promises and Blessings...* (New York: J. W. Harrison, 1842), 9.

3. Samuel Hopkins, for example, believed that the mass conversion of the Jews would resolve the great mystery of their survival: "The ends of their being preserved in such a state of distinction will then be answered.... When they shall become Christians, their name by which they are now distinguished will be lost, and they will be absorbed in the Christian Church, the true Israel of God . . . [where] all are one in Christ" (330). From "A Treatise on the Millennium," in *The Works of Samuel Hopkins*, vol. 2 (Boston: Doctrinal Tract and Book Society, 1852).

4. William Appleby, *A Few Important Questions for the Reverend Clergy to Answer, Being a Scale to Weigh Priestcraft and Sectarianism* (Philadelphia: Brown, Bicking & Guibert, 1843), 8.

5. Adams, *A Few Plain Facts*, 13.

6. Martin, *A Treatise on the Everlasting Gospel*, 50. The importance of the citations from Adams, Martin, and Appleby resides in their not being part of the inner circle of Smith's intimate colleagues and the front rank in the leadership of the church. They were lay missionaries who in their pamphlets

reflect the degree to which rank-and-file in the church agreed upon certain exegetical ground rules.

7. *Teachings of the Prophet Joseph Smith. . . .*, ed. Joseph Fielding Smith (Salt Lake City: Deseret Book, 1977), 9-10. From a statement made on 16 February 1832 while "translating" the Bible.

8. Adams, *A Few Plain Facts,* 13.

9. From Tract no. 598, *Mormonism* (London: Religious Tract Society, 1850?), 8.

10. "Joseph Smith—History: Extracts from the History of Joseph Smith, the Prophet," in *The Pearl of Great Price* (Salt Lake City: Church of Jesus Christ of Latter-day Saints, 1981), 48.

11. For studies of Smith's "Inspired Version," see Robert J. Matthews, *"A Plainer Translation": Joseph Smith's Translation of the Bible: A History and Commentary* (Provo, UT: Brigham Young University Press, 1975); Stephen R. Knecht, *The Story of Joseph Smith's Bible Translation: A Documented History* (Salt Lake City: Associated Research Consultants Publication, 1977); Reed C. Durham, Jr., "A History of Joseph Smith's Revision of the Bible," Ph.d. diss., Brigham Young University, 1965; *The Joseph Smith Translation: The Restoration of Plain and Precious Things,* eds. Monte S. Nyman and Robert L. Millet, Religious Studies Monograph Series, vol. 12 (Provo, UT: Religious Studies Center, 1985).

12. "We do not have the information or requisite tools . . . to obtain the information needed to establish empirically what parts are restoration, what parts commentary, and what parts simply the result of good judgments." Matthews, *A Plainer Translation,* 253.

13. Robert J. Matthews, "A Walk Through the Bible," 31st annual Joseph Smith Lectures, Utah State University, 9 Dec. 1973, 8, archives, Historical Department, Church of Jesus Christ of Latter-day Saints, Salt Lake City. See also *A Plainer Translation,* 256.

14. Collected in the Books of Moses and Abraham in the Pearl of Great Price. See Gen. 14:17, 22, 25-40 in *The Holy Scriptures: Corrected by the Spirit of Revelation, by Joseph Smith, Jr.* (Independence, MO: Herald Publishing House, 1936); hereafter JST.

15. See also Hugh Nibley, *Enoch the Prophet: The Collected Works of Hugh Nibley,* ed. Stephen C. Ricks, vol. 2 (Salt Lake City: Deseret Book Company, 1986).

16. Gordon Irving, "The Mormons and the Bible in the 1830s," *Brigham Young University Studies* 13 (Summer 1973): 475.

17. Marvin S. Hill, "Cultural Crisis in the Mormon Kingdom: A Reconsideration of the Causes of the Kirtland Dissent," *Church History* 49 (Sept. 1980): 286-97.

18. Charles Wordsworth, *Mormonism and England: A Sermon Preached in Westminster Abbey on Sunday, July 28, 1867* (London: Gilbert & Rivington, 1867), 17-18.

19. Having survived the first winter in the valley of the Great Salt Lake, Parley P. Pratt, one of the twelve apostles and early Mormonism's most important pamphleteer, used the occasion of his eldest son's birthday to underscore LDS particularism: "After dinner, in presence of the assembled family, I related the circumstances of his being a promised child, with an account of his birth, his history, and the death of his mother. . . . I rehearsed to him my own sufferings, and the sufferings of my family, and of the Church while in the States—telling him of the murder of our prophets and Saints, and how we had been driven to the mountains, robbed and plundered of a very large amount of property and possessions. The day was spent most pleasantly and profitably by all." *Autobiography of Parley P. Pratt,* ed. Parley P. Pratt, Jr., 8th ed. (Salt Lake City: Deseret Book, 1976), 362.

20. Wordsworth's felicitous title; Wordsworth, *Mormonism and England,* 9.

21. Orson Pratt, "The Absurdities of Immaterialism," *Millennial Star* 11 (15 May-15 Oct. 1849).

22. For an account, see Joseph Smith, *History of the Church of Jesus Christ of Latter-day Saints,* ed. B. H. Roberts, 7 volumes (Salt Lake City: Church of Jesus Christ of Latter-day Saints, 1927-32), 1:196-99; hereafter cited as HC. See also JST Matt. 21 and JST Luke 23:31.

23. JST Matt. 21:48; see also JST Luke 23:3.

24. Midrash Rabbah on Exodus reads, "Do not grieve about the first tables. They only contained the Ten Commandments, but in the two Tablets I am about to give thee now, there will

also be laws, Midrash and Haggadah." *Midrash Rabbah: Exodus*, ed. H. Freedman and Maurice Simon, vol. 3 (London: The Soncino Press, 1961), 427.

25. Letter to N. E. Saxton published in *The Personal Writings of Joseph Smith*, ed. Dean C. Jessee (Salt Lake City: Deseret Book, 1984), 274.

26. See Warder Cresson, *The Key of David* (1852; reprt. New York: Arno Press, 1977).

27. Revelations dated 22 Sept. 1832, 24 Feb. 1834, 12 July 1843.

28. On "adoption" and Mormon ties to Ephraim and Joseph, see Melodie Moench, "Nineteenth Century Mormons: The New Israel," *Dialogue: A Journal of Mormon Thought* 12 (Spring 1979): 42-54. For a twentieth-century working of this subject along quasi-official lines, see *Doctrines of Salvation: Sermons and Writings of Joseph Fielding Smith*, comp. Bruce R. McConkie (Salt Lake City: Bookcraft, 1972), 2:250-51, 3:246-53.

29. "Joseph Smith—History," Pearl of Great Price, 49.

30. D&C 45 (7 Mar. 1831); 133:8-10, 16, 18, 35 (3 Nov. 1831); *The Latter Day Saints' Evening and Morning Star*, Aug. 1832.

31. Richard Bushman, *Joseph Smith and the Beginnings of Mormonism* (Urbana: University of Illinois Press, 1984), 170.

32. From "Prophetic Conjectures on the French Revolution," cited in Leroy Edwin Froom, *The Prophetic Faith of Our Fathers: The Historical Development of Prophetic Interpretations*, 4 vols. (Washington, D.C.: Review and Herald, 1946), 3:108.

33. Robert Flanders, "To Transform History: Early Mormon Culture and the Concept of Time and Space," *Church History* 40 (1971): 108-117.

34. From Joachim of Fiore's "Book of Concordance" in Bernard McGinn, *Visions of the End: Apocalyptic Traditions in the Middle Ages* (New York: Columbia University Press, 1979).

35. See Froom, *Prophetic Faith of Our Fathers*, 4:139.

36. Ibid., 3:279-81; 4:56-99, 394-95.

37. Letter to W. W. Phelps, 31 July 1832; cited in *Personal Writings of Joseph Smith*, 249.

38. *Personal Writings of Joseph Smith*, 273.

39. Smith in *Messenger and Advocate* 1 (Nov. 1835): 209.

40. Ibid. Smith writes "see book of Mormon, page 566"—Ether 12 of current Book of Mormon edition.

41. Smith's single foray into prophetic chronological specificity was an isolated, rather timid affair, which yielded an uncertain conclusion. See D&C 130:14-17.

42. HC 2:259-62.

43. Froom, "Prophetic Conjectures," 180-81. See also Ernest Sandeen, *The Roots of Fundamentalism: British and American Millenarianism* (Chicago: University of Chicago Press, 1970); W. H. Oliver, *Prophets and Millennialists: The Uses of Biblical Prophecy in England from the 1790's to the 1840's* (Auckland: Auckland University Press, 1978).

44. Oliver Cowdery, "Letter VI" to W. W. Phelps in *Messenger and Advocate* 1 (Apr. 1835): 111.

45. Sidney Rigdon, "The Millennium," *Evening and Morning Star*, Jan. 1834, 126.

CHAPTER FOUR

Joseph Smith and Modern Israel

Scriptural exposition and prophetic charisma were not sufficient for assembling the Saints and building a city for the righteous. The exigencies of the gathering demanded rational planning for an ordered economy and a trained labor and missionary force. These daunting tasks underscored the necessity of education, especially for Joseph Smith and others within the church's leadership who were handicapped by abbreviated formal schooling. While searching for teachers for a ministerial school where church leaders could be properly instructed, Smith and others encountered contemporary American Jews for the first time. These meetings were to have a significant impact on Smith, the development of his theology, and his understanding of the Jewish people.

In response to explosive church growth and an agenda of this-worldly kingdom building, "Joseph," Fawn Brodie writes, "began to make learning a personal ideal. . . . [H]idden under the guise of mysticism in Joseph was an insatiable curiosity and hunger for knowledge."[1] This hunger was shared by many Mormons similarly deprived of the rudiments of education.[2] The public ideal of learning was given its first authoritative expression in a revelation dated 27 and 28 December 1832 and 3 January 1833 and later published as Doctrine and Covenants 88. Known as the "Olive

Leaf," this revelation instructed the Saints first that they should "Teach one another the doctrine of the kingdom. Teach ye diligently and my grace shall attend you. That you may be instructed more perfectly . . . Of things both in heaven and in the earth, and under the earth; things which have been, things which are, things which must shortly come to pass; things which are at home, things which are abroad; the wars and perplexities of the nations . . . and a knowledge also of countries and of kingdoms." Topics sacred and secular came within the domain of the kingdom; their study was an act of worship which would be attended and illumined by divine grace.[3] The sacrality of the pursuit of knowledge was underscored by the locality of its undertaking: a temple consecrated unto the Lord. In the same revelation the Saints were bidden to "organize yourselves, prepare every needful thing; and establish a house of prayer, a house of fasting, a house of learning . . . a house of God."[4]

Beginning with the laying of foundation stones on 25 July 1833, the Saints in Kirtland were to work two and a half years on their first temple.[5] In the spring of 1836, a contemporary observer described the newly completed "huge stone temple" built on a site with a commanding view of the Chagrin Valley: "Its dimensions are sixty by eighty feet, and fifty feet high. It is of no earthly order of architecture, but the Prophet says it is exactly according to the pattern showed him. It appears to be of two stories, having two rows of gothic windows running round it, besides windows projecting from the roof for the attic story. The first floor is the place of worship, and is completed in a very showy style . . . the second floor, and the attic loft are designed for a seminary, literary and theological!"[6]

Thus "according to the pattern"[7] of the divine template, the configurations of the overall structure and the articulation of its parts manifest the temple's conjoined purpose as house of worship and study. The "order of the house" mandated that fully more than half of its "inner court" be devoted to a "school of the prophets established for . . . instruction in all things" (D&C 95:15-17; 88:127). In four winter sessions from 1833 through 1837 (excluding the winter of 1834), "elders" were instructed in doctrine, which included not only revelations and "lectures on faith" but also orthography, arithmetic, grammar, geography, Hebrew in the winter term of 1836, and Latin and Greek in the winter of 1837. By 1835 hundreds of Saints were drawn to the curriculum of the school and enjoined to "seek ye diligently and teach one another. . . . seek ye out of the best books words of wisdom; seek learning even by study and also by faith" (D&C 88:118; also 109:14).

According to John Corrill, a visiting elder from Missouri, the Kirtland Saints were inspired with an "extravagant thirst after knowledge."[8] James H. Eells grudgingly admired Kirtland's education mania: "Mormons appear to be very eager to acquire education. Men, women and children lately attended school . . . and about seventy men in middle life, from twenty to forty years of age, are most eagerly engaged in the study [of Hebrew]. They pursue their studies alone until twelve o'clock at night, and attend to nothing else. . . . They are by no means, as a class, men of weak minds. Perhaps most fanatics and visionaries have intellects peculiarly though perversely active."[9]

Accounts of the 23 January 1833 inaugural session of the school over which Joseph Smith presided suggest the conjunction of learning and worship sought by the Saints. Before two dozen close associates, Smith invested the pursuit of knowledge with all the solemnity, reverence, and intensity which the completed House of the Lord was later designed to instill. The Kirtland Council Minute Book records: "Opened with Prayer by the President and after much speaking praying and singing, all done in Tongues proceeded to washing hands faces feet in the name of the Lord . . . after which the president girded himself with a towel and again washed the feet of all the Elders wiping them with a towel."[10] Zebedee Coltrin, one of the inaugural members of the school, recounted almost a half century later that "before going to school we washed ourselves and put on clean linen."[11] The Lord's Supper was administered "after the ancient order," and members of the school came fasting at sunrise and continued throughout the class.

Although James Eells had in his account of Kirtland "noticed some fine looking and intelligent men among them," for the most part he found these freshmen students "exceedingly ignorant."[12] Excluded from educational opportunities through tradition, class, and poverty, these "elders," "Saints," and incipient "prophets" celebrated learning like priests celebrating the cult in the Tent of Meeting.

Later in a letter to Isaac Galland written on 22 March 1839, Smith articulated the formative dynamic of knowledge in the lives of the Saints: "The first and fundamental principle of our holy religion is, that we have the right to embrace all, and every item of the truth, without limitation or without being circumscribed or prohibited by the creeds and superstitious notions of men."[13] It was in pursuit of this "first and fundamental principle" that the Saints made their first recorded acquaintances with Jews.

In the autumn of 1835 it had been decided to add Hebrew to the curriculum of the School of the Prophets. Oliver Cowdery had corresponded with Lucius Parker of Southborough, Massachusetts, seeking to engage him as a Hebrew instructor.[14] But when it became clear Parker knew little beyond the rudiments of the language, the Saints began to look elsewhere.

The solution seemed close at hand. At the nearby Willoughby College, a forerunner to Case Western Reserve University, Dr. Daniel Levi Madura Peixotto (1800-

43) was a faculty member. Previously Peixotto had been editor of the *New York Medical and Physical Journal* and a founder of the New York Academy of Medicine. An active Jacksonian Democrat, he had also served as *hazzan* of New York's Congregation Shearith Israel.[15] Having just rejected Parker as an instructor, Smith along with Sidney Rigdon, Oliver Cowdery, Frederick G. Williams and others went to Willoughby to hear Peixotto lecture.[16] Ostensibly the purpose of this 2 November trip was to hear Peixotto lecture on "physics," but as a result of their meeting, he was engaged "to teach us in the Hebrew language, when we had our room prepared."[17]

As the Saints worked to complete their temple and to begin at the school, Smith sent his "second elder" Cowdery to New York "to make arrangements respecting a book bindery"[18] and to purchase dictionaries, grammars, and lexicons for the school. Cowdery departed that very week.

At about the same time on the morning of 9 November, "Joshua the Jewish Minister" appeared on the streets of Kirtland.[19] Unknown to the Saints, this Joshua was better known in New York state as "Matthias the Prophet," or Robert Matthias, religious eccentric and perpetual litigant and defendant in criminal and civil lawsuits.[20] His unannounced arrival at the door of Joseph Smith was at first met with curious interest. Matthias's appearance, Smith remembered, "was something singular, having a beard about three inches in length, quite grey: also his hair was long and considerably silvered with age . . . tall, straight, slender built, of thin visage, blue eyes, and fair complexion, wore a sea-green frock coat and pantaloons, black fur hat with narrow brim; and while speaking, frequently shut his eyes, with a scowl on his countenance." Smith inquired about the elderly man's name, but he received no definite reply. Instead the two "soon commenced talking on the subject of religion." Gossip about the aged "Jew" of rather remarkable mien at Smith's house soon brought a stream of visitors to his door. Smith later noted that "curiosity to see a man that was reputed to be a Jew, caused many to call during the day, and more particularly in the evening" during "Joshua's" first day among the Kirtland Saints.

During a three day period, the twenty-nine-year old prophet and leader of the Latter-day Saints boarded and conversed at length with this man he welcomed as a Jew. After some preliminary introductions and conversation, a brief "relation of the circumstances connected with the coming forth of the Book of Mormon," and dinner together, Smith urged "Joshua" to freely speak his mind on "the subject of religion" and to describe in length his belief and practice.

For the rest of that evening and throughout a good portion of the following day, Matthias obliged. He interpreted the prophecies of Daniel and of John's Apocalypse, commenting on the relationship of those enigmatic books to contemporary political and industrial affairs. He went on to expound the doctrine of resurrection, the nature of "light" described in the Genesis account of the world's formation, the assumption of priestly names by virtue of the "transmigration of soul or spirit from father to son." Smith's scribe, Warren Parrish, was present during Matthias's wide ranging remarks and dutifully recorded the visitor's "doctrines" at length. Smith throughout refrained from arguing or contradicting, "wishing," he noted, "to draw out all that I could concerning his faith." When Matthias's comments became too obscure, Smith requested the elderly man to more clearly disclose their meaning.

The point for Smith was that here was an immediate opportunity for a presumed "Jewish minister" to "enlighten my mind more on his views respecting the fundamentals of his belief." The Saints were in the midst of building a temple without Christian precedent.

Smith was seeking a vernacular proper to the "restoration of all things" and had turned to Hebraic institutions, categories, and practices to distance his church from "apostate" Christianity and to underline their continuity with covenant Israel. Smith had encouraged the Saints to "embrace all, and every item of the truth, without limitation . . . [whether] written in the old or new testament, or anywhere else, by any manifestation." Now in the same week, Smith had enlisted Peixotto as Hebrew instructor, sent Cowdery off in search of Hebrew texts, and met at length with Matthias.

Unfortunately, other events combined to discourage the Ohio Saints just at the point when they were so receptive to outside influence from Jewish sources. First, "Joshua, the Jewish Minister," was a fraud. His Christian prophetic preoccupations soon made clear that his "Jewish" credentials were fabricated, and he was compelled to confess his deceit. Although he candidly remarked that Matthias "made some very excellent remarks," Smith was forced to admit that Matthias's "mind was evidently filled with darkness. . . . [H]e was in reality in possession of a wicked and depraved spirit. On the morning of the eleventh Matthias was requested to leave the city."

Oliver Cowdery did encounter an authentic Jewish witness before he returned to Kirtland from New York City. He wrote to his brother Warren, "I became quite intimately acquainted with a learned Jew, with whom I held several conversations *one* very interesting."[21] However, out of all the members of the Mormon hierarchy, with the possible exception of Sidney Rigdon, Cowdery was the least open to such an encounter. For Cowdery the Jewish people represented an instance of a broken covenantal community. The only lesson to be learned from it was negative: how to avoid their ignominious demise and exile.

For the next six weeks the assembled elders stumbled through the Hebrew alphabet, translations, and pronunciation, manifestly in need of professional instruction. Joseph's impatience and desire to learn the language can be glimpsed in the following diary entry, typical of these winter days: "Tuesday, 22.—At home. Continued my studies. O may God give me learning, even language; and endue [endow] me with qualifications to magnify his name while I live."[22] The upper room of the temple stood ready for the Hebrew class: only Peixotto himself was wanting until the 4 January date set for the formal opening of Hebrew instruction.

A third event intruded in this season of learning and anticipation. On the last day of 1835, Smith entered into his journal an extract entitled "Heathen Temple on Lake Erie" from Mordecai Manual Noah's Jewish newspaper, the *New York Evening Star*. For Smith this entry summed up outside opinion about "the cause of God, which I have fearlessly espoused": "That bold-faced imposter, Joe Smith, of Gold Bible and Mormon memory, has caused his poor fanatical followers to erect on the shores of Lake Erie . . . a stone building . . . denominating the same 'The Temple of the Lord.' We should think this work of iniquity extorted out of the pockets of his dupes, as it reflects its shadows over the blue Lake, would make the waters crimson with shame at the prostitution of its beautiful banks to such unhallowed purposes."[23]

In an essay, "How to Become a People: The Mormon Scenario," American historian R. Laurence Moore suggests that Mormon distinctiveness and the religious persecution which dogged the Mormon community throughout the nineteenth century were cultivated by the Saints themselves through a "rhetoric of deviance": "Mormons were different because they said they were different and because their claims, frequently advanced in the most obnoxious way possible, prompted others to agree and to treat them as such."[24] According to Moore,

Latter-day Saints deliberately fostered an identity through distinction and opposition. Outside opposition confirmed this sense of uniqueness and legitimated the LDS move away from an "apostate" Christian world.

In the case of Mordicai M. Noah, Smith's strategy of opposition worked against his openness to Jewish influences. Noah had attempted to foster his own "gathering" at "Ararat" on Grand Island, New York, a decade earlier. The Mormon undertaking no doubt seemed a poor coin in comparison to his own scheme and detracted from his dream of a gathered Israel. Joseph rose to Noah's bait: "Thus much from M. M. Noah, a Jew, who has used all the influence in his power, to dupe his fellow Jews, and make them believe that the New Jerusalem for them was to be built on Grand Island. . . . The Lord reward him according to his deeds."[25]

In December 1835 and January 1836, a final blow came to an LDS opening to Jewish sources. Peixotto failed to appear on the appointed day of instruction, although informed that the room, texts, and students waited. The members of the class voted "that his services were not wanted." The school would "do the best we could until we obtained a teacher."[26]

Smith's frustration can be seen in his journal history. The elders no longer "would submit to such treatment" in future dealings. The following day "unpleasant feelings" and "controversy" broke out in the teacherless classroom as strong-willed students such as Orson Pratt and Smith himself strove over "so small a matter as the sound of a Hebrew letter."[27] For men seeking to acquire "a pure language, and [an] earth . . . filled with sacred knowledge," the unfortunate experiences of the previous two months must have seemed too familiar, their relations with outsiders again compromised through misunderstanding and acrimony.

However, William McLellin returned from the Hudson Seminary, where he had been sent to look for an instructor, with good news: a teacher was hired for a "term of seven weeks, for three hundred and twenty dollars." With revived hopes Smith wrote, "He is highly celebrated as a Hebrew scholar, and proposes to give us sufficient knowledge during the above term to start us in reading and translating the language."[28] By engaging Joshua Seixas, the Saints obtained the service of what one scholar has called "the best Hebraist, Jew or not, whom Kirtland could have hoped to attract in the 1830's." This was the same "James Seixas" who in 1833 produced the *Manual of Hebrew Grammar for the Use of Beginners,* a work second only in quality at that time to that of Moses Stuart at Andover Seminary. Not only was Seixas acquainted with Stuart's work, he was also a "friendly correspondant" with the elderly Hebraist."[29]

Seixas was the son of America's most prominent Jewish civic and religious leader, Rabbi Gershom Mendes Seixas. The elder Seixas had been "minister of Shearith Israel" in New York City, one of the thirteen clergymen to participate in Washington's 1789 inauguration, a trustee of Columbia College, and member of the first Board of Regents of the state university.[30] Like Smith, Joshua Seixas was also in his early thirties. He was teaching Hebrew and working from his *Manual* in several newly founded seminaries and colleges in the frontier state of Ohio. Before teaching at Hudson Seminary, he had passed a brief period at Oberlin College, where Lorenzo Snow, later to become an apostle and president of the LDS church, had been one of his young students.

The seven years of labor lavished on the production of his *Manual* and his work as a teacher were motivated, he wrote, by "a desire to benefit others and promote the best of all studies, the study of the Bible."[31] He rekindled hopes among the brethren in Kirtland, hopes which would not be disappointed.

On 26 January the first term officially began with about forty adult pupils attending. Instruction took place five days a week, with hour-long sessions meeting at ten in the morning and two in the afternoon.[32] After the first week thirty more adults presented themselves as pupils. And by mid-February, Seixas found himself teaching four separate classes.[33]

Smith took to Seixas immediately. Seixas's "instruction pleased me much," he wrote of their first day in class. On 30 January Joseph observed, "He is a man of excellent understanding, and has a knowledge of many languages which were spoken by the ancients, and he is an honorable man, so far as I can judge yet."[34] Joseph in company with Rigdon, Cowdery, and others often visited Seixas in the latter's private rooms in the evening to converse on the subject of the school, their want of books, particular questions about Hebrew, and religious subjects. Smith remarked that Seixas "conversed freely," that he was "an interesting man," cordial, intelligent, and pleasant.[35] Smith lent his own horses and sleigh so that his instructor could visit his wife and children in nearby Hudson during the cold winter months.

The sympathetic treatment accorded Seixas by the Saints in Kirtland and their manifest dedication to the study of Hebrew contributed to an excellent working relationship between students and scholars and rapid progress at the school. By 15 February translating exercises had begun, and Seixas remarked that his Kirtland pupils "were the most forward of any class he ever instructed for the same length of time."[36] The *Ohio Atlas* printed a letter from a visitor to the city on 16 March 1836, reporting that the elders "are now studying Hebrew with great zeal, under the instruction of Mr. Seixas."[37] John Corrill noted at about the same time, "Schools were instituted for the use of the elders and others. Some studied grammar and other branches; they also employed the celebrated Hebrew teacher, Mr. Seixas, who gave them much insight, in a short time, into that language. They had been previously commanded to seek learning and study the best books, and get a knowledge of countries, kingdoms, languages, etc., which inspired them with an extraordinary thirst after nowledge."[38]

A special class of the most advanced pupils was rganized to study in additional sections besides the usual two-hour daily meetings. This group included Smith, Rigdon, Cowdery, and apostles Orson Hyde, Orson Pratt, and others. They started translating Genesis 17 and 22 with the fired-up Smith "retiring to the printing office" after class, where he "translated ten verses of the 3rd of Exodus, which, with the first and second Psalms, are our next lesson."[39]

For Smith this was a season of great activity and happiness. He was simultaneously supervising the completion of work on the temple for its 27 March dedication, instructing priesthood quorums in their duties, receiving visitors, "attending to family concerns," speaking to numerous congregations, officiating at marriages, daily laboring on "my studies as usual," and attending school. Amidst this flurry of activity, Smith paused to exclaim, "my soul delights in reading the word of the Lord in the original, and I am determined to pursue the study of the languages, until I shall become master of them, if I am permitted to live long enough. At any rate, so long as I do live, I am determined to make this my object; and with the blessing of God, I shall succeed to my satisfaction."[40] Events momentous and tragic were later to deflect this pursuit.

Seixas was contracted to another term of instruction and had even brought his family to Kirtland, but for reasons not entirely clear, the expected spring session never took place, and formal, organized study of Hebrew among the Saints came to an end. However, the spirit of those seven weeks was framed by Seixas in the certificate he awarded Smith on completing his first course in biblical Hebrew. Dated 30 March 1836, the document included the following appraisal of the student and host: "Mr. Joseph Smith Junior . . . has been indefatigable in acquiring the principles of the sacred language of the Old Testament Scriptures. He has so far accomplished a knowledge of it, that he is able to translate to my entire satisfaction. . . . I take this opportunity of thanking him for his industry and his marked kindness towards me."[41]

The American Jewish historian, Moshe Davis, commenting on this document in particular and on this interlude in Kirtland in general, notes that this "help[s] to explain much . . . at a crucial moment in the evolution of [Mormon] theology and program." Thereafter "some of the implications of the later relationship between Mormons and Jews become logical." Essentially, it was through this kind of experience that the inseparable bond of Mormons, Hebrew, Bible, and Holy Land was consecrated. Davis further suggests that the keen interest of the Latter-day Saints in "the divine tongue" was completed by the desire to more "fully understand the new revelations" promised and issuing forth from the Lord as his house, his temple, approached its dedication.[42]

Indeed those bonds were manifestly consecrated in the revelatory events and words attending the dedicatory ceremonies of the Saints' first temple, which occurred at the same time Seixas was issuing Smith's certificate.[43] Smith's dedicatory prayer of 27 March is of particular significance. Coincident with completing their tutorial with Seixas, Smith included the following words in this priestly invocation upon the house of learning and worship: "Now these words, O Lord, we have spoken before thee, concerning the revelations and commandments which thou hast given unto us, who are identified with the Gentiles. But thou knowest that thou hast a great love for the children of Jacob, who have been scattered upon the mountains for a long time, in a cloudy and dark day. We therefore ask thee to have mercy upon the children of Jacob, that Jerusalem, from this hour, may begin to be redeemed; And the yoke of bondage may begin to be broken off from the house of David; And the children of Judah may begin to return to the lands which thou didst give to Abraham their father" (D&C 109:60-63).

From Smith's earliest revelations, gentile and Israelite are intimately associated by an imperative to gather to lands of covenant. A host of Book of Mormon passages etch the Saints' commission to "further the cause of the recovery of God's covenant people," first by gathering out a righteous people of covenant from the Gentiles; and second, to assist the independent gathering of the Lord's "ancient covenant people" to Jerusalem through material and sacramental means. The "sacramental" aspect of the Latter-day Saint commission found tangible, concrete expression in the rendering of the "keys" of the gathering to Smith by revelation on 3 April 1836 and, four years later, by sending Apostle Orson Hyde to Palestine. But in acknowledging the Lord's "great love for the children of Jacob," Smith expressed an additional sensibility to the unique status of Israel, its homeland, and of the Lord's unimpaired steadfastness to Israel's redemption. The "yoke of bondage . . . of the house of David" henceforth must be "broken off" and Israel recovered from its exile.

It is tempting to speculate further about the influence Joshua Seixas had on these developments. But for the past half dozen years and more, Smith had been dealing with "ancient" covenant texts which record the stormy but persistent love affair between Israel and its God. Until his acquaintance with Seixas, Smith had never known a living nineteenth-century Jew, Robert

Matthias's claims notwithstanding. Smith's work on the text of the Book of Mormon, even with the christologizing filter of its editors and "translator," and also his "revised" manuscript of the Hebrew Scriptures, provided the foundation for Smith's recognition of the "great love" of Jacob's God and for his belief in Israel's imminent gathering to Palestine.

In spite of Matthias's imposture, the disappointment over Peixotto's non-appearance, Cowdery's tense encounter with the "learned Jew" in New York, and Seixas's polite rebuff of Smith's over-zealous friendship (discussed below), the fact remains that Smith wanted to learn from and listen to the voices and opinions of living Jews. This might appear to be a small matter. But during this period of American history, the attitude was rare.[44]

Smith's New Testament revision frequently demonstrated his ignorance of first century Judaism and of the subsequent development of Jewish texts, scholarship, institutions, and movements up to 1836. In this he shared much with the majority of his contemporaries inside and outside the Mormon church. Rigdon, Smith's first counselor in the church presidency, echoed traditional theological perspective in his two-and-a-half-hour sermon on Matthew 18:18-20 at the Kirtland temple dedication. He reasoned that because "the Son of Man hath not where to lay His head," Israel's God "did not put His name there [the Jerusalem temple] nor did he accept the worship of those who paid their vows and adorations there." He expanded the condemnation from this passage to all first century Jewish parties, all depicted as dysfunctional and rent with schism except in their opposition to "The Savior."[45]

At the same sacred service, Smith followed Rigdon's jeremiad with his dedicatory prayer and its more sober and informed appraisal of Israel. From this point on

Smith's views on Israel diverged publicly from those of many of the senior figures in the church.

In another setting Smith condemned that "spirit which hath so strongly riveted the creeds of the fathers . . . upon the hearts of the children," calling it "an iron yoke . . . a strong bond, [the] fetters of hell" (D&C 123:7-8). All early Latter-day Saints were drawn into their covenant community from other Christian churches. The process of conversion was not so profound or the break so radical with customs and creeds of the past that inherited anti-Jewish prejudice was eliminated.

Seixas's cordiality and intelligence initially elicited from Smith an inclusive, conversionist impulse. Oliver Cowdery's "Sketch Book" records that Smith, Rigdon, and Cowdery prayed together two weeks after the commencements of their studies that Seixas "may embrace the gospel and believe the Book of Mormon . . . that he may become our brother in the faith of the gospel."[46]

However, from first to last, as Louis Zucker has observed, Seixas "shunned all theological controversy" and met all of the brethren's leadings "with a graciously polite reserve." In his "Mormon and Jew: A Meeting on the American Frontier," Zucker points out that "Seixas apparently cultivated the traditional Jewish attitude, namely: a desire neither to proselytize nor to be proselyted, a desire not to reawaken acerbity between Jew and non-Jew."[47] Early on in February 1836, Joseph related to Seixas "some of the dealings of God with me, and gave him some of the evidence of truth in the work of the latter days." The good teacher, he records, "Listened cordially and did not oppose."[48] On another occasion Seixas "listened with attention, and appeared interested" when Smith spoke to him on "the subject of religion."[49]

The contrast between Seixas's considered reticence and Smith's high hopes for this "chosen vessel unto the Lord" that "he will eventually embrace" the gospel began to make Joseph feel self-conscious about his efforts. After waxing optimistic about his instructor's future among the Saints in his journal, Smith breaks off and self-mockingly states, "but I forebear lest I get to prophesying upon his head."[50] Time and proximity transformed their relationship. Seixas the "stranger" became the "neighbor"; Seixas the Jew ceased to be a theological abstraction. The "ancient" covenant people were embodied in a lively contemporary dialogue.

Seixas's quiet composure when evangelized, his evident devotion to the foundational text and holy language of his people, his intelligence and sincerity tested Smith's uncritical assumptions about the rules of encounter between Jew and Mormon. Seixas was far from supine before what Mormons saw as their religious authority; he was in no way tempted to embrace the aggressive faith of his gentile admirer. Smith's Hebrew instructor lived a meaningful and productive life without the "restored" gospel. In Seixas, Smith had finally made the first-hand acquaintance of another "peculiar people, distinct and separate . . . a light and an example to all surrounding nation," a people of what Smith would later call "true piety [and] real religion."[51] For a man who claimed that he was told by divine revelation that "all the sects . . . were an abomination" in the sight of the Lord, such adjectives as "true" and "real" for another religious community were hardly trivial.

During the final six weeks of Seixas's tenure in Kirtland, Smith never again mentioned conversion. Instead his journal history focused on Seixas as acquaintance and mentor. He savored their evening tutorials, exulting as the language disclosed its bounty. He brooded over the dearth of texts and materials cramping the progress of nearly 120 pupils crowding Seixas's four classes. Smith tried to extend Seixas's contract to a second term and mediated a dispute between instructor and a group of pupils over the sale of some Bibles.

Above all he labored over the passages singled out by Seixas for translation in his "select class." Those texts all dealt with covenant: its singularity and renewal, its stipulations and promises. The transcendent God, creator of heaven and earth, enters into a binding pact with a mortal son, Abraham, in Genesis 17; the covenant is imperiled and then rescued in the "binding of Isaac" in Genesis 22; finally in Exodus 3 the Lord hears captive Israel's cries, remembers his covenant with Abraham, and calls Moses to lead Israel's hosts from bondage and into a land of promise.

By any reckoning the three years following the dedication of the Kirtland temple were turbulent ones for Smith and the Latter-day Saints. The well-documented woes which afflicted Kirtland during the "panic" year of 1837 precipitated divisive controversies and schisms within the church and pressed against Kirtland's season of temple building, schooling, and endowment.

During the Kirtland sojourn Smith had increasingly absorbed both "religious" and "secular" responsibilities in the office of the presidency, much to the consternation of many Saints who wanted a prophet disentangled from worldly affairs. Ironically it was a modern Orthodox Jewish scholar who commented that Smith "was now, in every historical sense of the Hebrew word, a *nabi* [a prophet]."[52] But for many of his associates in the hierarchy and for a faction from the rank and file of the church, the all too-human face of prophecy was insufficient. They expected infallibility in Smith's words and actions.

When a militant faction of dissenters threatened the life of Smith and his supporters, he fled to Mormon settlements in Missouri, where he was warmly received.[53] But flight to Missouri in January 1838 brought him little respite from controversy. Frontier Missourians had never welcomed the influx of Mormons, who came for the most part from northern, non-slave states.

Suspicion and animosity—religious and political, cultural and economic—erupted sporadically into violence and reprisal. Dozens of Latter-day Saints died, and hundreds were forcibly expelled from one western county to another by mobs and regular militia alike.

In 1838 the influx of Kirtland Saints and their prophet into the tense Missouri back country only exacerbated already poisoned Mormon-gentile relations. A 6 August 1838 election day disturbance at Gallatin, where Mormons were harassed and prevented from voting, set off more disorder which led to an "extermination order" by Governor Lilburn Boggs on 27 October 1838 and, finally, Mormon expulsion from the state.[54] In the fall of 1838, Smith and others were arrested and left to rot in Liberty Jail in Independence, Missouri. The fractured, hounded, and demoralized Saints continued their forced hegira yet again, seeking a haven from violence and a place for their "gathering."

Illinois temporarily welcomed the Saints, and on its western border they began laying the foundations of a city and a new temple. Smith and companions were never formally charged or tried and finally escaped imprisonment in the spring of 1839. They too gathered to the new city rising from the marshlands above the banks of the Mississippi. The months of confinement, disastrous to the health of the ailing Rigdon, were a torment to Smith but also a period of reflection. It was in Liberty Jail that Smith sketched the contours of much of what was distinctive in his theology in the final years.

Smith's experiences in Kirtland and Missouri combined to leave him repulsed by dogmas—religious, cultural, or political—which fostered prejudice and violence. In Liberty Jail he wrote: "We have been made to bow down with grief, sorrow, and care, under the most damning hand of murder, tyranny and oppression, supported and urged on and upheld by that spirit which hath so strongly riveted the creeds of the fathers . . . upon the hearts of the children, and filled the world with confusion" (D&C 123:7). Smith would counter "unrighteous dominion" with the "virtue of the priesthood" (D&C 121:41-42). In this vein Smith wrote his March 1839 letter which embraced truth from whatever source as "the first and fundamental principle of our holy religion."

Interest in education had not been lost in the chaos and disappointment of Kirtland. Following in the spirit of the School of the Prophets, a regularly constituted lyceum for adult "continuing education" was organized in the new center of gathering at Nauvoo, Illinois, and a system of common schools was being established by 1841.[55] At the apex of a planned educational system was a "University of the City of Nauvoo," whose charter was a centerpiece of the city's incorporation along with that of the Nauvoo Legion. In a prospectus issued to "the Saints Scattered Abroad," Smith wrote that "We hope to make this institution one of the great lights of the world, and by and through it to diffuse that kind of knowledge which will be of practicable utility, and for the public good, and also for private and individual happiness."[56]

A corollary to the system of education was Smith's openness to the numerous travelers who began to include Nauvoo in their circuit. Josiah Quincy, visiting from Boston, provided this description of Nauvoo: "The curve of the river enclosed a position lovely enough to furnish a site for the utopian communities of Plato and Sir Thomas More; and here was an orderly city, magnificently laid out, and teeming with enterprise."[57]

Frequently these travelers arrived to criticize, propound, and convert. They were often invited to lecture and preach, usually to sizeable assemblies. One astonished Methodist minister, Samuel Prior, "sat in breathless silence" during one of Smith's sermons "waiting to hear that foul aspersion of other sects . . . that rancorous denunciation of every individual but a Mormon." To his amazement, instead he "was invited to preach, and did so." "The congregation was large," he wrote, "they paid the utmost attention. This surprised me a little, as I did not expect to find any such thing as a religious tolerance among them."[58] Nauvoo hosted and often heard out Masons, socialists, Unitarians, and mainline denominational representatives either in private homes, lecture halls, or open air congregations.

The legacy at work in the streets, halls, and school rooms of Nauvoo was twofold. Negatively the lessons of persecution had been forced upon the Saints. Positively through the tutelage of figures such as Seixas, the distinctive integrity of individual minds and the collective commitment of covenantal communities were being impressed upon the Mormons gathered at Nauvoo.

On 27 June 1839 Smith addressed questions concerning a "vast number [of the] Keys of the Kingdom"[59] which had been discussed the previous day in a study group comprised of some of Nauvoo's leading citizens. Included in Smith's discourse, according to his scribe, Willard Richards, were such subjects as the "Doctrines of Faith . . . Repentance . . . Baptism . . . Tongues . . . Resurrection and Election."[60] The focus of the doctrine of "election" was the question of the relationship of gentiles—Latter-day Saint converts—to Israel's covenant inherited from Abraham.

How can a gentile be of the seed of Abraham and thus a co-heir within the patriarch's household? William Marks, who was to become president of the Nauvoo stake, had written an article in a July 1837 *Messenger and Advocate* called, "Behold the Good and Severity of God." Here Marks etched this dilemma of election in the following words, "we remark again that the Law, the covenants and promises, were to Israel, and the Gentiles, as such, had no claim in any promises that had been made."[61] Marks's solution was congruent with that of Smith's later discussion of election in 1839: "if ye be

Christ's, then are ye Abraham's seed and heirs of the promise."

According to Smith, all nations would worship the God of Abraham, Isaac, and Jacob which Jesus and his disciples preached and thus make Abraham the father of many nations. Smith also believed that the effect of conversion and the "Gift of the Holy Ghost" was a material one, which "upon a Gentile is to purge out the old blood and make him actually the seed of Abraham."[62] As in Paul's epistles, the life of Jesus was the goal, the *telos*, of the Law; Israel's eternal covenant was never in question.

In the spring of 1841, Smith returned to "the subject of election" in an assembly of the Saints on the "Meeting Ground" in Nauvoo. As it was reported in the *Times and Seasons*: "The speaker . . . read the 9th chap. in Romans, from which it was evident that the election there spoken of was pertaining to the flesh, and had reference to the seed of Abraham, according to the promise God made to Abraham, saying, 'In thee and thy seed all, the families of the earth shall be blessed.' To them belong the adoptions, and the covenants &c. . . . election of the promised seed still continues."[63]

During the mid-1830s in Kirtland, Sidney Rigdon and Oliver Cowdery, the two men second in power and authority among the Latter-day Saints, similarly addressed the question of covenant and election. In these years, 1834 and 1835, both men were at the height of their authority within the community. Their articles, letters, and pronouncements dominated the pages of the major periodicals, the *Evening and Morning Star* and the *Messenger and Advocate*. But Rigdon's essay on "The Millennium," in which his views on the covenant and election were featured, and Cowdery's sixth letter of historical reminiscences about the founding of the Latter-day Saint church, which also touched on covenant and election, varied significantly from Smith's later pronouncements.

In their writings both men interpreted Jeremiah 31:31-34. According to Rigdon the restoration of Israel's standing and fortune was to come "not by virtue of any previous covenant with the House of Israel but by [another covenant] which was to be made with the House of Israel and the House of Judah in the last days," one "which was to be different from all other covenants." That covenant would be taught from "the stammering lips" of the Gentiles, who in the "latter days . . . were to enlighten them [Israel]."[64]

Cowdery wrote to the editor of the *Messenger and Advocate* that Israel's covenant had been broken and could be substituted only by one wholly new, a covenant "put . . . in their inward parts" and written "in their hearts."[65] It was clear from the text of Cowdery's letter that the Latter-day Saints, the favored remnant after two general "apostasies," one Jewish and one gentile, were to be the heralds of the new "perpetual covenant." In Cowdery's parlance that covenant was synonymous with the Latter-day Saint gospel.

But in Nauvoo several years later when Smith picked up the subject of election and covenant again and referred to the same Jeremiah prooftext, his writings avoided his associates' preoccupations and conclusions. Jeremiah was called up by Smith only in reference to the knowledge of the Lord shared by all who crossed the threshold of faith and inherited the covenant. It is not verses 31-33 of chapter 31 which beckoned to Smith but rather verse 34. Christian exegetes and apologists had been drawn to the former passage as a text forecasting the church, the "new covenant" and the "new Israel."

Smith's concern was epistemological not supersessionist, about knowing and understanding about salvation, not overcoming and replacing the Jewish people. How can the Saints, gentile disciples of a first century

Palestinian Jew, "Know the Lord"? How could they be sure of their "calling & election"? Joseph's concern was for "the twelve [apostles] & even the least Saint." He looked forward to "the day . . . when no man need say to his neighbor know ye the Lord for all shall know him . . . from the least to the greatest."[66] That Israel's covenant would be replaced by a "perpetual one" according to Latter-day Saint terms is not mentioned.

A fitting prologue to his June 1839 discourse was entered into Smith's journal history dated 21 May. It begins, "To show the feelings of that long scattered branch of the house of Israel, the Jews, I here quote a letter written by one of their number, on hearing that his son had embraced Christianity."[67] What follows is an impassioned letter quoted at length without editorial comment, purportedly written by "A. L. Landau, Rabbi," of Breslau.[68] The rabbi pleads with his son in Berlin: "Do not shed the innocent blood of your parents. . . . Do you think that the Christians . . . will support you and fill up the place of our fellow believers? . . . [Do] not change our true and holy doctrine, for that deceitful, untrue and perverse doctrine of Christianity. What! will you give up a pearl for that which is nothing. . . ? Why hast thou forsaken that holy law which shall have an eternal value; which was given by my servant Moses, and no man shall change it?" The letter goes on to call the prospective convert to his senses and his duty; it charges "the Lord be with you!" and then concludes abruptly "because of weeping."

Why does this letter appear in Smith's historical narrative? The entry leaps out from among one sentence summaries of Smith's work week: "Saturday. May 18—Finished my business at Quincy for the present. . . . Monday 20—at home attending to a variety of business."[69] Then comes Tuesday's entry and a flood of emotions from a devastated Jewish father a continent away.

Perhaps the letter echoed Smith's own troubled feelings over the denouement of the Missouri persecutions. He had only two months before escaped imprisonment. The violence and constant threats to the security and lives of the Saints and their property had elicited acts of courage and devotion, cowardice and defection. Stung by apostasy and criticism, Smith could have been drawing a parallel to his anguish and hopes over those who had left: "Will you give up a pearl for that which is nothing?"

Or Smith could have recorded this letter solely because he approved of the reference to "that deceitful, untrue and perverse doctrine of [apostate] Christianity" and its ministers, who also considered Mormons and their Christian restorationism "as a thing of naught." The case could be made that as traditional Christian apologetics depended on its "controversy" with the "old" Israel, so the Latter-day Saint identity was beholden to its opposition to "apostate" Christendom. Mormons were certainly not above resorting to polemics borrowed from non-Christian sources for ammunition in their own assault upon orthodox Christianity.

However, neither of these interpretations can fully account for this dramatic addition to Smith's historical record. The most telling argument against such conjectures is the short introduction added by Smith to the letter. Neither wayward Mormons nor Missouri persecution nor Mormonism's controversy with Christendom figure in Smith's commentary. The entry is made, Smith writes, "To show the feelings of . . . the Jews."[70] He lets them speak for themselves without Christian censorship.

Smith's attitude immediately affected the tone of the *Times and Seasons*, the bi-monthly church publication, when he took over its editorial responsibilities in 1842. The paper's first number had appeared in November 1839; Ebenezer Robinson and Smith's brother, Don Carlos, were its editors. Subsequent issues appeared under the editorship of various individuals, including Robert B. Thompson and John Taylor.[71] In the hands of these editors, the position of the paper was straightforward in denouncing persecution of Jewish communities. It covered stories which tended to coincide with the basic contours of LDS predictions about movements and events leading to the millennial advent of Christ. But it also featured theological or biblical articles which in the main reflected traditional Christian assessments of Jewish religion and the exile of the Jewish people.

The first editorials opposed religious persecution, especially by Slavic and Oriental despots. The paper found itself in good company heaping editorial outrage on the notorious "Damascus blood libel" along with *Niles' Weekly, Frazier's Magazine,* and the *New York Herald,* from whose columns the *Times and Seasons* borrowed liberally. Similarly it could exult in "the truly gratifying intelligence that Sir Moses' [Montefiore] efforts obtain release of 7 Jews on charge of being party to the death of Father Thomas."[72]

The Mormon press reported letters of appeal being sent from the German Jewish population in Jerusalem "To our Brethren the Israelites of Europe and America" for assistance in building their dwellings. These settlers promised "to devote a portion of your wealth as a sacred tribute" towards erecting "the temple of the most holy king." "It is with great pleasure," the Mormon editors wrote, "[that] we lay before our readers the proclamation of the Jews from the land of inheritances."[73]

Any movement towards Jewish gathering to Jerusalem or efforts to rebuild and restore its former glory were greeted enthusiastically. "[T]he judgements which the Lord denounced against that people, in consequence of their repeated transgressions," one editorial read, "have indeed been fulfilled to the very letter; and the promises of their restoration, to the land of their

Fathers, with their ultimate splendor and glory, now remains to be accomplished." "Surely," Ebenezer Robinson and Don Carlos Smith concluded, "the work of the father, as spoken . . . has commenced, which shall roll forth with power . . . until Jerusalem shall be built up . . . and Zion be established to be thrown down no more forever."[74]

Ultimately according to these editors, the "judgements which the Lord denounced against that people" were a "manifestation to the religious Jews, that they had departed from the principles delivered unto them through the messengers who God inspired." "Every person in every degree acquainted with the Jewish history," an unsigned article on "The Gospel" argued, "knows that God, previous to the days of the Savior's coming in the flesh, was withdrawn from that people."[75] The "whole world," the author opines, "apostatized from the living God. . . . there was not a sufficiency of righteousness to save one creature in all the world."[76]

This position reflects a theological commitment common among pre-millennialists in the nineteenth and twentieth centuries. A gathering of Judah, a restored Jerusalem, even an independent polity in an "unconverted" nation were concessions required by a "literal" reading of the prophecies. However, events had to proceed according to a Christian, pre-millennial script. Accordingly, the roads and seas Jews travelled to return to their homeland, the fields they cultivated, the foundations they laid, the walls they erected, the blood spilled, the infants born, all would ultimately confirm Christian divination and adventist expectation. Jewish lives were not their own but were lived at the behest of Christians who alone knew their story.

With the 15 February 1842 issue of the *Times and Seasons,* Smith made his debut as editor. Comparing two numbers of the paper, one from 15 December 1841 and the first issue under Smith's direction two months later, the changed perspective is evident. The 15 December issue featured an article on "Charity" taken from Benjamin Winchester's LDS magazine, *The Gospel Reflector,* which had been produced independently in Philadelphia.[77] Written by Winchester, the "presiding elder" in Philadelphia, the article extolled Christian charity in contrast to Jewish ethics in first-century Palestine. Jews "at the time of Christ," Winchester wrote, were broken into "sects" and had "apostatized" from its ordinances and covenant by vaunting "traditions over law."[78] Their acts of charity, he assumed, were the grudging concessions of legalists, performed not with the benevolent intent of a disinterested heart but mechanistically with an eye to perfunctory service and quantifiable merit.

With the 15 February number of the *Times and Seasons,* Smith began publishing letters and articles culled from sources written by and apparently for Jews. Unlike the presentation of the Winchester article, Smith presented these items unadorned. Jews directly addressed Christian readers.

Thus an article dealing with the status of Jews living among gentiles is presented simply, Smith writes, to show "the feeling of one of the seed of Abraham upon this subject." It is entitled, "A Word in Season from an Israelite, to His Brethren."[79] The anonymous author of the letter asserts that as a result of Jewish fidelity to God's truth, "We are as completely a nation as when first established as such for we acknowledge ourselves now, as then, as being under the immediate government of the Sovereign of the universe, with the same law for our obedience as was vouchsafed to our ancient fathers."

The constitutive intent of that law had produced, the writer explained, a concrete historical fact—a chosen people, an independent "nation"—and at the same time furnished that people with its restless, creative raison d'etre. "We are," the article continues, "a separate people from all the nations of the earth. . . . [T]he greatest object of our selection was to constitute us the instrument to work out the redemption of mankind, from the darkness, and unhappiness of a false worship." With such a calling and agenda he asks: "shall we cast aside our real law at the bidding of the 'London Society?' [The London Society for Propagating the Gospel Amongst the Jews] and the written law at the command of Deists, and self styled philosophers? Ought we merely to accommodate our religion's observance to suit our convenience? . . . What, if we were so lost to a sense of our own dignity, would become of the trust reposed in us by the Supreme being? What of our religion?—of ourselves as a people, of our offspring?"

It is uncertain whether Joseph Smith was informed of the debates, hinted at in this letter, raging at that time within the Jewish community in America and Europe over basic and wide ranging reform. Possibly either Seixas or Alexander Neibaur, a German Jew who in England converted to Mormonism and worked in Nauvoo as a "surgeon dentist," described the Orthodox or Reform parties and their respective platforms.

From Smith's record and Neibaur's diary, it is evident that the two often met for German and Hebrew tutorials.[80] However, Neibaur's single contribution to the pages of the *Times and Seasons* was an article on Jewish belief concerning the resurrection, where he cites only traditional Jewish sources and outlines traditional arguments for the doctrine.[81] There are no explicit indications by either Smith or Neibaur that the state of contemporary Jewry was ever a topic of discussion. The articles Smith was to cite later, though originating from proponents of Reform and Orthodoxy, were presented without reference to controversy. Smith does not demonstrate knowledge about intra-Jewish affairs, but still the break from obtrusive theologizing and commentary is abrupt and clear.

The 15 March issue of the *Times and Seasons* featured an extract from modern Orthodoxy's "founder" and earliest prominent exponent Sampson Raphael Hirsch's *Essays on Israel's Duties in Dispersion,* which included a discussion of "tsaadekau."[82] By printing this selection, Smith hoped to show how "Jews . . . maintain principles of benevolence and charity which many of our professedly enlightened Christians would do well to imitate."[83] The attention of the LDS reader is directed to the words and "feelings of the Jews" in their own right.

The subject of the anonymous "Word in season" letter, published on 15 February, also accorded well with Smith's analogous preoccupation: how to forge a collection of diverse individuals into a holy nation and kingdom of priests, a distinct people. The Jewish writer's appeal for fidelity to Israel's redemptive and covenantal commission in the face of Christendom's cultural solvents would have no doubt addressed some of Smith's central concerns. Having translated the Book of Mormon which told of the law and doctrine proceeding "in purity" from the Jews and being distorted by the machinations of gentile Christians, Smith now seemed to be providing a limited forum for Israel's voice to again speak unmediated to the Saints.

He followed up the 15 February letter by affirming the "literal gathering of Israel" as one of thirteen essential Latter-day Saint beliefs[84] and by printing an extract from S. R. Hirsch's *Essays on Israel's Duties in Dispersion.* Prefacing the latter column, Smith again underscored his intention to "show what the feelings of the Jews are, in regard to moral rectitude, and that although persecuted, afflicted, robbed and spoiled, they still adhere with great tenacity to their ancient moral code, and maintain principles. . . . Christians would do well to imitate."[85]

The next issue of 1 April 1842 included a reprint of the extraordinary "dedicatory prayer" offered by Elder

Orson Hyde from the summit of the Mount of Olives.[86] In that prayer Hyde expressed Mormon hopes for both the gathering and the restoration of the Jewish people in Palestine, and he blessed and dedicated the land to flourish politically, spiritually, and agriculturally with the return of exiled Judah. "Rabbi" Landau's impassioned letter to his son was quoted in its entirety in the next bi-monthly number. [87] Unlike the terse introduction it received in Smith's journal history, the *Times and Seasons's* preface ran to several dozen lines.

The preface was polemical, with Smith blasting the Christian world for its persecution of Jews. Christians have created of themselves a "merciless" adversary to the Israel of God and a "religion . . . so at variance with the principles of righteousness" that Jews have little recourse but to "cherish in their bosoms, feelings of disgust and abhorrence at the idea of their children embracing it."[88] He laments this destructive and alienating visage of Christianity: "What a pity that the glorious precepts of the Redeemer should be so misrepresented." But he declined to deliver the expected resolution to this criticism: convert the Jews.

Editorially Smith complemented the work of his distant apostle, Orson Hyde. The attention of both men focused on contemporary Jewry, but unlike their Christian peers in this most evangelical of periods, neither advocated Jewish missions. In the very next issue of the *Times and Seasons,* Smith roundly criticized contemporary Christians. "Did God," he asks, "ever tell the London Society, to send out missionaries?" Commenting on the pathetic spectacle of the attempts by "Mr. Ewald, London Missionary" to convert a "Rabbi Judea," Smith concluded, "What consummate ignorance is displayed in missionaries quoting the New Testament to the Jews. . . . As if the Rabbi was going to be damned by not bowing with deference to his [Ewald's] ipse dixit."[89]

After publishing several more letters from Hyde during the summer months of 1842, Smith abruptly resigned as the journal's editor. The last "Jews" column he was to edit featured an extract in English translation from Michael Creizenach's *Schulhan Aruch, oder Enzyklopaedische Darstellung des Mosaischen Gesetzes.* In that multi-volume work, Creizenach attempted to show "that talmudic Judaism was a reform of Biblical Judaism, and, thus, that the Reform Judaism of his own time was a legitimate approach."[90] The *Times and Seasons* included Creizenach's plea for a revival of education and of an informed piety which would continue the work of "reform" begun by the Talmud. Smith's final, terse comment summed up the intent of the "Jews" columns over which he had presided as editor. He concluded that the subject of the column, the Jewish people, "inculcate attendance on divine worship" and manifest to any "disinterested reader" what can be seen as "true piety, real religion, and acts of devotion to God."[91]

With the passing of editorial duties from Smith to former English dissident Methodist lay preacher John Taylor, now Mormon apostle, the editorial slant of the *Times and Seasons* resumed a more conventional approach to contemporary Jewry. Subsequent "Jews" columns comprised uncredited notices about Jewish emigration plans in Europe and population statistics from the popular press. The major exception was a 1 February 1843 article, "Both One in Christ," written by a converted Jew, "Alfred Morris Myres," and taken from a Christian religious publication. The article focused on the "Church of Rome" as the greatest obstacle to missionary endeavor. The author invokes sympathy for Jews and hope that the Jewish "miracle" will soon be crowned with the "future blessings for them in store," the blessings of Christ and his Protestant church.[92]

The step from Hirsch and Creizenach to Myres signalled the demise of the "Jews" column as a conduit of Jewish expression to a Mormon readership. Entries continued to be fairly frequent but inconsequential until Smith's death in the summer of 1844. His assassination marked a new round of violence, which climaxed in yet another mass expulsion from dearly won homes and temple. Smith's halting approach to God's Israel was waylaid by the challenges of a greater order of magnitude forced on his successors.

The leadership of the early LDS movement was not of a single mind. The Mormon hierarchy was comprised of several dozen men of fierce will and belief yoked roughly together in the common pursuit of the "restoration." But what was the restoration to look like? Mormon leaders came from different denominations, sects, and schools of thought and brought with them as converts to the LDS church beliefs and agendas which were often profoundly at odds. Smith's leadership provided the glue which bound his associates together, but it is clear from the writings and actions of many of them that the force of Smith's personality and ideas did not always insure unanimity.

Thus it is not surprising to read that Rigdon and Cowdery in propounding their ideas would draw on their own resources, background, education, and religious world view. What is singularly important to note is that Smith disagreed fundamentally with their views on Jewish people. From the first decade of Mormonism, distinct and divergent views about Jewish people were expressed by Mormon leaders—Smith and disciples such as Brigham Young and Orson Hyde on one side, and Sidney Rigdon, Oliver Cowdery, and Orson Pratt on the other. It is possible that these men were not consciously aware of how antagonistic their views were. If they were conscious of it privately, opposition was not expressed publicly nor were antagonists named.

NOTES

1. Fawn Brodie, *No Man Knows My History: The Life of Joseph Smith,* 2d ed. rev. and enlarged (New York City: Alfred A. Knopf, 1971), 169.

2. "Most of the people called the Latter-day Saints have been taken from the rural and manufacturing districts of this and the old countries, and they belonged to the poorest of the poor. . . . There are but few in this Church who are not of the laboring class, and they have not had an opportunity to cultivate their minds. . . . Brother Heber and I never went to school until we got into 'Mormonism': that was the first of our schooling. . . . What are we here for? To learn to enjoy more, and to increase in knowledge and in experience." These statements by Brigham Young taken from the *Journal of Discourses* are quoted in "Educating the Saints," *Nibley on the Timely and the Timeless: Classic Essays of Hugh W. Nibley,* Religious Studies Monograph Series, vol. 1 (Provo, UT: Religious Studies Center, Brigham Young University, 1978), 234-35.

3. "Mormons, then, possess a theology which . . . embraces the concept that the processes of salvation, the steps to sanctification, are profoundly and inseparably connected with the acquisition of knowledge and intelligence. . . . this concept of learning, even commandment to study, underscores the idea for Latter-day Saints, too, learning may be thought of as an act of devotion to God, an action which possesses transcendent meaning." S. Kent Brown, in Jacob Neusner, *The Glory of God Is Intelligence: Four Lectures on the Role of Intellect in Judaism,* Religious Studies Monograph Series, vol. 3 (Provo, UT: Religious Studies Center, Brigham Young University, 1978), xviii-xix.

4. For an account of the reception of this revelation, see Lyndon W. Cook, *The Revelations of the Prophet Joseph Smith: A Historical and Biographical Commentary of the Doctrine and Covenants* (Provo, UT: Seventy's Mission Bookstore, 1981).

5. For a description of the Kirtland temple, see Laurel B. Andrew, *The Early Temples of the Mormons: The Architecture of the Millennial Kingdom in the American West* (Albany: State University of New York, 1978), 35-53.

6. From a letter to a Br. Leavitt by James H. Eells, extracted from the *Christian Journal* of Exeter, New Hampshire, 21 Apr. 1836, quoted in *Among the Mormons: Historic Accounts by Contemporary Observers,* eds. William Mulder and A. Russell Mortensen (New York: Alfred A. Knopf, 1958), 88. "When the Lord commanded this people to build a house in the land of Kirtland, he gave them the pattern by vision from heaven, and commanded them to build that house according to the heavenly pattern that he by his voice had inspired to his servants," according to Orson Pratt, *Journal of Discourses,* 14:273.

7. For an account of the "pattern" given in revelation, see D&C 95:13-17.

8. John Corrill, *Brief History of the Church of Christ of Latter-day Saints . . . with the reason of the Author for leaving the Church* (St. Louis: Printed for the Author, 1839), 23.

9. Eells, in *Among the Mormons,* 88.

10. Kirtland Council Minute Book (1832-37), 7, archives, Historical Department, Church of Jesus Christ of Latter-day Saints, Salt Lake City, Utah; hereafter LDS archives.

11. From *Salt Lake School of the Prophets Minute Book 1883* (Palm Desert, CA: ULC Press, n.d.).

12. Eells, in Mulder and Mortensen, *Among the Mormons,* 88.

13. Joseph Smith to Isaac Galland, in *The Personal Writings of Joseph Smith,* ed. Dean C. Jessee (Salt Lake City: Deseret Book, 1984), 420.

14. Parker was a cousin of Brigham Young. See Joseph Smith et al., *History of the Church of Jesus Christ of Latter-day Saints,* ed. B. H. Roberts, 7 vols. (Salt Lake City: Church of Jesus Christ of Latter-day Saints, 1927-32), 2:470; hereafter cited as HC.

15. "Peixotto," in *Encyclopedia Judaica* (Jerusalem: Macmillan Co., 1971), 13:213.

16. HC 1:299-300.

17. Ibid., 2:355.

18. Ibid., 2:300.

19. For the complete account, see ibid., 2:304-307.

20. Accounts of the career of Matthias included Theodore Schroeder, "Matthias the Prophet, (1788-1837)," *Journal of Religious Psychology* 6 (Jan. 1913): 59-65; and William L. Stone,

Matthias and His Impostures: or, the Progress of Fanaticism (New York: Harper & Brothers, 1835).

21. 22 Nov. 1835, Oliver Cowdery Sketchbook, 1 Jan. 1836-27 Mar. 1836, LDS archives.

22. HC 2:344.

23. Ibid., 2:351.

24. R. Laurence Moore, *Religious Outsiders and the Making of Americans* (New York: Oxford University Press, 1986), 31.

25. HC 2:351.

26. Ibid., 2:355.

27. Wed., 6 Jan. 1836, ibid., 2:356.

28. Ibid.

29. Louis C. Zucker, "Joseph Smith as a Student of Hebrew," *Dialogue: A Journal of Mormon Thought* 3 (Summer 1968): 45.

30. See article on Seixas in *Encyclopedia Judaica*, 14:1117-18.

31. Zucker, "Student of Hebrew," 45.

32. HC 2:385-86.

33. Ibid., 2:391. Milton V. Backman, Jr., has estimated the number at about 120 people; Backman, *The Heavens Resound: A History of the Latter-day Saints in Ohio, 1830-1838* (Salt Lake City: Deseret Book Co., 1983), 271.

34. HC 2:388.

35. Ibid., 2:390, 393, 398.

36. Ibid., 2:396.

37. Subsequently cited in the 20 May 1836 issue of the *Painesville Telegraph* (Ohio).

38. Corrill, *Brief History of the Church*, 22-23.

39. HC 2:405.

40. Ibid., 2:396.

41. Certificate dated Kirtland, Ohio, 30 Mar. 1836, J. Seixas, Joseph Smith Collection, LDS archives.

42. Moshe Davis, "The Holy Land Idea in American Spiritual History," in *With Eyes Toward Zion: Scholars Colloquium on America-Holy Land Studies*, ed. Moshe Davis, vol. 5 (New York: Arno Press, 1977), 151-53.

43. For an account of the temple dedication, see HC 2:410-33, 435-46; and M. Backman, chap. 16.

44. HC 2:325.

45. For an account of this sermon, see ibid., 2:413-15.

46. Jessee, *Personal Writings of Joseph Smith*, 661-62.

47. Zucker, "Mormon and Jew: A Meeting on the American Frontier," typescript of lecture in LDS archives, 45.

48. HC 2:390.

49. Ibid., 2:397.

50. Ibid.

51. *Times and Seasons* 3 (1 June 1842): 810.

52. Zucker, "Joseph Smith as a Student of Hebrew," 42. In a note responding to a critical letter from one of *Dialogue*'s readers attacking his estimation of Smith, Zucker wrote: "Although I limit Joseph Smith to genius and transcendental intuition and see him not above occasional charlatanry, yet I will not yield to RFS's thinking-for-me and categorize Joseph Smith as a nebi sheker. . . . When Joseph Smith seems to me to be a nebi emet, a genuine prophet, I regard him as being of the mould of Moses, Isaiah, Jesus—a mould created cumulatively by the succession of Hebrew prophets. . . . All learned to prophesy from the Hebrew prophets. Were there no Hebrew prophets for them [gentile religious and social critic-prophets] to imitate, they would have criticized their countrymen, their times, in far different ways." Louis Zucker Papers, Marriott Library, Special Collections, University of Utah, Salt Lake City, Utah.

53. HC 3:8-9.

54. Leonard J. Arrington and Davis Bitton, *The Mormon Experience: A History of the Latter-day Saints* (New York: Alfred A. Knopf, 1979), 51.

55. The lyceum met every Tuesday at different locations in Nauvoo for several months beginning 5 January 1841. Andrew F. Ehat and Lyndon W. Cook, eds., *The Words of Joseph Smith: The Contemporary Accounts of the Nauvoo Discourses of the Prophet Joseph*, Religious Studies Monograph Series, vol. 6 (Provo, UT: Religious Studies Center, Brigham Young University, 1980), 82, 263. See also Robert B. Flanders, *Nauvoo: Kingdom on the Mississippi* (Urbana: University of Illinois Press, 1965), 52.

56. HC 4:269 (4 Jan. 1841). See also section 24 of "An Act to Incorporate the City of Nauvoo," HC 4:243.

57. From Quincy's *Figures of the Past,* in Mulder and Mortensen, *Among the Mormons,* 137.

58. See Prior's letter to *Times and Seasons,* 4 (15 May 1843): 198.

59. From Wilford Woodruff's journal, in Ehat and Cook, *The Words of Joseph Smith,* 17.

60. Ehat and Cook, *The Words of Joseph Smith,* 3-6.

61. *Messenger and Advocate* 3 (July 1837): 542. William Marks, born in Rutland, Vermont, 15 November 1792, was president of the "Nauvoo Stake of Zion" from 1839-44. Elected alderman for Nauvoo in February 1841, he also served as a regent of the University of the City of Nauvoo. See Andrew Jenson, *Latter-day Saint Biographical Encyclopedia,* vol. 1 (Salt Lake City: Andrew Jenson History Company, 1901), 283-84.

62. Ehat and Cook, *The Words of Joseph Smith,* 4.

63. *Times and Seasons,* 2 (16 May 1841): 430.

64. *Evening and Morning Star* 2 (Jan. 1834): 126.

65. *Messenger and Advocate* 1 (Apr. 1835): 110.

66. Ehat and Cook, *The Words of Joseph Smith,* 4.

67. HC 3:356-57.

68. In Smith's *History,* the letter is dated 21 May 1839 and entered into his history of 1839 of the same date. It is most likely that Joseph learned of this letter after May 1839 and inserted it after it was published in a second source.

69. HC 3:356.

70. This approach contrasts with that of Brigham H. Roberts, twentieth-century editor of Joseph Smith's multi-volume *History,* who appended a prolonged editorial to the 21 May 1839 letter.

71. For a brief description of the *Times and Seasons,* see Peter Crawley and Chad Flake, *A Mormon Fifty: An Exhibition in the Harold B. Lee Library in Conjunction with the Annual Conference of the Mormon History Association* (Provo, UT: Friends of the Brigham Young University Library, 1984), number 2.

72. *Times and Seasons* 2 (1 Mar. 1841): 341-42.

73. Ibid., 1 (Aug. 1840): 157-59.

74. Ibid., 154.

75. Ibid., 2 (1 Nov. 1840): 197-98.

76. Ibid., 199. See also "Jewish Apostasy," by "B" in ibid., 2 (1 Apr. 1841): 368.

77. For a description, see Crawley and Flake, *A Mormon Fifty*, no. 20.

78. Cited in *Times and Seasons* 3 (15 Dec. 1841): 628-29.

79. Ibid., 3 (15 Feb. 1842): 692-93.

80. See 24 May 1844, diary entry, Alexander Neibaur Journal 1841-61, LDS archives; also "Had the honor of instruction [sic] the Prophet Joseph Smith until he went [to Carthage] in the German (and Hebrew) from which text he Preached several times to large Congregations," from Alexander Neibauer, *Reminiscences*, Mar. 1876, LDS archives.

81. *Times and Seasons* 4 (1843): 233-34.

82. Tzedekah, what Smith called "essential righteousness" or "charity."

83. *Times and Seasons* 3 (15 Mar. 1842): 725.

84. These "articles" were first formed as a statement of essential Mormon beliefs to newspaper editor John Wentworth. The letter was published in ibid., 3 (1 Mar. 1842): 710.

85. Ibid., 3 (15 Mar. 1842): 725.

86. Ibid., 3 (1 Apr. 1842): 739-42.

87. Ibid., 3 (13 Apr. 1842): 754-55.

88. Ibid.

89. Ibid., 3 (2 May 1842): 781.

90. "Michael Creizenach," *The Jewish Encyclopedia*, ed. Isidore Singer, vol. 4 (New York: Funk and Wagnalls, 1903), 341-42.

91. *Times and Seasons* 3 (1 June 1842): 810.

92. Ibid., 6 (1 Feb. 1843): 85-89.

Joseph Smith, Jr.

Orson Hyde

A VOICE FROM JERUSALEM,

OR A

SKETCH

OF THE

TRAVELS AND MINISTRY

OF

ELDER ORSON HYDE,

Missionary of the Church of Jesus Christ of Latter Day Saints,

TO

GERMANY, CONSTANTINOPLE, AND JERUSALEM,

CONTAINING A

DESCRIPTION OF MOUNT ZION, THE POOL OF SILOAM,
AND OTHER ANCIENT PLACES,

AND SOME ACCOUNT OF THE

MANNERS AND CUSTOMS OF THE EAST, AS ILLUSTRATIVE OF SCRIPTURE TEXTS, WITH A SKETCH OF SEVERAL INTERVIEWS AND CONVERSATIONS WITH JEWS' MISSIONARIES, ETC., WITH A VARIETY OF INFORMATION ON THE PRESENT STATE OF THAT AND OTHER COUNTRIES WITH REGARD TO

COMING EVENTS AND THE RESTORATION OF ISRAEL.

COMPILED FROM HIS LATE

LETTERS AND DOCUMENTS,

The last of which bears date at Bavaria, on the Danube, Jan. 18, 1842.

LIVERPOOL:
PUBLISHED BY P. P. PRATT,
STAR OFFICE, 36, CHAPEL STREET.

PRINTED BY JAMES AND WOODBURN, 14, HANOVER STREET.

Orson Hyde's account of his visit to Jerusalem

Oliver Cowdery

Orson Pratt

Brigham Young

signature of Joshua Seixas

Jerusalem as it probably looked to Orson Hyde

Jerusalem as it probably looked to Orson Hyde

Jerusalem as it probably looked to Orson Hyde

CHAPTER FIVE

Joseph Smith and Oliver Cowdery: Identity of Israel and the Church

Not all of Joseph Smith's associates shared his willingness to hear out the few Jews who happened to cross their paths. Among that number was Oliver Cowdery, "assistant president" and "second elder" of the church. Cowdery's doctrinal opinions, scriptural interpretations, and actions illustrate the deep theological rift in the Mormon leadership over the issue of the Jewish people. They also point out, by contrast, how far Joseph Smith had travelled away from traditional Christian anti-Judaism. In the weeks following the Saints' encounter with Dr. Peixotto on 2 November 1835, Smith sent Oliver Cowdery to New York City on publishing business and to "purchase a quantity of Hebrew books for the benefit of the school in Kirtland." On this trip Cowdery was to meet and speak at length with a "learned Rabbi."[1] Cowdery's reconstruction of that meeting discloses the extent to which he and Smith perceived the Mormon/Jewish encounter in fundamentally different terms.

Cowdery was born nine months after Smith on 3 October 1806. He arrived in Manchester, New York, to fill a vacancy as schoolmaster in the town's log schoolhouse a mile east of the home of Joseph Smith, Sr., and his family.[2] Within a short time he became the principal scribe to Smith who was working on the Book of Mormon in the spring and summer of 1829. In addition he was among the six charter members of the "Church of Jesus Christ" founded in New York under Smith's leadership.[3] For seven years he was second only to Joseph Smith in the church's leadership.

Cowdery's background in education, rudimentary as it might have been, assured his place within the first ranks of those men put in charge of the church's early efforts to publish its cause with its own press. He was at various times charged with publication of the *Evening and Morning Star,* the *Messenger and Advocate,* the *Northern Times* (a local Ohio political newspaper), and the "printing . . . selecting, and writing of books for schools in this church" (D&C 55:4). Cowdery also played an important role in determining early Mormon political theory when Mormons in Missouri became the object of state-sanctioned terrorism.[4] His letters displaying opinions on doctrinal matters and biblical interpretation were featured prominently in the pages of the church's earliest periodicals. They also provided Latter-day Saint readers with one of the earliest accounts of events and personalities central to the "restoration of the gospel."[5]

As editor of the *Messenger and Advocate,* Cowdery either personally penned or supervised the inclusion by other authors of numerous articles dealing with the gathering of the house of Israel. In the premier number of the *Messenger and Advocate* published in October 1834, Cowdery outlined six principles of faith of the near creedless four-year-old religion for the benefit of readers and included the "gathering" among them: "We believe that God has sent his hand the second time to recover the remnant of his people, Israel; and that the time is near when he will bring them in from the four winds, with songs of everlasting joy, and reinstate them upon their own lands which he gave their fathers by covenant."[6]

Cowdery as editor of the *Messenger and Advocate* left no doubt in the minds of readers that Israel would be gathered into particular places and under particular circumstances. He was certain that the curtain had already risen on this luminous millennial drama.[7]

Cowdery's articles provide important commentary on the cast and script of the last days as he understood them. First in this "latter-day glory" were those who had "found a key to the holy prophets . . . and begun to unfold the mysteries of God."[8] To them "the Father of mercies has . . . caused his voice to be heard, has shown to his faithful ones that Israel is about to be gathered [and] the indignation toward the Jews is also to cease."[9] These faithful ones were the Latter-day Saints. In Cowdery's reading, both Jews and gentile Christians of an "apostate" church had been endowed with and then cut off from covenant and kingdom.

Cowdery and the early Saints read the history of covenant, including the history of their own covenantal community, through the normative interpretive frame of the author of Deuteronomy. Although celebrating Israel's election, this writer had manifested a concern that Israel even after being chosen, might yet forfeit its salvation through violation of its covenant with the Lord.[10] As Cowdery and others interpreted it, the legitimacy of a contract between two willing parties depended on fidelity to the stipulations of their agreement. Honoring the terms of the agreement would mean that Israel would be "blessed," that it would be constituted as a holy nation before God, dwell upon covenant soil, and be sanctified by the House of the Lord on Mt. Zion. Transgression of the articles of the covenant would abrogate the agreement and make Israel liable to the daunting curses of Deuteronomy 30.

The destruction of Israel's national polity, the dismemberment of its patrimony, and the forced dispersion of its people among the gentile nations were read by many Latter-day Saints as testimonies to what must have been, by the force of this logic of blessings and curses, Israel's transgression. Thus Cowdery declares: "the house of Israel has forsaken the Lord, and bowed down and worshipping other Gods, which were no gods, [and has] been cast out before the face of the world. . . . the Lord has poured upon them his afflicting judgements, as he said by the mouth of Moses. . . . After reproving them for their corruption and blindness, he prophecies their dispersion."[11] Cowdery laid the reason for their dispersion during the era of Christendom's triumph on Israel's so-called "rejection of Jesus": "There has ever been an apparent blindness common to men. . . .[E]ven the Jews, whose former principles had become degenerated, and whose religion was a mere show, were found among that class who were ready to build and garnish the sepulchres of the prophets . . . and follow the directions of heaven as delivered to the world by them; but when one came teaching the same doctrine . . . they would not hear. [Then] shamefully they betrayed, and crucified the Savior of the world."[12] The subsequent heirs of covenant Israel were the citizens of the newly constituted gentile Christian kingdom established by Jesus' apostles. Cowdery wrote, "In consequence of the transgression of the Jews at the coming of the Lord, the Gentiles were called into the Kingdom."[13]

But as blessings and curses lay to the right and left of "ancient" Israel, so too were the "new Israelites" similarly bounded, and the fall of the latter after the death of the apostles was more precipitous than the Jewish dispersion. "Nothing," wrote Mormon apostle Orson Hyde in 1836, "is more plain than, that the Gentiles have not continued in the goodness of God; but have departed from the faith and purity of the gospel. . . . [A] great apostacy, from the true apostolic order of worship, has taken place."[14]

The apostasy of the churches was a central assertion made by the Latter-day Saint movement. It ranked second only to Israel's restoration as subject for Mormon exegetical attention.[15] "Reformatio Christianae" was no longer a viable option for the community of Latter-day Saints. The gentile Christians of the post-apostolic period had, according to a Doctrine and Covenants text echoing prophetic Hebrew indictment, "strayed from mine ordinances, and have broken mine everlasting covenant; they seek not the Lord to establish his righteousness, but every man walketh in his own way, and after the image of his own God . . . whose substance is that of an idol, which waxeth old and shall perish in Babylon" (D&C 1:15-16).[16] In effect the "new Israel" had become "mystic Babylon." The "times of the gentiles," according to Mormon millennial preaching, was at an end along with the "corrupt systems and discordant factions, at present so mysteriously interwoven."[17] Coincident with the descent of Christendom was a change of Israel's fortunes. It was time for fugitive Israel to return both to its territorial and spiritual patrimonies.

According to Cowdery, the houses of "Israel and Judah," broken off through transgression of covenant, would be reestablished under the terms of a new one: "not according to the one which he made with their fathers." This last time God's law would be indelibly inscribed within Israel's "heart" and "inward parts." A retooled Israel bound "in a perpetual covenant" would be fully gathered by "many fishers and . . . many hunters" bearing "glad tidings of great joy, with a message of peace, and a call for their [Israel's] return."[18]

The "many fishers and hunters" were none other than the Latter-day Saints, bearers of the restored gospel. Only they would "understand the plan of salvation and restoration for Israel." Not revealed until the last act of the prophetic drama, the role of the Saints was to be decisive for resolving the epic of Israel's salvation. It was through "their [the Saints'] obedience to the faith" that "they shall see the house of Jacob come with great glory, even with songs of everlasting joy, and with him partake of salvation." However, Cowdery noted, even though Israel's children were yet "worshipping other gods," they would not recommit the error once made in the "meridian of time." For "daily reading the ancient prophets, and . . . marking the times and seasons of their fulfillment . . . they will know the voiçe of the Shepherd when he calls upon them. . . . [They] will be willing to harken to his counsel."[19]

Cowdery and his fellow Saints alone understood the meaning of the successive scenes of the "plan of salvation and restoration for Israel" and the identity of the actors in this economy of events leading to the reign of Jesus Christ. And like the teacher in a log cabin school, which he had once been, Cowdery was determined to school Jews and Saints alike. He would cut the enigmatic knot of prophecy with the authority given him through multiple canonical texts and by virtue of his calling and office as "first preacher unto the church" (D&C 21:12).

After the twenty-nine-year-old Cowdery had visited New York City to purchase Hebrew texts, he chronicled his foray into America's largest metropolis in letters to his brother Warren. Of particular interest is the account of his conversation with a "very learned and intelligent Jew" who had been recommended by a New York bookseller. Dated 1 February 1836 and published in an issue of the *Messenger and Advocate,* Cowdery's letter fulfilled a promise made earlier to his brother to give a more detailed description of his final encounter.[20]

Cowdery's description is a typical Christian construction of a "dialogue" between Christian and Jew. Since Justin's *Dialogue with Trypho,* the annals of Christian apologetic literature have seen many additions to the genre.[21] Cowdery's letter is in fact a carefully constructed soliloquy. Behind it stands no doubt a conversation which did in fact take place between Cowdery and the rabbi.[22] But it is readily apparent that his letter is a great deal more than a raw stenographic report of an exchange of ideas and commentary. Its structure and confidence benefitted from the hindsight of two months' elapse, the return of Cowdery to familiar turf, and the demands to satisfy the Saints' curiosity about his journey to New York City.

The marks of self-conscious doctrinal demands and literary aesthetics can be detected throughout the text. There is the cautious balancing of scriptural prooftext and "common sense" argument. In the final half Cowdery's words crowd those of his adversary from the frame of the text. The account is seamless and effortless. It wastes little time in drawing the lines of disputation: "You being a Jew by birth . . . of course do not believe that that personage, who by many was called the Messiah . . . who was on the earth some eighteen hundred years since, was the one spoken of by the prophets, for whom the house of Israel looked, and through whom, or by whose power, they expected redemption." In response to the negative reply, Cowdery counters with the "infallible evidence" of personal testimony, "I know him to have been and to be, the true Messiah." But realizing that such a statement is hardly conducive to "dialogue," he then seeks to make his case through the warrant of scripture. Accordingly Cowdery cites prooftexts from Zechariah 12 and 14; Isaiah 7:14, 9:6, and 53; Psalm 2:7; and Micah 5:2.

The venerable rabbi responds firmly by pointing out the flaws in the standard Christian translation of Zechariah (a point Cowdery deigns not to contest "as [I] was unacquainted with that language") and of the unwarranted lifting of the "Suffering Servant" passage from the context intended by its author. At this point, having raised his objections to the young man's exegesis, the "learned Rabbi" basically drops from the narrative and Cowdery progresses unopposed to the conclusion of his letter. To engage in a frank exchange of scholarship and ideas, to be taught rather than to teach, was out of the question. To allow variant readings would mean, Cowdery confesses, that all would be "immersed in mystery." Therefore Cowdery insists on the right "to interpret them [the scriptural texts] as I have been accustomed." The texts which he cites are, he claims, "plain declarations . . . from ancient inspired men" who teach facts and whose "figure of speech . . . is a plain one." Thus "it appears to me, and ever has," Cowdery confidently asserts. He promises that "all who will not turn from the plain declarations of the prophets, (as the great day of God's power is near) will be watching for the glorious time long since shown to the fathers."

Cowdery then simply insists on a christological interpretation of his Old Testament proof texts. He describes the "learned Rabbi" as incapable of objecting to his scriptural argument. The older man is reduced to silence and thus, in effect, delivers possession of the texts and their interpretation to his adversary. Cowdery, the former school master and young publicist of the Mormon church, determined that this otherwise obscure encounter bear the combined weight, not only of the tradition of anti-Jewish "dialogue," but also of the developing myth of a new religious tradition.

Seven years prior to Cowdery's trip, an early disciple of Joseph Smith had similarly ventured to New York City entrusted with an important task bearing on the legitimacy of the work of the young prophet. Martin Harris, an upstate New York farmer and neighbor of the Smiths, had been one of Smith's principal followers and his only financial resource for publishing the Book of Mormon. Wishing to deflect family criticism of his generous aid to Smith and his "gold Bible" and seeking as well to substantiate the young man's prophetic gifts, Harris sought out the scholarly opinion of professors

Samuel L. Mitchell of Rutgers and Charles Anthon of Columbia College. Harris took with him characters written down by Smith, who claimed to have copied them from the ancient record he was translating. Harris hoped the scholars would authenticate Smith's project.

Fawn Brodie has termed what took place "one of the minor conundrums facing a student of Mormon documents."[23] Accounts by the various parties involved are at odds. For the Saints Harris's account was the crucial one. In his story the rustic goes into the heart of America's greatest metropolis and seeks the advice of those vested with the authority of worldly prestige. When the professors learn of the miraculous provenance of the characters, Mitchell protests that he cannot verify the document without seeing the source text, and Anthon agrees that he cannot read a hidden or "sealed" book.

The farmer returns to his prophet with the depressing account. But Smith turns the incident into one of the foundational narratives of his infant religion. He directs Harris to Isaiah 29. Under Smith's direction, the enigmatic prophecy of Isaiah yields itself. In Isaiah's prophecy the "learned" and "prudent" with their "wisdom" and "understanding" perish because they cannot read a "sealed book." In contrast the "meek" and the "poor among men," those previously "deaf" and "blind," "hear the words of the book" and "see out of obscurity." The obscure rather than those vaunted by the world will "sanctify my name, and sanctify the Holy One of Jacob, and fear the God of Israel." For what had been entrusted to an itinerant laborer-prophet from upstate New York was nothing less than that "sealed book"—the Book of Mormon, harbinger of the "marvelous work and a wonder" to be carried off by the Lord in the last days. Mitchell and Anthon, the learned professors, thus become the unwitting instruments of prophecy and the means through which an improbable religious undertaking received significant warrant in the eyes of its followers.[24]

This passage from Isaiah was critical to early Mormon self-perception and was knit into the fabric of some of its earliest historical accounts, in particular one written by Oliver Cowdery. W. W. Phelps, Joseph Smith's hand-picked publisher in Independence, Missouri, requested of Cowdery an eyewitness history of the signal events of the Restoration. Through 1834 and 1835 Cowdery duly sent Phelps occasional letters on "The Origin of the Book of Mormon and the Rise and Progress of the Church of Jesus Christ of Latter-day Saints."[25]

The Isaiah passage surfaces in Cowdery's account of the Latter-day Saint restoration. In Cowdery's casting of Joseph Smith's 1823 vision, Isaiah's words are rehearsed: "I will proceed to do a marvelous work and a wonder; the wisdom of their wise shall perish, and the understanding of their prudent shall be hid." Oliver follows with an observation: "You will notice an item like the following, 'God has chosen the foolish things of the world and things which are despised, God has chosen', &c. This I conclude to be an important item. Not many mighty and noble, were called in ancient times, because they already *knew so much* that God could not teach them."[26]

Martin Harris's encounter with prominent American scholars proved then that wisdom would not come from the mighty and noble of the age. In November 1835 Cowdery, the once obscure village school teacher, would similarly help legitimize his religion. This time it would be at the expense of the "ancient covenant people" embodied in the "aged and learned Rabbi" from the same city stormed seven years earlier by Harris and Smith. The crucial dichotomies—foolish versus wise, meek and versus mighty, old versus new—organize Cowdery's narrative. In its opening lines Cowdery expresses thanks that he and his brother, and all Latter-day

Saints, have been given "*both* hearts and minds which were willing to forsake that which was old and ready to vanish away, or rather to exchange it for that which is *new* and everlasting."[27] The meeting comes about because an elderly man heeds the impulses of the heart. Cowdery points out his host's "kindness and warmth" and the "feeling manner" with which he then presses the younger man to consent to one final meeting.

Though the heart leads to the meeting, Cowdery takes pains to point out that it is not the heart but the mind that the elderly man relies on in drawing from the fund of traditional learning. As presented by Cowdery, this imbalance prohibits the rabbi from being won over to the younger man's passionate reasoning. The old man's erudition, his knowledge of Hebrew, and his interpretation of the prophets are insufficient to enable him to pass over from an old, vanishing order to the new one. The rabbi represents those men who "build and garnish the sepulchres of the prophets"[28] but cannot acknowledge a young prophet in their midst.

In his published letter Cowdery frequently pleads in contrast his own ignorance and lack of training. He is "unacquainted with that language" [biblical Hebrew] and thus incapable of textual debate. He begs falsely, "I do most sincerely hope, that some one, more wise than myself, will instruct me in the way of truth and convert me from the error of my way."[29] In order to stand in the mythic roles of prophecy, Cowdery must feign such ignorance and emphasize his lack of education. But at the same time he marshals prooftexts and reasoned arguments to prove his case and win his interlocutor. The reader has been informed before the "scholar's debate" begins that the careful discipline of learning and tradition will not prevail in his encounter with the Jew. The Lord "could not teach" the wise and prudent. Cowdery relies on a "literal" reading of the "plain declarations of the prophets" along with the sure guide of a "contrite heart" and the "infallible evidence" of testimony borne by the Holy Spirit."[30]

In Cowdery's selective reconstruction, the aged Jew, like Anthon before him, had been called to stand as a symbolic witness at a pivotal moment in the divine drama. Previously Anthon unwittingly testified that the Lord's work had passed from the "mighty and noble" to the itinerant laborers, farmers, and village school teachers. In the late autumn of 1835, a son of "old Israel" is portrayed as acquiescing in silence to the new order, ceding exegetical rights of his own scriptures and his covenantal birthright to Cowdery.

Smith and Cowdery represent, even today though in ways largely unrecognized, twin claims on the paternity and hence in part the identity of the Latter-day Saints. The two men through their lives and work put forth distinct and variant models of Mormonism, models which, among other things, proposed differing ways for understanding and relating to the Jewish people.

The distinction between Smith and Cowdery arises to a great extent from their differing arrangements of scriptural symbols and texts.[31] Cowdery's principal religious focus was reclaiming church structure and rite from the corrosive effects of apostacy. His vision was of a sanctuary fully embodying its "primitive" or "apostolic" past. Mormonism was formulated by Cowdery as a repetition of the church of Jerusalem: a church of visible Saints awaiting the imminent end of the world and the demise of the ungodly. This church was an embattled, exclusive sect of the righteous set apart by its apocalypticism and its confrontation with a hostile "host" religious culture. The bitterness of the siege years was sweetened by Cowdery's confidence in the future. In the Millennium the church would rule with Jesus Christ at its head for a thousand years. Thus Cowdery's vision of Mormonism was fundamentally hostile to rival covenant traditions and communities. Others had no real or autonomous future in Cowdery's view of the "last things." His theological orientation was therefore hostile to the autonomy and integrity of the Jewish people.

For Smith, in contrast, Israel's example and integrity loomed large and led him to foster its covenantal role in the redemption of the world. Redemption, according to Smith, depended on "New" Testament acts of the "restoration of all things" and the doctrine of the "gathering," redemptive tasks which had been conferred on the righteous to perform. Cowdery's restricted conception of a church made again pristine was insufficient for Smith. To realize his vision, Smith turned to the whole depository of scripture, as well as the wisdom of humanity's experience, for his blueprint. In particular, he appropriated and revised Israel's categories of priest/temple, scribe/sacred text, Messiah/messianic kingdom. These key categories in Israel's experience corresponded to Smith's preoccupation with the temporal, spatial, and textual landscape of the Saints and their program. With other righteous gentiles, they were to gather, to lay the foundations of the earthly kingdom of God, and to sanctify themselves. The decades which followed witnessed the oft-repeated attempts of the Saints to reorder their world spatially and temporally.

The task was formidable. It was Smith who recognized that the "restoration of all things" depended not on what one scholar has called the evangelical era's "aimless love affair" with Jesus Christ. Instead "a viable life in towns and settlements" had to be created, a "non-Augustinian construction of God's plan for human history in the world—the time and space of man."[32] In the doctrine of the gathering, Smith explicitly acknowledged that, as Walter Harrelson put it, "there can be no hope for a people unless that hope includes the gift of land in which to live."[33] Thus the Saints set about laying streets and foundations, planting vines, trees, and grains, pursuing knowledge of arts and sciences, human and divine, and begetting and rearing children "in the covenant." To many of the Saints, the tangibility and continuity of belief expressed in these acts and memorials proved more compelling than a revival, a mission society, or a dignity conferred only beyond the grave.

The Saints' labor was disrupted by a successive loss of fields, home, friends, and family due to religious persecution. Because of what the Saints lived through, Smith recognized the aptness of Israel's response to the demands of time and space in their historical experience. His appropriation, arrangements, and revision of Israel's categories and history were crucial not only for his own identity and that of the church, but for his views of the Jewish people as well.

Cowdery seemed unable to share Smith's crucial reworking of the patriarchal and historical narratives of Hebrew scriptures and Israel's experience. His preference for the Apostolic Writings ("New" Testament) and the Mormon church's earliest doctrine, to which he contributed, ill-disposed him to accept the integrity of covenant Israel outside of the Latter-day Saint church. Cowdery's theology reflected the acrimonious feelings held by "New" Testament theologians toward emergent rabbinical Judaism.

On the issue of learning and worship, the distinction between Smith and Cowdery was acute. The magnitude of the restorationist task confronting Smith required recovering truths hidden, lost, or widely diffused. Smith's sanctification of learning encouraged forays into religious, scientific, and cultural domains beyond sectarian conviction. As a student, translator, and interpretor of sacred texts, Smith augmented God's words with new books of scriptural narrative and covenantal ordinances and passed on a priceless heritage of inquiry into the origin, nature, and limits of knowledge. It was the pursuit of this symbolic cluster of text, scribe, and study that led to Smith's encounter with Seixas and to his subsequent attention to the words of other living Jewish scholars and commentators the importance of which, for the Mormon community, has yet to be explored and understood.

Cowdery's loyalties were irredeemably suspended between two objects of affection. He possessed a passionate conviction in the apocalyptic triumph of the modern church over other religions and secular institutions. But he was also devoted to the expansive pretensions of Jacksonian America. Cowdery's scruples of church/state separation and his allegiance to the offices and authority of the United States reined in his support of a people and kingdom beyond parochial national interests and discrete loyalties. Until the Advent, Cowdery could attend to the presumably separate worlds of secular and religious affairs. He preferred law, the intrigue of local party politics, and non-regulated entrepreneurialism to a planned social and economic order directed by the global needs of a heterogeneous church membership supervised by a prophet and a lay theocratic order.

Although sharing much of Cowdery's mystical adventism, Smith believed the foundation of the messianic kingdom was to be laid in mundane time and space. Redemption required a community wielding the prosaic, complicated, and complicating tools of statecraft upon a covenanted and territorial patrimony designated by the Lord for the assembly of the Saints. Smith preached that there would be no peace but in "Zion and her stakes,"[34] and he sent out the elders of the church to preach the gathering of Israel "as set forth in Holy scripture."[35] It was to Israel's prophets and to Israel's perennial aspirations for an independent homeland that Mormon elders naturally turned for the terms, symbols, and syntax of their own gathering. Israel's gathering had been affirmed in Latter-day Saint scripture and in one of Smith's "Articles of Faith"—"We believe in the literal gathering of Israel and in the restoration of the Ten Tribes." It is hardly surprising then that the Saints were interested in modern Israel's national aspirations.[36]

A final, crucial distinction between Smith and Cowdery appears in their differences about what one scholar has called the "physical as well as symbolic heart of Smith's restoration,"[37] the temple at Nauvoo rising on the bluffs above the city and river. Again their diverging views about temple building were related to their views of Judaism. In October 1840 Smith spoke of the necessity of building a "House of the Lord"[38] in Nauvoo. Land was dedicated and plans laid for building a temple "unto the Lord." Only one other temple had been built (although other sites had been dedicated), and that had been in Kirtland above the Chagrin River in Ohio.

This earlier structure's purpose, function, and rites had posed no problem to Cowdery's scruples. Its design and ornamentation borrowed eclectically from an established vernacular in American church building. It served the Kirtland community as a house of assembly and worship in its open lower floors and in its attic rooms as offices for administration, translation, and study. A long promised "endowment from on high"[39] was intended to instruct and equip the priesthood to serve the church and carry the "new and everlasting covenant" to "all nations" which were "bowed down and worshipping other gods, which are no gods"—which Cowdery understood to refer to both Jews and gentiles (D&C 38:33). This endowment celebrated this priesthood in terms and rituals congruent with New Testament accounts where the solidarity of Jesus with his disciples was commemorated.[40]

The temple served as a material, public sign of the location of the divine presence in the last days, a tabernacle which distinguished the Latter-day Saints from other nations on the earth.[41] By combining so many functions within one edifice, the Kirtland temple was different from protestant church buildings in America, however much it resembled them in style. But its use was still largely coined in terms and symbols reassuring to those who perceived the Latter-day Saint movement as a restoration of the church of Jerusalem, an answer to the apostacy which had undermined the legitimacy of the churches. Purpose, objects, and symbols were derived almost entirely from the world and texts of Christianity without reference to other religious traditions and communities of past or present.

The new Nauvoo temple focused Smith's vision in the final years of his life. He found architectural and textual sources for the temple in a variety of symbolic vernaculars. Working from an "inspired" template, the temple's architects and craftsmen groped to express Mormonism's "restoration of all things" by means of external symbolic motifs and jarring stylistic combinations of structure and decoration. Rituals were introduced to underline the religious and historical continuity of the Saints and previous covenantal dispensations. That continuity was underlined by use of institutions, kinship lines, and myths adopted from those periods.[42] In particular, sacred instruction and rites created a tradition connecting Mormonism with Hebrew scriptures and Israel's experience. As one scholar of Nauvoo has written, Smith "seemed also to grasp the profound significance that the ancient temple had for Jewish culture—the unique role that it played in the Jewish concept of divine history."[43]

Commenting on the significance of the institution of the temple for "ancient" Israel, Jacob Neusner points out that "for eleven centuries and more the Jewish people had organized its entire life—social, metaphorical, natural and super-natural—around sacrifices organized in the Jerusalem Temple. . . . The Temple stood at the very center of the order of Israelite society."[44] Its imposing presence over the city of David dominated and oriented the behavior of the nation. It marked the Divine Presence and signalled Israel's unique status among nations. It was a symbol in stone of Israel's independent political and cultural identity.

It is no accident then that a temple became the focus of a "latter-day" prophet in the western reaches of American territory. Smith pressed for construction of the temple in the center of Mormon gathering and for the celebration of its endowment by a sanctified nation of priests. One American historian has observed with some wonder that "given his rustic, western, practically unchurched Protestant background, Smith's insight about the role of a temple in the Mormon restoration is impressive. . . . In light of the rootlessness of American life in general . . . the temple, rooted in cosmic time and space, was an anchor of great significance, a tangible center for a new sacred lifestyle."[45] This new order and sacred lifestyle, at once national and priestly, dominated Smith's sermons and writings in his final years. The building of temples became the cornerstone in Smith's understanding of a restored church and an independent, renewed, and gathered Israel.

Thus on the day after announcing plans for construction of the Nauvoo temple on 5 October 1840, Smith turned to the question of the priesthood which would serve the restored temples of Mormonism and Israel.[46] In particular he turned to the restoration of priestly sacrifice and the Levitical order. First, he stated that "God will not acknowledge that which he has not called, ordained, and chosen." Next, he affirmed that consonant with the breadth of the restoration, "all the ordinances and duties that ever have been required by the priesthood under the direction and commandments of the Almighty . . . in any of the dispensations, shall all be had in the last dispensation," including the rite of sacrifice. In response to those Saints acquainted with the Epistle to the Hebrews and with Third Nephi in the Book of Mormon, he acknowledged that it "is generally supposed that Sacrifice was entirely done away when the great sacrife [sic] was offered up." But his reply to this objection was direct and blunt: "these sacrifices [referring to Leviticus 2-3, for example] as well as every ordinance belonging to the priesthood will when the temple of the Lord shall be built and the Sons of Levi be purified be fully restored and attended to then all their powers ramifications and blessings—this . . . ever was and will exist when the powers of the Melchisid [sic] Priesthood are sufficiently manifest. Else how can the restitution of all things spoken of by the Holy Prophets be brought to pass[?]"

In a lyceum meeting six months later, Smith returned to this theme of priesthood and restoration. Commenting on Malachi 2:7, Smith is reported as saying, "Now it was written that the priests lips should keep knowledge and to them should the people seek for understanding and above all the law binds them and us to receive the word of the Lord at the hands of the Levites." Again in referring to this restoration, Smith remarks, "Yes brethren the Lord will purify the sons of Levi good or bad for it is through them that blessings flow to Israel . . . and then shall the offering of *Judah & Jerusalem* be pleasant unto the Lord as in days of old and as in former years."[47]

In these citations several affirmations stand out. Smith positively valued Israel's temple and the ceremonial cult it housed. Israel's restoration depended, the Mormon prophet came to believe, on a restored temple and a renewed and reconstituted priesthood. Christian theological opinion about Jesus' crucifixion as the final, consummate high priestly offering erected insuperable barriers to the latter-day undertaking of the restoration of Israel directed by its own priesthood, celebrating its renewal through a restored sacrificial cult in the temple.

No Mormon temples have ever been designed to function as houses of sacrifice along "Levitical" lines. When Smith speaks of "election," "sons of Levi," and "the offering of Judah & Jerusalem" in these passages, he is speaking about a temple, priesthood, and people constituted independently from the church. Knowing little of the beliefs, history, and institutions of rabbinic Judaism and living before the rise of modern Jewish denominational movements and political Zionism, Smith used the only metaphors available to him as he sought to understand Israel's gathering and national restoration.

By physically gathering the Saints, by reviving a priestly order and temple, by dispatching an apostle to dedicate Palestine for the return of Israel, Smith sought to realize the part scripted for the church in the days leading up to the messianic age. These steps were envisioned as providing sympathetic assistance to a "modern" and "scattered" Israel and its longing to realize an end to exile and the renewal of its own national existence in its land of covenant.

What emerges from these assembled texts and sketches is a picture both clear and strange. On the American frontier in the 1840s, a Christian religious leader was editing a newspaper which featured articles on modern Jewry and its concerns. Mormons were eavesdropping on conversation scripted by Jews, not for the purpose of disputation and demolition but for imitation and instruction. At the same time, this leader was affirming in the scriptural language available to him a renaissance of Jewish institutions and national life independent of any necessary connection to the Church of Christ. By focusing on such notions as a city, a temple, a renewed priestly order, and acts of sacrifice, and by insisting on their literal restoration, Smith calibrated his rhetoric to jar assumptions about present-day Israel and the assumed homogeneity of the coming millennial kingdom ruled by the universal church. At the heart of Smith's vision was an affirmation "that the election of the promised seed still continues . . . according to the promise made to Abraham." That promise had room for both the Israelite whose "election was pertaining to the flesh" and the gentile to whom "belonged the adoption, and the covenants &c."[48] It was the vindication of God's promises, not the Saints' presumptions, which Smith sought in this work. Those promises included gathered peoples, nations administering justice, and acknowledging the sovereignty of the God who had established an eternal covenant with a "wandering Aramean."

Oliver Cowdery too had pressed for a doctrine of gathering and restoration. But his scenario for the future scripted the church's complete and universal victory at Christ's advent. He was thus unable to share Smith's affirmation of Israel's national and covenantal independence.

Smith feared that Israelites and Latter-day Saints would balk at the prerequisites of the promise. As early as 1835, drawing from a text in Revelation 23, Smith had asserted that before the "tabernacle [of God] can be with man, the elect must be gathered from the four quarters of the earth."[49] In June 1843, according to a contemporary account, "he exhorted the people in impressive terms to be diligent—to be up and doing lest the tabernacle pass over to another people and we lose the blessing."[50] He asked: "What was the object of gathering the Jews together or the people of God in any age of the world[?] . . . the main object was to build unto the Lord an house whereby he could reveal unto his people the ordinances of his house and glories of his kingdom & teach the people the ways of salvation."[51] In gathering the Saints and rearing a temple in their midst, Smith sought to realize his longing that his people would become heirs to the "promise made to Abraham." When he proclaimed in an April 1843 conference at the foot of the unfinished temple in Nauvoo that "Jerusalem must be rebuilt. & Judah return . . . [and] build the walls & the Temple,"[52] he expressed the Saints' sympathetic affirmation of Israel's own hopes and of the covenant which binds Israel to its Lord and his promises.

NOTES

1. In his "Mormon and Jew: A Meeting on the American Frontier," Louis C. Zucker speculates that "To help Cowdery select the best books, the bookseller (in New York City) had referred him to a 'learned Jew' with whom Cowdery, in his own words, 'became intimately acquainted.' This 'learned Jew' could well have been 'Israel Baer Kursheedt, lay luminary of Congregation Shearith Israel in New York . . .' the 'aged and learned Rabbi' who was so gracious and helpful to Oliver Cowdery; and who gently but firmly maintained the Jewish belief about the Messiah and . . . Israel's captivity, as against the Christian interpretation" (typescript, 6, archives, Historical Department, Church of Jesus Christ of Latter-day Saints, Salt Lake City, Utah; hereafter cited as LDS archives).

2. Stanley R. Gunn, *Oliver Cowdery: Second Elder and Scribe* (Salt Lake City: Bookcraft, Inc., 1962), 29.

3. Joseph Smith et al., *History of the Church of Jesus Christ of Latter-day Saints,* ed. B. H. Roberts, 7 vols. (Salt Lake City: Church of Jesus Christ of Latter-day Saints, 1927-32), 1:76; hereafter cited as HC.

4. See D&C 134; Lyndon W. Cook, *The Revelations of the Prophet Joseph Smith: A Historical and Biographical Commentary of the Doctrine and Covenants* (Provo, UT: Seventy's Mission Bookstore, 1981), 296.

5. That account appeared in letters printed serially in the *Messenger and Advocate* and was later published in pamphlet form as *Letters by Oliver Cowdery, to W. W. Phelps, on the Origin of the Book of Mormon and the Rise of the Church of Jesus Christ of Latter-day Saints* (Liverpool: Thomas Ward and John Cairns, 1844).

6. *Saints' Messenger and Advocate* 1 (Oct. 1834): 2.

7. See Cowdery's "Prospectus" for the third volume of ibid., 3 (Oct. 1836): 385.

8. Ibid., 1 (Sept. 1835): 178.

9. Ibid., 2 (Oct. 1835): 204.

10. See this theme discussed in Gerhard von Rad, "Deuteronomy," in *The Interpreter's Dictionary of the Bible*, vol. 1 (Nashville: Abingdon Press, 1962), 837.

11. *Saints' Messenger and Advocate* 1 (Apr. 1835): 110.

12. Ibid., 1 (Nov. 1834): 22.

13. Ibid., 1 (Apr. 1835): 111.

14. Ibid., 2 (July 1836): 344. This was written by Elder Orson Hyde with the approbation of the editor, Cowdery.

15. Grant Underwood, "Book of Mormon Usage in Early LDS Theology," *Dialogue: A Journal of Mormon Thought* 17 (Autumn 1984): 46.

16. Revelation given by Smith at a conference of elders at Hiram, Ohio, 1 Nov. 1831.

17. Cowdery, in *Saints' Messenger and Advocate* 3 (Oct. 1836): 385.

18. Ibid., 1 (Apr. 1835): 111.

19. Ibid.

20. For the full text see *Saints' Messenger and Advocate* 2 (Feb. 1836): 268-71.

21. See David P. Efroymson, "The Patristic Connection," in *Antisemitism and the Foundations of Christianity*, ed. Alan Davies (New York: Paulist Press, 1979), 98-117; John G. Gager, *The Origins of Anti-Semitism: Attitudes in Pagan and Christian Antiquity* (New York: Oxford University Press, 1983), chaps. 8-9.

22. See Zucker, "Mormon and Jew," 6.

23. Fawn Brodie, *No Man Knows My History: The Life of Joseph Smith*, 2d ed., rev. and enlarged (New York City: Alfred A. Knopf, 1971), 51.

24. HC 1:19-20. See also Richard Bushman's appraisal of this encounter in *Joseph Smith and the Beginnings of Mormonism* (Urbana: University of Illinois Press, 1984), 86-89, 219n.

25. As it was entitled when published in pamphlet form in Liverpool in 1844.

26. Cowdery, *The Origin of the Book of Mormon*, 21-22.

27. *Messenger and Advocate*, 268.

28. Ibid., 2 (Feb. 1836): 270.

29. Ibid.

30. Ibid., 269.

31. I am indebted to Jacob Neusner for this interpretive idea. See his *Judaism and the Beginning of Christianity* (Philadelphia: Fortress Press, 1984), 37. I also want to acknowledge his contribution to a modern Mormon, scholarly appreciation of the timely and timeless, the messianic and temple-hieratic, with Mormon doctrine, thought, and experience.

32. Robert B. Flanders, "To Transform History: Mormon Culture and the Concept of Time and Space," *Church History* 40 (Mar. 1971): 113.

33. Walter Harrelson, *From Fertility Cult to Worship* (Garden City, NY: Doubleday and Co., 1969), 38.

34. From an 8 Aug. 1839 sermon, in Andrew F. Ehat and Lyndon W. Cook, eds., *The Words of Joseph Smith: The Contemporary Accounts of the Nauvoo Discourses of the Prophet Joseph*, Religious Studies Monograph Series, vol. 6 (Provo, UT: Religious Studies Center, Brigham Young University, 1980), 11.

35. 8 Apr. 1840, Ibid., 36.

36. See Eldin Ricks, "Zionism and the Mormon Church," in *The Herzl Year Book*, 5 (1959).

37. Flanders, "To Transform History," 116.

38. *Words of Joseph Smith*, 38.

39. The first reference to the endowment appeared in a revelation dated 2 January 1831 (D&C 38:32). The promise of the endowment was frequently reiterated. For several citations, see D&C 43:16; 95:8; 105:11-12; 110:9.

40. The endowment ceremony included the washing of feet and the celebration of the Lord's supper. "Pentecostal" occurrences, strikingly reminiscent of "primitive church" phenomena, accompanied the Kirtland temple dedication and included a public display of speaking in tongues, the appearance of patriarchal figures associated with Christ's "transfiguration," and a visitation of the resurrected Christ himself accepting the offering of the temple; see HC 2:410-436.

41. See R. E. Clements, *God and Temple* (Philadelphia: Fortress Press, 1965).

42. See Thomas F. O'Dea, *The Mormons* (Chicago: University of Chicago Press, 1957), 56-60.

43. Flanders, "To Transform History," 116.

44. Jacob Neusner, *Ancient Israel After Catastrophe: The Religious World View of the Mishnah* (Charlottesville: University Press of Virginia, 1983), 11-12, 13.

45. Flanders, "To Transform Mormon History."

46. *Words of Joseph Smith*, 38-44, 50-55.

47. Ibid., 66.

48. Ibid., 73.

49. *Messenger and Advocate* 2 (Nov. 1835): 210.

50. Eliza R. Snow Diary, 11 June 1834, in *Words of Joseph Smith*, 216.

51. Wilford Woodruff Journal, 11 June 1834, in ibid., 212.

52. Joseph Smith Diary, recorded by Willard Richards, ibid., 180.

Chapter Six

Orson Hyde and Israel's Restoration

In April 1840 Orson Hyde, a charter member of the LDS church's Quorum of Twelve Apostles, left his family and associates in Nauvoo, Illinois, for a "quite peculiar and extraordinary mission" to Jewish communities in western Europe and to Palestine.[1] Hyde's mission was to be the most explicit expression of Mormon beliefs and hopes about God's Israel in the nineteenth century.

The contours of Hyde's early life followed lines similar to many of his contemporaries joining the LDS church in its first years.[2] Born on 8 January 1805 in Oxford, Connecticut, Hyde was orphaned when he was seven and passed the next two decades migrating west. Passing fitfully from job to job, he sought solace from a succession of new religious movements, including Methodism and the Campbellites, and finally joined the Mormons on 30 October 1831.

In the summer of 1831, Hyde had begun to examine the claims and doctrines of Joseph Smith. He attended meetings and debates and "often heard the Prophet talk in public and in private upon the subject of the new religion." He recorded that "after three months of careful and prayerful investigation, reflection and meditation, I came to the conclusion that the 'Mormons' had more light and a better spirit than their opponents." He was baptized by the former Campbellite leader, now Mormon, Sidney Rigdon.

Hyde spent the rest of his life in service to the church, beginning with his ordination as apostle in 1835. He was a successful missionary, serving thirteen missions for the church. When the Saints relocated to the Great Basin, he filled terms as associate judge in the Utah supreme court and as territorial legislator.[3]

Hyde had briefly left the church and was dropped from the Twelve during the height of the Missouri persecutions in 1838. Though he was later restored to his former position after what he described as a "long, sad repentance" and joined the Saints in Illinois, he was still troubled, restless, and in his own words uncertain about "the field of my ministerial labours."

In March 1840, these uncertainties were cleared away when "the vision of the Lord, like clouds of light, burst upon my view." According to Hyde, "the cities of London, Amsterdam, Constantinople, and Jerusalem all appeared in succession before me; and the Spirit said unto me, 'Here are many of the children of Abraham whom I will gather to the land that I gave to their fathers, and here also is the field of your labours. . . . Speak comfortably to Jerusalem, and cry unto her that her warfare is accomplished—that her iniquity is pardoned. . . ."[4]

Writing to Hyde after his departure, Joseph Smith spoke of the significance he attached to his apostle's undertaking: "It is a great and important mission. . . . Although it appears great at present, yet you have but just begun to realize the greatness, the extent and the glory of the same."[5] Several years earlier in Kirtland, Ohio, Smith had provided a key to interpreting his later emphasis on Hyde's mission when he wrote: "One of the most important points of the faith of the Church of the Latter-day Saints . . . is the gathering of Israel . . . when it shall be said that the Lord *lives* that brought up the children of Israel in from . . . all the lands whither he has driven them. That day is one, all important to all men."[6] Along with many of the Saints, Joseph believed that Hyde's mission represented the first rays of that "all important day."

As early as 1833 Hyde had been marked by Smith to perform an important role in what Mormons believed to be that reciprocal relationship which inhered between the Latter-day Saints and the Jewish people. At the prophet's hands, Hyde had received a special blessing and was promised: "In due time, thou shalt go to Jerusalem . . . and be a watchman unto the house of Israel; and by thy hands, shall the most high do a good work, which will prepare the way and greatly facilitate the gathering together of that people."[7]

Events crucial for Saints and for Hyde's mission were to transpire in Kirtland in 1836. First came the winter term of the School of the Prophets when Mormon elders learned Hebrew. An advanced class of ten men, promoted above the other sections, started to translate from the Hebrew Bible three weeks after Joshua Seixas's arrival. Hyde was among the members of this "first class," which included Joseph Smith, Sidney Rigdon, and Orson Pratt.[8] At the end of that term Hyde wrote a letter to Seixas "thanking him for the skillful and whole-hearted teaching which advanced us in the knowledge of the Hebrew Scriptures . . . [beyond] our expectations."[9]

The end of their term of studying Hebrew was marked by certificates and letters from both teacher and students filled with expressions of respect, gratitude, and satisfaction. During this same period, preparations for the dedication of the Saints' first temple at Kirtland were concluded. The dedication of the temple capped a brief season of progress which was to be bitterly overturned only a few months later. But dissension and disappointment were the furthest from anyone's mind during those final days of March and first week of April 1836, when the impressive dedicatory ceremonies were attended by an outpouring of spiritual gifts and visionary manifestations.

Smith's prayer of 27 March 1836 sanctifying and dedicating the edifice reflected the persistent identification of the Saints with the "gentile" commission to "further the cause of the recovery of God's covenant people." Acknowledging the "great love . . . thou hast . . . for the children of Jacob, who have been scattered upon the mountains for a long time, in a cloudy and dark day," Smith invoked the Lord's "mercy upon the children of Jacob, that Jerusalem, from this hour, may begin to be redeemed; and the yoke of bondage may begin to be broken off from the house of David [that] the children of Judah may begin to return to the lands which thou didst give to Abraham, their father" (D&C 109:60-64). Scattered among the gentile nations, exiled from a homeland, and lacking the requisite power and means to express national aspirations, the Jews of the first half of the nineteenth century were seen by Mormons as suffering under the yoke of bondage. Their redemption had been decreed by prophets in the past and now reiterated by one in the present. Their ingathering was perceived as the remedy, the key to unlock the shackles by which they were controlled and their birthright denied.

This priestly prayer on behalf of Israel and its restoration was followed a week later by a divine manifestation to Joseph Smith and Oliver Cowdery, wherein "the keys of the gathering" were rendered to them. "After this vision closed, the heavens were again opened to us; and Moses appeared before us, and committed unto us the keys of the gathering of Israel from the four parts of the earth, and the leading of the ten tribes from the land of the north" (D&C 110:11). This question of authority was of central importance to the Saints' plan of restoration. Smith wrote, "all things had under the authority of the Priesthood at any former period, shall be had again, bringing to pass the restoration spoken of by the mouth of all the Holy Prophets."[10]

The "keys of the gathering," according to Joseph Smith, had been formerly possessed by Moses, who had been "raised up to deliver the house of Israel from Egypt" (2 Ne. 3:9-10). Following the logic of the Restoration, it was appropriate for Moses to appear and bestow the keys of the gathering on the Saints. Once authorized, the Saints could work to effect conditions favorable to Smith's prayer that "the children of Judah may begin to return to the lands which thou didst give to Abraham."

For Orson Hyde divine sanction conferred on the Lord's church was the crucial test of the validity of his undertaking to Europe and Palestine, the linchpin in all his arguments with Christian divines and missionaries who crossed his path and repudiated his goal. It was the touchstone of his confidence that his work would produce historically attested results.[11]

In a letter dated 15 June 1841 and written in London to "President Smith," Hyde refers to a "book" he had written. He explained, "a snug little article upon every point of doctrine believed in by the Saints. I began with the Priesthood." He continued, "God has sent his holy angel directly from heaven with his seal and authority, and conferred it upon men with his own hands."[12] Good intentions, an inner light, a compelling idea or desire, seminary training—none were sufficient authorization to work in the name of the Lord. As Hyde explained years later in Salt Lake City: "We profess that he has spoken to us from heaven, and revealed unto us his mind and will touching our duties and the course of life that we should pursue in order to build up his kingdom and spread the light of truth throughout the world. . . . Where is the man who is authorized to go forth and act in the name of the Lord Jesus Christ? If I obey my own will—my inclination or burning desire to go and preach what I believe to be the gospel, that does not authorize me to go in the name of the Lord. Now we, in the sacredness of that name, bear testimony unto you that the Priesthood has been given to man, and we do it with the assurance that God will respond to the deeds done in his name, and by the authority of that Priesthood which he has given."[13]

In letter, discourse, and disputation, Hyde returned again and again to this warrant of his faith and work: no divine sanction means no authority to work efficaciously in the Lord's name. But Hyde was convinced that "An angel, yes an angel sent by the Almighty descended to take away the veil of darkness."[14] This angel endowed the Saints with heavenly power and commissioned them "to proceed according to the letter of instructions that he has given to us."[15] For Hyde the instructions outlining the "field of his ministerial labors" had been emphatic and clear. As an apostle in the church, he had been expressly directed to help the Saints in their part in rescuing the dispersed of Israel.

Hyde addressed a semi-annual conference of the Saints in Nauvoo on 3 April 1840. According to contemporary accounts, more than three thousand Saints attended the open-air meeting. Hyde's impression impressed his auditors. After hearing Hyde, John E. Page, another apostle, had stood in the conference and forcefully expressed his interest in and approval of Hyde's vision and intent. Carried away by the high spirits of the meeting, the conference recruited Page to accompany and assist the senior apostle on his journey.[16]

In his conference address Hyde disclosed the nature of his vision of the previous month and how it fit in with the prophecy pronounced upon him seven years earlier. Smith at that time had mentioned the "great work" Hyde was to perform "among the Jews." Hyde then described in more detail the revelation he had received. According to the minutes included in Smith's Journal History: "Elder Orson Hyde addressed the Conference at some length. . . . [H]e had recently been moved upon by the Spirit of the Lord to visit that people [the Jews], and gather up all information he could respecting their movements, expectations, &c., and communicate the same to this Church; and to the nation at large, stating that he intended to visit the Jews in New York, London, and Amsterdam, and then visit Constantinople and the Holy Land."[17]

A pamphlet, *A Voice from Jerusalem, or a Sketch of the Travels and Ministry of Elder Orson Hyde. . .*, was published by the church in England as Hyde's mission came to an end. The preface elaborated more about the revelation. In this "evening vision," Hyde was instructed that "many of the children of Abraham" resided in the cities opened up to Hyde's prophetic "sight." These, the Lord instructed Hyde, "I will gather to the land I gave to their fathers."[18]

Part of the task was to make a "strict observance of the movements of the Jews, and a careful examination of [the Jewish] faith relative to their expected Messiah [and] the setting up of his kingdom among them." This latter event would be accompanied, Hyde understood, by "the overthrow of the present kingdoms and governments of the Gentiles." By relating all this information, Hyde would serve "to open the eyes of many of the uncircumcised . . . that the great day of the Lord comes not upon them unawares." Hyde was then instructed to obtain "credentials" from "your brethren" as well as the governor of the state of Illinois. He was subsequently issued "credentials" from Smith, which expressly enjoined him "to transmit to this country nothing but simple facts . . . entirely disconnected with any peculiar views of theology, leaving each class to make their own comments and draw their own inferences."[19]

However, Hyde's commission as revealed in his vision[20] entailed a message to be delivered to Jewish communities as well. "[G]o ye forth to the cities which have been shown unto you," he was told, and call "unto Judah": "Assemble yourselves . . . Retire! stay not . . . the lion is come up from his thicket, and the destroyer of the Gentiles is on his way . . . to make thy land desolate, and thy cities shall be laid waste without inhabitant." He was also commanded: "Speak comfortably to Jerusalem, and cry unto her that her warfare is accomplished—that her iniquity is pardoned, for she hath received at the Lord's hands double for all her sins." Finally Hyde was specifically enjoined to "let your warning voice be heard among the Gentiles as you pass" and to let them aid and assist him in his undertaking.[21]

As reconstructed by Hyde, this vision had two distinct messages for two separate audiences. For gentiles, Hyde has a predominately dark and apocalyptic message. The "times of the gentiles" was at an end; the "movements" and "faith" of the Jews to return to their kingdom would mean "the overthrow of present kingdoms and governments." A new, messianic order was coming—a millennial kingdom with two capitals an ocean apart in Jerusalem and Zion. "Blow ye the trumpet in the land: cry gather together. . . . let us go to the defended cities."

Parley P. Pratt, an important publicist, apostle, and theologian for the Mormon church, was publisher of Hyde's pamphlet and intimately acquainted with the terms and intent of Hyde's mission. Pratt was working in England when Hyde passed through on his way to Palestine, and it was Pratt who received Hyde's correspondence. Not long after Hyde's brief sojourn in England, Pratt penned a broadside directed at the empire's young queen, in which the apocalyptic theme of Hyde's vision was forcefully reiterated. "A letter to the Queen of England: touching the signs of the times, and the Political destiny of the World"[22] is dated 28 May 1841 and was written from the office on Chapel Street, Liverpool. Pratt told the monarch that her reign would probably be a brief one: "Know assuredly that the world . . . is on the even of a *revolution* . . . a revolution [for which] heaven itself has waited with longing expectation for its consummation." "Connected with the ushering in of this new era," the Mormon apostle confidently prophesied, "will be the restoration of Judah and Israel from their long dispersion. They will come home to their own land, and rebuild Jerusalem and the cities of Judea, and rear up the temple of their God" while at the same time "the destruction of all other kingdoms" was inevitable.

This prophecy, Pratt opined, need not herald the devastation of Victoria's young rule. She had only to become an instrument for "revolution" herself. "I must close this letter," Pratt wrote, "by forewarning the Sovereign and the people of England, in the most affectionate manner, to repent and turn to the Lord with full purpose of heart. . . . Let them deal their bread to the hungry, their clothed to the naked, —Let them be merciful to the poor, the needy, the sick and the afflicted. . . . Let them set the oppressed free, and break every yoke. . . . Let them dispense with their pride [sic] extravagence, their luxury and excess; for the cries of the poor have ascended up to heaven . . . and his anger is kindled, and he will no longer suffer their sufferings to go unnoticed. . . . If [Queen and people] will not hearken to the words of the prophets and apostles, they will be overthrown with the wicked, and perish from the earth."

Hyde's message had an impact on associates within the church and occasionally on uninitiated gentile readers. The sweep of Hyde's vision propelled John E. Page from his seat in the April conference to travelling companion and second witness to Hyde. A young missionary on his way to England by the name of George J. Adams accompanied Hyde across the Atlantic. Once disembarked, Adams became an indefatigable propagandist for the gathering and restoration of the Jews and the imminent downfall of the current political order.[23] In a conference in Manchester, England, Hyde "appealed powerfully to the meeting and covenanted with the Saints present in a bond of mutual prayer during his mission to Jerusalem . . . which was sustained on the part of the hearers with a hearty Amen."[24] After hearing Hyde speak, William Appleby, either at a conference in Philadelphia or New York prior to his departure for England, was moved to pen a "Farewell Address to Orson Hyde." Appleby rhapsodized: "And as you go your warning voice/ Lift up to Jew and Gentile too,/ The poor in spirit will rejoice/ At tidings that are borne by you. . . . O how your heart will then rejoice,/ To see the outcasts' flocking home;/ The chosen seed of Israel's race,/ No more in foreign climes to roam."[25]

The Crown no doubt ignored the apocalyptic warnings issuing from Chapel Street, Liverpool, but the same message overturned the world of a small-time entrepreneur and farmer in Quincy, Illinois, named E. T. Benson. The twenty-nine-year-old Benson heard the message of the approaching millennial order and the ascendancy of Israel from Elders Hyde and Page while the pair were making their way slowly across the country to the Atlantic seaboard.

Their resonate message touched on signal topics of the day: William Miller's predicted apocalyptic year approached and anxious souls waited for the signs of the times to point to the Lord's advent. Miller's imminentism was bolstered by Israel's seeming disarray and irreversible exile, or so it seemed to Miller and his followers.

Six years later Benson, in "A brief history written by himself,"[26] explained his conversion to Mormonism: "Elder Hyde preached, in the morning, a rich discourse upon the gathering of the Jews and the rebuilding of Jerusalem, and called upon Elder Page to pray and I never heard the like before. They took up a collection to assist them on their mission. . . . This was the first time I had ever helped any missionary. . . ." Benson described the effect of Page's discourse: "Elder Page . . . preached upon the gathering of the house of Israel, which was very interesting to me. He spoke so loud that he broke up a Presbyterian meeting close by and upon coming out of their meeting he called upon the college bred missionaries to shew him where the Lord led the ten tribe[s], but none came forward. . . ." Soon after, both Benson and his wife were baptized in the Mississippi River.

By preaching in "rich discourse upon the gathering of the Jews and the rebuilding of Jerusalem," Hyde both affirmed the Mormon doctrine of gathering and refuted the imminentist, anti-Jewish apocalyptic of Millerite adventists. Page's unusual prayer, his loud sermonizing, and taunting questions were gauged, furthermore, to distinguish the identity of this missionary undertaking from those of the established competition, here represented by the Presbyterians. Benson's reconstruction of the event and its effects emphasize both the distinctiveness of the message and the fact that the question of Israel's restoration was a topic of lively interest. If convincingly "answered," it could persuade men and women to embrace a new Christian sectarian identity.

Gentiles were not the primary audience intended to welcome the message Hyde received in his March 1840 vision. It was principally the Jewish community that needed to escape the "destroyer of the gentiles." The words of Hyde's vision, part of which were reconstructed from Isaiah 40, were meant to be a joyful announcement that the streets of Jerusalem would soon resound to the clamor of the return of scattered Israel. But that joy was accompanied by an ominous oracle. Hyde's message included a warning that the merciless hand of an enemy was raised against the Jews and posed a mortal peril for their whole household in Europe. Hyde cited Jeremiah 4: "The lion is come up from the thicket and . . . is on his way . . . to make thy land desolate."

Hyde was also sent on an embassy of peace and reconciliation. This was a necessary part of the Restoration. The latter half of 3 Nephi in the Book of Mormon relates the ministry of the resurrected Jesus Christ among his messianic disciples in the New World. Perhaps the climax of that account is Christ quoting the words of Isaiah: "Sing O barren . . . break forth into singing . . . for thou shalt break forth on the right hand and on the left, and thy seed shall inherit the Gentiles and make the desolate cities to be inhabited. . . . [T]hou shalt forget the shame of thy youth. . . . For thy maker, thy husband, the Lord of Hosts is his name. . . . For a small moment have I forsaken thee, but with great mercies will I gather thee . . . with everlasting kindness will I have mercy on thee, saith the Lord thy Redeemer" (22:1-8). The preaching of this message is singular among Christians in ante-bellum America—a representative from a Christian church visiting Jewish people with words of peace and pardon. Nowhere in Hyde's account of his vision was Christian conversion or baptism attached to this message of reconciliation.

It was not until 13 February 1841 that Hyde set sail for London. Page's enthusiasm had already waned, and the two had separated; Page never reached New York or points east. After a routine crossing, Hyde arrived in Liverpool on 3 March and was greeted there by members of the Quorum of the Twelve, who were laboring in what was for Mormons a fertile mission field.[27] Hyde and Heber C. Kimball[28] had opened up this mission in 1837 after Smith told Kimball that "something new must be done for the salvation of . . . the Church."[29]

That "something" was the LDS church's first overseas mission. In the next several decades, tens of thousands of Britons were to hear and accept the message preached by itinerant Mormon apostle/missionaries. At first the prospects of opening a mission in England struck unlettered apostles such as Kimball with dread. Kimball marveled, "How can I go to preach in that land, which is famed throughout Christendom for learning, knowledge and piety; the nursery of religion; and to a people whose intelligence is proverbial?"[30] Dread, however, was soon replaced with disgust at the abject conditions to which the British industrial class had been reduced. Mormon apostle Wilford Woodruff recorded: "The streets were crowded with the poor, both male and female, going to and fro from the factories with their wooden clog shoes which makes a great rattling on the pavement. The poor are in as great bondage as the children of Israel in Egypt."[31]

Modern historians have analyzed the effectiveness of Mormon proselytizing in the mid-1800s in Great Britain. The distinctive attractions of the Mormon millenarian program, which included immigration and financial and material assistance to remove to the American west, converted many Britons. What Mormon elders preached, in the words of British historian H. F. C. Harrison, was a "kingdom of this world . . . it offered practical, material benefits here and now."[32]

However, Hyde did not tarry long with his brethren in their proselytizing endeavors on this trip to England. He left for London determined to labor for the "other" gathering. W. H. Oliver, in his study of prophets and millennialists in England between 1790 and 1840, pointed out the bifurcated spatial focus of Latter-day Saint millenarian hopes: "this characteristically Mormon gathering [of the English Saints] did not preclude a vital interest in the gathering of the Jews to their ancient homeland. . . . [T]he early numbers of the *Millennial Star* [the church's official publication in England] as a whole contain plenty about the gathering of the

Jews. . . . The Mormon teaching depicted two future and cosmic gatherings. Each was part of the prophetic world picture upon which the new religion rested."[33]

In London Hyde immediately sought an audience with "Solomon Hirschel, President Rabbi of the Hebrew community in this country." The seventy-eight-year-old Hirschel informed the Mormon apostle, the latter reported, that he would be unable to receive Hyde "in consequence of a very severe accident" which left him "confined to his room" with a broken leg.[34] Undaunted Hyde wrote a lengthy letter to Hirschel on the subject of his mission. Feeling that its contents "may not be altogether uninteresting to the Saints and friends in America," Hyde mailed a copy to Joseph Smith, which was subsequently published in the *Times and Seasons*.[35]

Hyde's message to Hirschel was essentially two-fold. His letter addressed the issue of Jewish exile and proposed a means to contrive its end. Though "not being able, by any existing document or record, to identify himself with your nation," Hyde expressed the hope that owing to his "affections" for the "writings of the Jewish prophets" and the "finest sympathies of my heart" for the "scattered and oppressed condition" of the Jewish people, his message might yet obtain a favorable reading from England's chief rabbi.

As an apostle of the "gathering," Hyde argued that the bitterness of exile was due to an absence of "security . . . and honor . . . light . . . and knowledge" which "Kingdom," "country," and "standard" provide. The remedy to this "yoke of bondage" lay in the contemporary renewal of the appropriate institutions, terms, and boundaries from Israel's past as a nation state. In the past when "they possessed a kingdom," Hyde wrote, "a land of milk and honey—then the strong arm of Jehovah taught the surrounding nations . . . to pay homage to them. . . . [T]heir standard was raised high . . . and under its shade, the sons and daughters of Israel reposed in perfect safety; and the golden letters of light and knowledge were inscribed on its fold."

Hyde rehearsed his blessing at the hands of Smith for this "mission," and also the particulars of his March 1840 vision which addressed the issue of Israel's return to its covenant home. Averring that he was "completely untrammeled from every party interest and from every sectarian influence," Hyde urged Hirschel and the Jewish community to, "Arise! Arise! and go out from among the Gentiles; for destruction is coming from the north to lay their cities waste. Jerusalem is thy home. There the God of Abraham will deliver thee." Israel's gathering would not only contribute to the realization of Jewish national aspirations, it would also, Hyde warned, provide the alternative to an all-consuming, proximate catastrophe which would otherwise overtake covenant Israel.

When Hyde explained the reason for the dispersion, Hirschel could hardly have been impressed. Hyde's traditional use of biblical and theological sources led him to assign Israel's condition to their collective responsibility for the death of Christ: "The fiery storm that burst upon your nation at that time . . . too plainly declare[s] that the strong imprecation which they uttered on a certain occasion, has been fulfilled upon them to the letter. 'Let his blood be upon us and on our children.'" At least he, unlike Cowdery before him, did not also lay the charge of idolatry at contemporary Israel's door. Though his "pen," he wrote, "is pointed with friendship and dipped in the fountain of love and good will towards your nation," the collective charge of homicide could not have encouraged an appointment with Hirschel.

In fact Hyde's charge runs contrary to one of the most basic of Mormon doctrines. In what is now called the "Articles of Faith of the Church of Jesus Christ of Latter-day Saints," Joseph Smith expressed belief in the individual accountability of human beings. In a letter to newspaper editor John Wentworth, who had inquired about the fundamental beliefs of Mormons, Smith had replied in words which found their way into the LDS scriptural canon: "We believe that men will be punished for their own sins, and not for Adam's transgressions."[36] This belief was not qualified by reference to Jewish guilt for the death of Jesus. Building on such silence, W. D. Davies, in his article "Israel, Mormons, and the Land," has pointed out that "It is striking . . . that in the passage where the cross emerges in the Book of Mormon and in the Doctrine and Covenants the Jews are not explicitly mentioned as responsible for it; rather, the cross is dealt with in broad terms. . . . It is surprising how few references to the cross occur in the Book of Mormon. In the index to the Doctrine and Covenants no item entitled 'cross' occurs. . . . [T]here is again no specific reference to the role of Jews in the Crucifixion but concentration on the suffering of Christ for all men." After surveying the corpus of Mormon canonical writings, Davies observed that "all this may be significant as pointing to the absence of any anti-Judaism in Mormonism."[37]

The explanation for exile was not central to Hyde's epistle. The remedy for it was. So too was the warning of an approaching menace to Israel's people. The crux of Hyde's message was that the solution to oppression and exile was renewal of worship and an autonomous state. The two-pronged solution was punctuated by Hyde's call for repentance: "Now, there, O ye children of the covenant, repent of all your backslidings, and begin, as in days of old, to turn to the Lord your God. Arise! Arise! and go out from among the Gentiles. . . . Jerusalem is thy home."

This spirited passage alludes to Jeremiah 3:11-21. There the prophet calls Israel in the name of the Lord, "Return, thou backsliding Israel . . . and I will not cause mine anger to fall upon you," if only it "will acknowledge [its] iniquity." The result of this turning would be their return "to Zion," growth in "Knowledge and understanding, expansion in numbers and influence or power," and rapprochement between the various members of the household of Israel and between Israel and its Lord.

If Hyde's aim had been preaching repentance to the Jewish people in the traditional Christian sense of a "turning to God in Christ with faith,"[38] he surely would have mentioned it in his letter to Smith highlighting his successes. The Latter-day Saint message to gentile audiences was unabashedly sectarian and conversionist. To the Jews, Hyde's message was fundamentally supportive of Israel's autonomy and its hopes for an end to exile among the gentile nations.

As illustrated by his use of Jeremiah 3:29, Hyde attempted to construe Israel's autonomy and integrity, its security and renewal, from the fund of metaphors available to him from scripture and from the Latter-day Saint experience. Thus when he states, "Repent . . . and begin, as in days of old, to turn to the Lord your God," the modern reader must take into account the whole of Hyde's epistle and the terms and categories being employed to explicate Mormon and Jewish identities. He borrowed these terms from Smith, who increasingly turned to ancient Israelite institutions, including high priests and temples, to construe the identity and strength of both the Jewish and the Mormon covenant communities.

Hyde left England after writing his letter to Rabbi Hirschel and started for the Netherlands. According to a letter to "Bro. Joseph and all whom it may concern," dated 17 July 1841, Hyde arrived in Rotterdam and "called on the Hebrew Rabbi."[39] In this meeting Hyde began to gather the information he had been sent to find. Limited by language barriers from entering "into particulars with him," Hyde asked three questions: Would the Messiah come from a woman or "from

Heaven"? When would this take place? "Do you believe in the restitution of your nation to the land of your fathers, called the land of *Promise*?"

Hyde reported that there was neither disputation nor contentiousness in the exchange. Without comment Hyde recorded the man's responses: first, the Messiah would be born of mortal parents and from "the seed and lineage of David"; second, the event, long awaited, was believed to be near at hand; and finally, "We hope it [the awaited gathering] will be so. . . . we believed that many Jews will return to Jerusalem and rebuild the city—rear a temple to the name of the Most High, and restore our ancient worship." "Jerusalem," he reported, "shall be the capital of our nation—the centre of our union, and the Standard and Ensign of our national existence."

In parting Hyde promised to have a fuller communication of his mission translated into Dutch and received the rabbi's thanks for his "respect." Unable to contact "the President Rabbi" during his stay of "only one night, and a part of two days" in Amsterdam, Hyde made his way by river passage to the Adriatic. There he secured a berth in a vessel bound for the Levant.

On 21 October 1841 after an overland passage from Jaffa, Hyde entered Jerusalem.[40] His stay was brief, most of his task completed within days of his arrival. By 22 November, a month later, Hyde was writing to his fellow apostle, Parley P. Pratt, in England, from the harbor of Alexandria: "I have only time to say that I have seen Jerusalem precisely according to the vision which I had. . . . [And] that through the goodness of the Lord, I have been enabled to accomplish that which was told me prophetically, several years ago, by Brother Joseph. . . ."

The climax of Hyde's mission which took him far from Nauvoo came on the morning of 24 October 1841. He writes: "On Sunday morning . . . a good while before day, I arose from sleep, and went out of the city as soon as the gates were opened, crossed the brook Cedron, and went upon the Mount of Olives, and there, in solemn silence, with pen, ink, and paper, just as I saw in the vision, offered up the following prayer to him who lives forever and ever." In the lengthy prayer which followed, Hyde dedicated Israel's land of inheritance and consecrated it for the "gathering together of Judah's scattered remnants," for the rebuilding of Jerusalem, and the construction of the Lord's temple. Reminding God of his covenant with Abraham, Isaac, and Jacob and of the longing of Israel for a return to its home, Hyde blessed the earth of the Holy Land with water, flocks, and fields sufficient to provide for the return of Israel's exiled children.

He further invoked the Lord to "incline them [Judah's remnants] to gather" and spread abroad the spirit of return so even gentile rulers and nations would assist in the gathering. Blessings were sought for all parties assisting this work, "while the nation or kingdom that will not serve must perish according to thy word—'Yea, those nations shall be utterly wasted.'" Ultimately the goal of this solemn prayer with its blessings and cursings was to manifest the Lord's "good pleasure to restore the kingdom of Israel" and to "raise up Jerusalem as its capital, and constitute her people a distinct nation and government, with David thy servant, even a descendant from the loins of ancient David, to be their king."

His prayer and work now completed, Hyde fashioned a pile of uncut stones "according to the ancient custom" as a witness and memorial. Those words and stones capped the Saints often inarticulate but passionate conviction that Israel would be restored as a distinct people and nation. More particularly they testified to the vision of their prophet Joseph Smith and to his belief in the concrete and efficacious power which inhered in the restoration of gospel and priesthood. That priesthood and gospel, they believed, had been extended to "the righteous among the gentiles" in the latter days to bless and fructify lands of covenant, effect Israel's return from exile, and hence quicken the coming of Messiah and the messianic age.

Little within the literary deposit left by nineteenth-century missionaries to Palestine or by biblical/archaeological scholars, pilgrims, consuls, colonists, and travelers drawn to the Holy Land compares with Hyde's mission and prayer. Hyde's own account of encounters with American, British, and German missionaries working in Jerusalem underline his divergent path. While in Jerusalem, Hyde reports that he read the substance of the letter he penned addressing Jewish communities to some missionaries representing the American Board of Commissioners for Foreign Missions, which was supported by Presbyterian and Congregationalist denominations, and also missionaries for the Anglican church. He was answered with silence and incomprehension. The others preferred, he reported, to draw the Mormon apostle into debate over distinctions between Mormonism and established Christian doctrine.

Hyde himself questioned the efficacy and propriety of Jewish missions in Palestine.[41] "Your time is spent here to little or no purpose," Hyde contended. Though he may well have been unfair, Hyde criticized not only the inadequacy of the religious propositions they communicated to an unreceptive audience but also the salaries they drew from foreign-based societies. Hyde refers sarcastically to the missionaries' project to "gather Israel, convert the heathen and bring in the millennium . . . in our own way, and according to our own will." Israel's primary and pressing need was the restoration of its territory and polity. Those would be restored, Hyde opined, not by tract or sermon but by the "political power and influence" of some gentile nations.

The point was clear enough to both parties. The missionaries, who because of their longer residence and training were acquainted with the city, its languages, and important local personalities, refused Hyde's request for introductions.[42] Thereafter he quit their company and struck out alone to survey Jerusalem and pronounce the blessings he had been commissioned to bestow.

Hyde's account of his encounter and debates with Protestant missionaries in Jerusalem no doubt focused on differences and distinctions for the benefit of Mormons reading his public letters in the states and Great Britain. The narrative also benefits from its retrospective composition in Alexandria and Trieste. But the distinctiveness of Hyde's mission is underlined by contrasting it with accounts of other Christians drawn like Hyde to Palestine in order to articulate their proposals for the fate of Israel.

First, there were biblical scholars such as Edward Robinson, who began his archaeological work in Jerusalem in 1838.[43] Robinson's work was of the highest quality. At the same time his writings were couched in language geared to assist the pious in their reading of the scriptures. As one traveler put it, "a perfect knowledge of the Holy Land is needful to a perfect knowledge of the Hebrew Scriptures."[44] Robinson was also quite zealous to correct geographies and descriptions of the Holy Land "encrusted with Roman tradition" not corresponding with scripture and direct observation. Beginning with Robinson and continuing through Albright in our time, these works focusing on Israel's past material culture have been widely read and their findings followed by Christian readers both in America and Europe. In 1842 Robinson's work was cited in the *Times and Seasons*.[45]

Pilgrims and travelers comprised by far the largest group to visit the Holy Land. Whether traveling to renew their faith or taking in the Middle East as one more leg of the Grand Tour so popular in the nineteenth century (and wryly described in Twain's *Innocents Abroad*), accounts by pilgrims were legion. Reports of their travels in articles, speeches, letters, and books were also widely read. Many accounts ran through dozens of editions.

The reactions of such travelers were diverse. Herman Melville visited the Holy Land in 1857. In an epic poem *Clarel,* he wrote that the Holy Land was "in its mined state an outward and visible vision of the loss of religions among . . . men and, to some degree, the ruins of the world."[46] However, most did not share Melville's pessimism. The prominent millenarian Horatius Bonar visited just one year after Melville and found the land "possessed a magnetic power. . . . it wins the heart, and draws the steps towards itself, by a mighty and mysterious attraction." He noted approvingly the labors of Protestant missionaries approaching the "Jews of Jerusalem kindly yet boldly" in the hopes of winning them to Christ.[47]

The French Catholic father Becq had yet another vision. Becq realized a lifelong dream of visiting the Holy Land and his *Impressions d'un Pelerin de Terre-Sainte* is an ardent expression of his particular religious sensibilities. Becq's devotions are lavished on a land of shrines, pilgrimages, and sacred rites, the "land of Mary, my dear Mother, oh cradle, oh sepulchre of my God." The Jews of Jerusalem eat "their bread in affliction and tears," while non-Catholic Christians (*les schismatiques*) "are rich, ambitious, and hateful toward Catholics." His book ends with a prayer that one day he will return to salute the Holy City in its return to the Lord. He pleads for a "pacifistic crusade" within the Roman church to deliver Jerusalem by building up its numerous shrines and churches and by flooding its streets with a tide of pious pilgrims.[48]

Philip Schaff, the eminent church historian and theologian, journeyed to Palestine in the wake of a personal domestic crisis, seeking solace and better health. His account demonstrates a greater sympathy for the needs of the present-day inhabitants of Jerusalem than much of the Holy Land literature, but he still concludes: "The lands of the Bible are one vast mission field, which must be conquered with spiritual weapons for Christ and Christian civilization." In Jerusalem he perceives the makings of "a new Jerusalem . . . gradually springing up by the pious and benevolent efforts of foreigners, who labor for the revival of Bible Christianity in this Bible land."[49]

In addition to these pilgrims and travelers, small contingents of Americans and Europeans sought to reside in the Holy Land either as diplomats or colonists. Frank S. De Hass, Selah Merrill, Edwin S. Wallace, and Otis Overbrook were all Protestant ministers called by the American government to be its consuls in Jerusalem. It has been noted that their acceptance of consular appointments was less a matter of diplomatic credentials and experience than a desire to visit the lands of the Bible.[50] Often hopes for an inspirational tour of duty were smashed. Consul De Hass wrote, "You see nothing but ruin and desolation everywhere. The people are poor and ignorant, the land neglected and barren, and the towns filthy and cheerless."[51]

One exception was Warder Cresson, consul in Jerusalem in 1845. Cresson was a former Quaker/former Mormon who once in Palestine converted to Judaism and married a Jewish woman. Elden Ricks in his "Zionism and the Mormon Church" mentions that Cresson was instrumental in establishing an agricultural settlement there and raises the question of whether Cresson's interest in building up the country could be traced to his previous Mormon affiliation.[52]

Would-be-colonist George J. Adams's Mormon connection is in contrast well documented.[53] Having accompanied Hyde on the New York to London portion of the apostle's mission, Adams benefitted directly from

Hyde's sentiments concerning the restoration of the Jews. Much later in 1866 after having disaffiliated himself from the LDS church, Adams, now "President of the Messiah Emigration Association," led an ill-fated band of colonists to Palestine to witness the glorious events he believed would imminently unfold. Clorinda Minor, an American Millerite, also immigrated in anticipation of great events. Wanting to be a first-hand heir of Israel's regeneration, she had preceded Adams's group by thirteen years and established the Mt. Hope Colony in Jaffa in 1853.[54]

Other major groups to venture to Palestine were Protestant missionaries sent by the British Church Missionary Society, the "London Society," and the American Board of Commissioners for Foreign Missions. Founded in 1818 the American Board's first stated goal was the conversion and reformation of the Oriental Christian churches and the conversion of Muslims.[55] But in the words of Levi Parsons, who along with Pliny Fisk and Jonas King were the first to venture to Palestine, they also believed in the restoration of a Jewish Holy Land: "the outcasts of Israel will yet be gathered to their own land. . . . Surely the day so long desired by the people of God is beginning to dawn." To substantiate his claim, Parsons points to the success of Christian proselytizing among the Jews in Europe. He calls for the prayers of Christians and for an outpouring of charity in order to purchase New Testaments and train missionaries.[56]

William Jowett's reflections on his 1823-24 mission to Palestine, published in 1826 as *Christian Researches in Syria and the Holy Land*, is representative of the missionary assessment of Protestant Christianity's role in fashioning humanity's evangelical future. Jowett hoped that "the picture exhibited [in these pages] may be the means of rousing British public to a deeper sense of their obligations to prosecute Christian missions in this part of the world . . . and to visit all the dark places of the Earth." Jowett like Hyde indulged in descriptions of Jerusalem, its people, and environs. But unlike Hyde, he was compelled to describe the "meanness," "filth" and "misery" of the Holy City. All were manifest proofs, he concluded, "of the displeasure of that Great King resting upon his city." Visiting the Temple Mount, he mused on the destruction of the Second Temple. There would be no new temple except that which "He [Jesus] had rebuilt . . . of his own body . . . the wondrous work of raising a spiritual temple to his Father." Representing a more mundane, temple-building people, Hyde "erected" a pile of stones "on what was anciently called Mount Zion, where the temple stood." He no doubt believed this to be the site of the future restored temple of Israel.[57]

Jowett's only recorded personal encounter with the Jewish populace was with a Rabbi Mendel. As it appears in Jowett's memoirs, the meeting was designed to disparage the Talmud and to "prove" the superiority of Christianity. His general impression of the Jewish quarter and its inhabitants was that they were "pining away" and that their houses were "dunghills." While surveying his surroundings from the Mount of Olives, the British missionary was bombarded with impressions that the land was "suffering the vengeance of eternal fire" and that "God is a god of judgement." In his mind there was "no doubt as to the present sufferings and the eternal doom of the inhabitants of this once fertile plain of Jordan."[58]

As for oriental Christian and Latin churches and shrines, Jowett disparaged the "weight of their monastic piles." Their ceremonies were vain in the sight of God. For any truly Protestant missionary attempt to be successful, the "fulsome pageantry of the scene must first be removed. . . . this bustle of ecclesiastical apparatus must utterly vanish."[59]

Later on Jowett argues that the responsibility of Protestant missionaries is to prove to the Jews that Jesus is the Messiah and show them "Him whom they have pierced." Although "feelings of many devout Christians are, in the present day, wound up to the highest pitch in favor to the Jews," sentiments and expectations must be governed by a "wise and scriptural direction" given by Christian ministers from New Testament apostolic teaching alone. In contrast prophecy from the Old Testament leads to wild "conjecture catching at every probability." As for restoration of the Jews, Christians must desire to follow Providence and not lead.[60]

Talk of Jewish restoration in Palestine was purely a matter of business and politics, "How easily might multitudes of Christians be misled on topics of this nature." Christian efforts "in reference to the Jews, is none other than their spiritual conversion." On leaving Jerusalem Jowett reflects: "What good . . . has my visit done here? Who will be the better for it? I feel that I have done almost nothing. . . . Peace be within thy walls."[61]

The contrast between the sentiments expressed by missionaries, pilgrims, diplomats, and colonists and those expressed by Hyde and his prophet, Joseph Smith, is clear. At the same time many scholars and archaeologists staked out carefully boundaried academic territories for their labors and sought not to disturb the status quo for the sake of uninterrupted research. Those who went as pilgrims, Robert Handy has noted, "were really seeking the Holy Land of the first century . . . and hence were not . . . particularly concerned with the land as it had become."[62] Their letters and dispatches home often implicitly or otherwise deplored modernization or material renovation which upset biblical fantasies. Most of the missionaries pitted themselves against Israel's literal return and autonomous development. Their theological commitment could not make place for a politically sovereign Israel which did not have an organic relation to the church. As Jews and Muslims resisted proselytizing and Palestine became the site of *aliyah* or Jewish return and resettlement, mission accounts often expressed frustration that evangelists were mere observers not midwives to the great events they witnessed.

On the evening before Hyde's ascent of the Mount of Olives to invoke his prayer of dedication and consecration, he walked the darkened streets of Jerusalem highly agitated by the prospects of the coming morning's work. In contrast to the sentiments of his contemporaries, he wrote: "My spirit struggled within me in earnest prayer to the God of Abraham, Isaac, and Jacob, that he would not only revolutionize this country, but renovate and make it glorious. My heart would lavish its blessings upon it in the greatest prodigality in view of what is to come hereafter."[63]

NOTES

1. The description is by Parley P. Pratt, an associate of Hyde's in the quorum, from his introduction to Orson Hyde's *A Voice from Jerusalem. . .* (Liverpool: P. P. Pratt, 1842), 2.

2. The following character sketch comes from Hyde's own account, "History of Orson Hyde," *Millennial Star* 26:742-45, 760-61.

3. "Orson Hyde," in Richard S. Van Wagoner and Steven C. Walker, *A Book of Mormons* (Salt Lake City: Signature Books, 1982), 126-29.

4. Hyde, *A Voice,* ii, iii.

5. *Teachings of the Prophet Joseph Smith,* ed. Joseph Fielding Smith (Salt Lake City: Deseret Book, 1977), 163.

6. Joseph Smith, *History of the Church of Jesus Christ of Latter-day Saints,* ed. B. H. Roberts, 7 vols. (Salt Lake City: Church of Jesus Christ of Latter-day Saints, 1927-32), 2:357; my emphasis.

7. *Times and Seasons,* 2 (1 Oct. 1841): 553.

8. Orson Pratt (1811-81) was the younger brother of Parley P. Pratt and at twenty-three a member of the original twelve apostles. Pratt was a tireless evangelist, preacher, and publi-

cist. "To many Americans and Europeans in the nineteenth century, he was the best known Mormon besides Joseph Smith and Brigham Young. He was the foremost intellectual in the Church. . . ." "His influence on the doctrine and history of the Mormon people . . . can only be compared to Joseph Smith, Brigham Young, and his brother, Parley Parker Pratt." See Breck England's *The Life and Thought of Orson Pratt* (Salt Lake City: University of Utah Press, 1985). These assessments of Pratt are given by Leonard Arrington and Breck England (xv, xv).

9. Quoted in Louis Zucker, "Joseph Smith as Student of Hebrew," *Dialogue: A Journal of Mormon Thought* 3 (Summer 1968): 47.

10. *Teachings of the Prophet,* 171-72.

11. *Millennial Star,* 7 (Mar. 1842): 167-69.

12. *Times and Seasons* 2 (1 Oct. 1841): 551. This pamphlet, "Eine Stimme von der Wuste," was published by Hyde in 1842.

13. From a discourse dated 25 March 1860 as reported in *Journal of Discourses* (Liverpool: LDS Book Depot, 1855-86), 8:19-21; hereafter JD.

14. *Times and Seasons,* 3 (15 Oct. 1842): 950.

15. JD 8:21.

16. For an account of the conference, see HC 4:106, 112-13; and *Times and Seasons,* 1 (Apr. 1840): 92.

17. HC 4:106.

18. Hyde, *A Voice,* iii.

19. HC 4:113.

20. Hyde reports, "many other things were shown and told me in the vision which will be made public at the proper time and places. The vision continued open for a number of hours, that I did not close my eyes in sleep"; from Hyde, *A Voice,* iii.

21. Ibid., iii. iv.

22. Reprinted in the *Times and Seasons,* 3 (15 Nov. 1841): 591-96.

23. See ibid., 3:16; 3 (1 July 1842). See also George J. Adams, *A Few Plain Facts . . . also a short sketch of the rise, faith and doctrine of the Church of Jesus Christ of Latter-day Saints* (Bedford, England: B. Merry, 1841), 14-16; also *The Star in the East,* ed. Elder George J. Adams, 1:1, Boston 1846, 2.

24. Reported in the *Times and Seasons,* 2 (1 July 1841): 463.

25. Ibid., 1 (1 Dec. 1840).

26. Benson's "history" is recorded in the Journal History, 16 July 1846, archives, Historical Department, Church of Jesus Christ of Latter-day Saints, Salt Lake City, Utah; hereafter cited as Journal History. By 1846 Benson was the newest member of the Quorum of the Twelve and was making his way with the Saints from Nauvoo toward the Great Basin. He had been appointed to fill the vacant seat in the quorum left by John E. Page.

27. *Times and Seasons* 2 (15 July 1841): 483.

28. Heber C. Kimball (1810-68) was born in Shelton, Vermont. Kimball "was the third elder chosen to be a member of the original Quorum of the Twelve" in March 1835. Between 1832 when he was baptized a member of the LDS church and 1844, he served "eight missions and converted thousands." He was a member of the First Presidency of the church from 1847 until his death. Brigham Young and Kimball "were virtually inseparable." See Van Wagoner and Walker, *A Book of Mormons,* 136-40.

29. HC 2:489.

30. Quoted from Orson F. Whitney, *Life of Heber C. Kimball* (Salt Lake City: Stevens and Wallis, 1888), 116-17.

31. Scott Kenney, ed., *Wilford Woodruff's Journal,* 9 vols. (Midvale, UT: Signature Books, 1983), 1:405.

32. H. F. C. Harrison, *The Second Coming: Popular Millenarianism, 1780-1850,* 180.

33. W. H. Oliver, *Prophets and Millennialists,* 225.

34. *Times and Seasons,* 2 (1 Oct. 1841): 553.

35. Ibid., 551-55. Hyde's letters were published in occasional numbers of the *Times and Seasons* as a chronicle of his mission. They became one of the major marketing appeals of its editors and contributed to the appearance of "The Jews" column. The editors writing a review of volume two noted that "The interest of the succeeding volume will be greatly enhanced, from the fact that our being in the regular receipt of communications from Elder Orson Hyde, our missionary to Palestine. . . . [H]is letters will be perused with pleasure and deep interest by all the well wishers to the ancient covenant people of God—the children of Israel"; ibid., 2 (15 Oct. 1841): 574. In a "Prospectus for the third volume of the *Times and*

Seasons," the editor, E. Robinson, noted "the interest in the third volume," which, he promised, "will contain much information concerning the movements of the Jews, their belief &c, which is a matter of deep interest to all classes of community"; ibid., 3 (15 Nov. 1841).

36. Number two in "Articles of Faith," *Pearl of Great Price* (Salt Lake City: Church of Jesus Christ of Latter-day Saints, 1981), 60.

37. W. D. Davies, "Israel, Mormons, and the Land," in *Reflections on Mormonism: Judeo-Christian Parallels*, 94. Davies also points out an interesting variant conclusion in Apostle James E. Talmage's reading of the destruction of Jerusalem in *The Articles of Faith*, first published in Salt Lake City in 1899. Talmage writes, "the destruction of Jerusalem by the Romans, witnesses that every nation that fought against Israel, or in any way oppressed them, passed away." The accepted view, given out by New Testament writers themselves, was that the event was Jerusalem's just and due punishment for the death of Christ and the rejection of his movement.

38. Lewis R. Rambo, "Repentance" in *Westminster Dictionary of Christian Theology*, eds. Alan Richardson and John Bowden (Philadelphia: Westminster Press, 1983), 499.

39. According to his letter to the *Times and Seasons*, 2 (15 Oct. 1841): 570.

40. "My natural eyes, for the first time beheld Jerusalem. . . . a storm of commingled emotions suddenly arose in my breast, the force of which was only spent in a profuse shower of tears"; Hyde, *A Voice*, 7. The account of his experience in Jerusalem comes from this pamphlet: 8-11, 28-32. But did Hyde in fact travel to and see Jerusalem or did his record instead render an account of some inner visionary or spiritual pilgrimage? The following leads me to conclude he actually traveled there.

Physical descriptions. Hyde's testimony that he debarked in Jaffa, travelled overland to Jerusalem, and entered by the "west gate" (7) fits well with Yehoshua Ben Arieh's descriptions of such an approach by pilgrim traffic in the early decades of the nineteenth century; see *Jerusalem in the 19th Century: The Old City* (Jerusalem: Yad Itzhak Ben Zvi Institute, St. Martins Press, 1984). His accommodations at the "Latin

Convent" most probably refer to the Franciscan Convent of St. Savior (Hyde, 7; Ben Arieh, 227-29). Hyde's observations on the recent increase in the Jewish population in Jerusalem (Hyde, 16, 32; Ben Arieh, 270-72) and his description of the situation and appearance of Jerusalem all accord well with what a traveller in the autumn of 1841 would have seen and encountered.

Individuals. Hyde's account abounds with references to people who were present in Jerusalem and the Levant at the time of his account. Knowledge of the whereabouts of all these individuals would have been extremely unlikely had Hyde not been physically present. There is his description of German Anglicans (Hyde, 12; Ben Arieh, "they constituted most of the active missionaries in Jerusalem," 252); the naming of "Commodore [David] Porter," the first minister of the American legation in Constantinople (Hyde, 19; A. L. Tibawi, *American Interests in Syria, 1800-1901: A Study of Educational, Literary and Religious Work* [Oxford: Clarendon Press, 1966]) and "Mr. Chassan" [Jasper Chasseaud], the first U.S. vice-consul in Beirut (Hyde, 19; Tibawi, 76, 89, 94); and Hyde's frequent references to the Protestant missionary "Mr. [George B.] Whiting" (Hyde, 7, 8, 10, 11, 21 and Edward Robinson, *Later Biblical Researches in Palestine and in the Adjacent Regions* [1856; reprt. New York: Arno Press, 1977]). All of these references argue for placing Hyde in Jerusalem and the Levant in the early 1840s.

Events. Hyde notes accurately the presence of the British consul in Jerusalem not Jaffa (Hyde, 10; Ben Arieh, 184) and describes in detail reports of Druse-Christian conflicts in Lebanon (Hyde, 19; Tibawi, "the first Druze-Marionite armed conflict broke out in the autumn of 1841," 95) and the diplomatic exchange between the Sublime Porte, Consul Porter, and American missionaries in "Syria" (Hyde, 19, 34; Tibawi, 93-94).

The cumulative effect of these observations and references makes a strong case that Hyde was either unusually conversant with Mission Society records, diplomatic mail and appointments, and Middle East geography, or, what seems more reasonable, was physically present to witness and record his observations of places, people, and events in Jerusalem in October 1841.

41. Hyde, *A Voice*, 29-32.

42. Ibid., 8-11.

43. See Robert T. Handy, ed., *The Holy Land in American Protestant Life, 1800-1948: A Documentary History* (New York: Arno Press, 1981), xiv, 6-7.

44. Ibid., xiii.

45. Ibid., 7. Robinson's work was even cited in the *Times and Seasons,* 3 (15 Sept. 1842).

46. Herman Melville, *Clarel, a Poem and Pilgrimage in the Holy Land,* ed. Walter Bezanson (New York: Hendricks House, Inc., 1960), 126.

47. Horatius Bonar, *The Land of Promise: Notes of a Spring Journey from Beersheba to Sidon* (London: James Nistat and Co., 1858), 120, 208.

48. Abbe Becq, *Impressions d'un Pelerin de Terre-Sainte au Printemps de 1855: Journal d l'abbe Becq* (Tours: Alfred Marne et Fils, 1882), 11, 176, 236-37.

49. Philip Schaff, *Through Bible Lands: Notes on Travel in Egypt, the Desert, and Palestine* (New York: American Tract Society, 1878), 391, 234.

50. Handy, *Holy Land in American Protestant Life,* xviii.

51. Frank S. De Hass, *Buried Cities Recovered, or Explorations in Bible Lands,* 10th ed. (Philadelphia: Bradley and Co., 1885), 130.

52. Eldin Ricks, "Zionism and the Mormon Church," in *The Herzl Year Book,* 5 (1959): 160.

53. Ibid., and *Times and Seasons,* 2:2, 220-21; 2:16, 826-27; 3:17.

54. Handy, *Holy Land in American Protestant Life,* xix.

55. Ibid., xv, 77.

56. Ibid., 80-81.

57. William Jowett, *Christian Researches in Syria and the Holy Land in 1823 and 1824: In Furtherance of the Objects of the Church Mission Society* (Boston: Crocker and Brewster, Cummings, Hilliard and Co., 1826), 4, 6, 157, 159. Hyde's descriptions of Jerusalem can be found in *Voice,* 16, 32. For an important study of the fascination and dread which afflicted Christians with regard to the temple in Jerusalem, see Hugh Nibley, "Christian Envy of the Temple," *Jewish Quarterly Review* 50 (1959): 97-123 and (1960): 229-240.

58. Jowett, *Christian Researches,* 173-75, 189, 200.

59. Ibid., 188-89.
60. Ibid. 312-15, 318, 319.
61. Ibid., 318, 320, 193-200.
62. Handy, *Holy Land in American Protestant Life,* xvi.
63. Hyde, *A Voice,* 19.

CHAPTER SEVEN

Eschatological Pluralism

By 1853 a majority of Joseph Smith's followers were settled in Utah under the leadership of Brigham Young. Scores of sermons, tracts, commentaries, and books of theology and doctrine written in the middle decades of the nineteenth century chronicle continuing Mormon inquiry into questions about the Jewish people. Both of the contrasting views about Judaism focused by the writings of Joseph Smith and Oliver Cowdery in the church's early years continued to find issue in the Great Basin.

That Joseph Smith's more inclusive view continued to find disciples is illustrated by the encounter of Solomon Nunes Carvalho with the Mormons. In 1853 General Charles Fremont embarked on his fifth survey of the Rocky Mountains on behalf of the United States government. He was commissioned to map out a favorable transcontinental railroad route. Among the members of his team was his photographer Carvalho, a thirty-two-year-old Jew born in Charleston, South Carolina. According to one scholar, Carvalho came from a family "which prized secular and Jewish culture." Well-read and trained as an artist, Carvalho was the first photographer ever "appointed to the staff of an exploring party anywhere in the world."[1]

The route of Fremont's survey took his expeditionary team through the high and rugged mountains of southern Utah in the dead of winter. Their passage was arduous, and they were rescued by Mormon settlers in the town of Parowan. Carvalho writes, "I was mistaken for an Indian. . . . My hair was long and had not known a comb for a month, my face was unwashed, and ground in with the collected dirt of a similar period. Emaciated to a degree, my eyes sunken, and clothes all torn into tatters. . . . My hands were in a dreadful state: my fingers were frostbitten, and split at every joint: and suffering . . . from diarrhea, and symptoms of scurvy." Taken in and cared for by a Mormon family, Carvalho recalls, "When I entered Mr. Heap's house I saw three beautiful children. I covered my eyes and wept for joy to think I might yet be restored to embrace my own."[2]

Carvalho was so sick that he was unable to continue with Fremont and was sent to convalesce in Salt Lake City three hundred miles to the north. In his weakened condition, he reports, "I had to be lifted in and out [of the wagon] like a child."[3] Carvalho, who was to stay among the Mormon pioneers in Utah for almost three months, made quite an impression on his hosts. In turn he was struck by what he observed among the isolated pioneer communities of the Saints settling into the mountain valleys of the Rockies.

The largest Mormon settlement, Salt Lake City, was at the time of Carvalho's arrival in the late winter of 1854 less than seven years old. What he found was a city of some four square miles "laid out at right angles" and watered by streams of fresh water descending from the canyons of mountains ringing the settlement. Individual dwellings, mostly of adobe, "appropriated an acre and a quarter of ground, for gardening purposes." A courthouse, theater, and tabernacle had already been constructed, and another temple was "in the course of building." Carvalho "was allowed to see the plan projected by a Mr. Angell, who by *inspiration* had succeeded in producing an exact model of the one used by the

Melchisedek priesthood, in older times." Forced to abandon Nauvoo and yet another of their temples, the Saints were trying again to express their connection with the temple culture of ancient Israel. Carvalho also pointed out that Mormon men, members of a lay priesthood, wear an undergarment with distinctive marks upon it in imitation of the Jews, "who wear fringes on the borders of their garments, 'that they may look upon them and remember the commandments of the Lord to do them.'"[4]

Carvalho noted that all of these buildings and indeed "all the real estate in the valley" was the "property of the church." During a general conference of the church which he witnessed in 1854, Carvalho reports that "thousands of property holders . . . deeded their houses and lands to the church, in perpetuity." Carvalho believed he discerned in this and other manifestations of Mormon faith and practice a "sincere" and "honest" people "imbued with true religious feelings." He also went on to point out the advantageous material effects of Mormon economic policy during this period of colonization. Pioneers upon their arrival were transformed "From being tenants at will of an imperious and exacting landlord [into] land holders, in their own right—free men, living on free soil, under a free and enlightened government."[5]

Brigham Young, accepted as successor to Joseph Smith by a majority of the Saints after Smith's assassination, welcomed the explorer-photographer. Carvalho reports that "I called on Governor Young, and was received by him with marked attention. He tendered me the use of all his philosophical instruments and access to a large and valuable library."[6]

Carvalho accompanied Young on one of the president's tours to the scattered settlements of the Saints. Among Young's entourage was E. T. Benson, now an apostle. Benson was the young Illinois plainsman converted to Mormonism through the sermons of Orson Hyde and John E. Page on their way to Jerusalem. During an evening encampment, Carvalho joined a religious service. After listening to "an eloquent and feeling exhortation to the people, to practice virtue and morality" by a "Mr. Ezra Parrish," Carvalho heard Benson "preached a sermon on the restoration of Israel to Jerusalem, which would have done honor to a speaker of the Hebrew persuasion."[7]

Not all Mormons shared Benson's enthusiasm for Jewish restoration. Mormons have both produced and inherited a complex and mixed body of doctrines and traditions concerning the Jewish people and the relations between Jew and Christian. Nineteenth-century Mormons were converts from other Christian churches and theologies and practices governing Christian perceptions of Jews and Judaism. Early Mormon leaders were not of one mind about how the restoration affected their theological understanding and practical dealings with other religous traditions. The diversity that still existed in Mormon theology on this topic from the earliest days of the church can be seen by the contrasting views of two priesthood holders preaching near the time of Joseph Smith's death. At about the same time Smith was assassinated in Carthage, Illinois, church minutes report that an "Elder Whipple" preached to an assembly of the Saints "on the subject of the kingdom being taken away from the Jews and given to the Gentiles and the great work of the last days."[8] In his view at least, the Jews would play little part in the final events. But Whipple's views contrasted with those of an Elder Norton. In a conference in Greenwood, Steuben County, New York, on the first Sunday of April 1845, a "spirited discourse was delivered by Elder Norton from Isaiah 24:1-6, showing that the covenant made with the Jews, had been broken, also proved from the scriptures, that God had promised to renew it in the last days . . . [and] that the work had already commensed."[9] In Norton's view the Jews were already assuming their central place on the stage of the last days.

Joseph Smith himself was not innocent of a certain invective against Jews. Smith made use of the standard stock of New Testament epithets against Hebrews as weapons in his defense against attacks from without and dissension and defection within the ranks of the church. Doctrinal innovations introduced in Nauvoo—among them the practice of polygamy—brought intense opposition from many chagrined Saints, including some of Smith's closest associates. He attacked their resistance by linking them with those who opposed "new revelations" introduced by Jesus of Nazareth: "The same principle [resistance to innovations] was signally manifest among the Jews when the Savior came in the flesh. These, then religious bigots boasted of the old revelations, garnished the sepulchres of the dead . . . but yet when the new revelation came fresh from the mouth of the great I Am . . . they could not endure it. . . . it showed the corruptions of that generation."[10]

Referring to those seeking Smith's life in the fall of 1842, the *Times and Seasons* followed in this tradition: "Fortunately for this generation, their fathers had not prophets to kill, but they show a disposition to tread in the footsteps of the Jewish nation, and to manifest their religion by seeking to destroy from off the face of the earth those whom God hath sent. Our Savior said of the Jews, 'Ye are of your father the devil. . . .'"[11]

Those who followed in this same vein after Smith's death included John Taylor, Wilford Woodruff, and Orson Pratt. John Taylor, Smith's successor as editor of the *Times and Seasons* and Brigham Young's successor as president of the LDS church, claimed in an April 1853 general conference in Salt Lake City: "We read [that] the Jews . . . were a nation that submitted only in part to his [God's] authority, for they rebelled against his laws and were placed under a schoolmaster until the Messiah should come."[12] Sixteen years later Taylor opined that the Law had been a curse not a blessing to Israel. After quoting Galatians 3:8, he remarked: "Now some people think the law of Moses . . . was given to the children of Israel as a peculiar kind of blessing; but it was a peculiar kind of curse, added because of transgression. It was as Peter said—neither they nor their fathers were able to bear it. . . . When Jesus came to do away with the law and to introduce the gospel which their fathers had lost because of transgression . . . the heavens were opened, the purpose of God was unfolded and His power made manifest among the people."[13]

Ordained an apostle in 1838, Wilford Woodruff was veteran of numerous missions in the eastern United States and Great Britain and along with Orson Pratt was also among the first company of Saints to enter the Great Salt Lake Valley in July 1847. Woodruff succeeded Taylor in 1889 as the fourth president of the church.[14] In an 1878 sermon typical of numerous pronouncements by him on this topic, Woodruff pointed out that the Jews of first century Palestine were "intently looking forward to the coming of their Shiloh in the person of King, a ruler who should possess great power. . . ."[15] Chafing under the "Romish yoke," they rejected the "gospel message" of Jesus of Nazareth "and the words of life he taught them." Due to their "vanity and pride," they "despised him and persecuted him, and at last shed his blood." For this act the Jewish people "have been paying the penalty of their misdeeds for the past 1800 years. It costs something to shed innocent blood."[16] A "Gentile judge" was willing to release him, but "those that took part in the deed and those who sanctioned it, said, 'Let His blood be upon us and our children after us.'"[17]

Woodruff protested his good will towards the Jewish people: "I do not say this [their 'rejection' of Jesus] because I wish to find fault with them. I have a great love for them as a people."[18] And he pronounces evil tidings on their gentile persecutors, "Woe unto the Gentiles, who have administered afflictions to the Jews for these many years?"[19] Still the cumulative effect of Woodruff's preaching about the Jewish people was to cast them as justly suffering for venial and mortal crimes, as a cursed pariah community.

Orson Pratt was, along with his older sibling, Parley P. Pratt, a charter member of the first quorum of apostles organized in the spring of 1835. Both he and Parley were also prominent theologians and apologists for the church. Orson Pratt's published works were extremely influential in developing and articulating LDS church doctrine and theology.[20] With the exception of Brigham Young, Pratt was the most visible figure in the LDS church for the "gentile" world. Nicknamed the "Gauge of Philosophy,"[21] he was a singular intellectual force among frontier Mormons. He was conversant in mathematics, astronomy, surveying, philosophy, and theology, and his sermons were laced liberally with citations from Christian church fathers, Scottish philosophers, Unitarian biblical scholars, and Anglican ecclesiastical theoreticians as well as scriptural prooftexts from the Bible and the Book of Mormon.

In a major statement given on 2 January 1859 on the relationship of the Mormon canon to the scriptures of the Jewish and Christian communities, Pratt undertook a text-critical examination of biblical manuscripts and the history of their transmission. The intent of his sermon was to contrast the trust of Mormons in the Book of Mormon with the skepticism of "enlightened" scholars about the reliability of extant biblical manuscripts: "having learned that they are very imperfect in their present state, and that they have been translated from manuscripts that cannot be depended upon."[22]

In this examination of sources, Pratt accepted without hesitation the testimony of early church fathers riddled with anti-Jewish invective. Pratt concluded his survey of "ancient manuscripts" by stating that "All, therefore is uncertainty, not only in relation to the Hebrew manuscripts, but also the Greek."[23] In support of this contention, Pratt cites John Chrysostom (347-407 C.E.) and Justin Martyr (ca. 100-ca. 165 C.E.) as authoritative witness to the violence done to biblical manuscripts by Jewish leaders in the second and fourth centuries.

Chrysostom, author of the vituperative *Homilies Against the Jews,* was quoted as saying, "Many of the prophetical monuments have perished; for the Jews being careless, and not only careless but impious, have carelessly lost some of these monuments; others they have partly burned, partly torn to pieces." The reason behind this "impiety" had already been conveniently supplied by Justin, whose testimony Pratt cites: "We are also informed by St. Justin, another early Christian writer, that the Jews actually did destroy a great number of the prophetical books, in order that the world might not perceive the agreement between the ancient Prophets and the Old Testament and Christianity."[24]

It is clear from the whole text of Pratt's sermon that he did not intend to vilify Jews so much as undermine the exclusive scriptural authority of the Bible. For three decades Mormons had protested that the image of their church, beliefs, and leaders presented by journalists and observers was distorted. But when confronted with the testimony of ancient church fathers, who had no less an axe to grind against Jews than did opponents of the Latter-day Saints against Mormonism, Pratt uncritically depended on their narratives. Pratt's acceptance of these sources within the context of Judaism is even more striking given his otherwise constant criticism of the writings of a "fallen" Christian church.

The lapse in Pratt's critical faculty is less surprising when considered alongside his stated views on Judaism which were outlined in a major address given on 26

March 1871. Pratt was working from the text of Isaiah 4:1-5: "Speak ye comfortably to Jerusalem . . . that her warfare is accomplished, that her iniquity is pardoned." Pratt took pains to point out this was "a prediction not yet fulfilled."[25] In contrast, Orson Hyde had quoted these verses in order to deny any further corporate guilt of Jewish people for the death of Christ. Hyde insisted that this passage from Isaiah had been fulfilled.

In his 1871 discourse, Pratt either did not know of Hyde's pronouncement and mission or was preaching in conscious opposition to it. The Jews, Pratt sermonized, "were once in possession of all the miraculous fruits and blessings and gifts for the kingdom." But because they had "persecuted, hated, and reviled . . . [Christ] . . . and finally succeeded . . . in crucifying him," the "Kingdom was taken away from Israel and given to [the gentiles]." "In consequence of the wickedness of the people," Pratt continued, "and the great transgressions . . . in rejecting the Lord, their true Messiah, great and severe calamities and judgements came upon them. . . . In other words, all those curses which are pronounced in the Book of Deuteronomy upon the head of Israel have literally been fulfilled during the past 1800 years."

Thirty years after Hyde's mission of territorial dedication, healing, and blessing, Pratt went on to ask, "When will the time come for this great curse to be removed from the Jewish nation? When shall it be said that 'her iniquity is pardoned. . .?'" His own answer was in accordance with his reading of Luke 21:24—not "until the times of the Gentiles be fulfilled." "Until that is fulfilled," Pratt predicted confidently, "Jerusalem can never be rebuilt, and the Jews can never return as a nation."

At the same time there was another, more positively accented tradition which also found its roots in the pronouncements of Joseph Smith. This tradition favorably cited Jewish institutions, beliefs, concerns, and practices, especially when recommending variants of Jewish tradition to the Saints. Smith had begun this tradition when he lauded the "fervor and love and attachment to the Temple" displayed by Jews in "Solomon's and Nehemiah's days, which shed still greater lustre on the Jewish nation," an example Smith recommends that the Saints "in this age would do well to imitate."[26] Continuing in this tradition Brigham Young encouraged completion of the Nauvoo temple despite the setbacks posed by Joseph's assassination. Young pointed out to the devastated Saints: "If you leave this place [Nauvoo] for fear of the mob before God tells you to go, you will have no place to rest. . . . We want to build the Temple in this place, if we have to build it, as the Jews built the walls of the Temple in Jerusalem with a sword in one hand and the trowel in the other."[27]

The Mormon "exodus" from Illinois and other sites to the Great Basin of the Rocky Mountains was naturally compared to Israel's exodus from Egypt and its occupation of Canaan. In an article in the *Times and Seasons,* Brigham Young cited both the Exodus narrative and tale of Esther and Mordecai as precursors and parallels to the LDS "flight out of Babylon." Elsewhere he wrote, "A crisis of extraordinary and thrilling interest has arrived. The exodus of the Nation of the only true Israel from these United States to a far distant region of the west." Sam Brannan, a company "captain" in the Mormon hegira, proclaimed in the 31 January 1846 issue of the *New York Messenger,* "Come On O, Israel, it is time to Go!"[28]

At approximately the same time, Orson Spencer, the newly appointed president of the England mission for the LDS church, was searching for a more stately cadence to explain the Mormon doctrine of gathering. In a letter to the "Reverend W. Crowel, A.M.," Spencer invoked the authority of scripture: "The Bible, I trust . . . informs you not only how God *has* gathered his people in different periods of the world, but also, that He *will* gather them in the dispensation of the fulness of times." "Revelation," Spencer wrote, was given to Moses "to *gather* an oppressed people to a particular place." "When Jerusalem was about to be destroyed, Jesus instructed his disciples to flee to the mountain." "The ancient Jews were taught of God to build up Jerusalem as a place of *gathering*." In their capital city, "they could interchange hospitalities and friendships, and contract matrimonial alliances." Their records were "deposited in the archives of the great Temple of the Lord at Jerusalem."[29] The "commonwealth of Israel," Spencer continued, and the rites and festivals of the Jews all combined in a "great design" to bring "the righteous together in one place." "By these multiplied means," he concluded, "the union of the Jews became proverbially strong; and their attachments to their nation and kindred, and national rights and usages, became as enduring as their existence. If, perchance, they should be scattered amongst the remote nations of the earth, still the recollection of their journeyings to Jerusalem in social groups, their royal affinity with the great and good of God's people, vibrated through their minds with resuscitating power."[30]

One of the earliest and most important of Latter-day Saint tracts, Apostle Parley P. Pratt's *A Voice of Warning* published in 1837, made clear how Mormonism's positive accent on the Jewish model was pitted against traditional Christian agendas for the Jews.[31] In this pamphlet Pratt denigrated Christian mission societies and their plans for the conversion of Jews: "Behold ye flatter yourselves that the glorious [millennial] day spoken of by the Prophets will be ushered in by your modern inventions and your moneyed plans, which are got up in order to convert the Jews . . . and you expect when this is done, to behold a Millennium after your own heart. But the Jews . . . never will be converted as a people to any other plan than that laid down in the Bible, for the great restoration of Israel." Later in the book he continued: "[A]ny man who says that the Jews, as a nation, have been commanded to repent and be baptised for the last seventeen hundred years; says that which he cannot prove. . . . [N]either will any generation of Jews, which have existed since inspiration ceased, be condemned, for rejecting any message from God [via Christian missionaries], for he has sent no message to them; consequently they have rejected none. . . ."[32]

In the same tract Pratt also turned his attention to the "restoration of Israel to Jerusalem." Citing Deuteronomy 28:33-38 and 36, he concluded, "On the subject of this restoration, the Prophets have spoken . . . fully and . . . repeatedly." The cumulative effect of these prophecies had meant that "Now in [their] long captivity, the Jews have never lost sight of the promises respecting their return. Their eyes have watched and filled with longing for the day when they might possess again that blessed inheritance, bequeathed to their forefathers; when they might again rear their city and temple, and reestablish their priesthood, and worship as in days of old."[33]

There are common threads which stitch all of the preceding comments together and which begin to focus the radical differences which ultimately make of Mormonism an independent Christian tradition. But there are also important differences which amount to two divergent traditions within Mormonism. The differences ultimately have to do with how closely tied various interpreters remain to traditional Christian views. Radically severing such interpretative ties becomes critical then to enabling the crucial differences of Mormonism's separate tradition to stand forth.

Whether it is E. T. Benson's sermon "which would have done honor to a speaker of the Hebrew persuasion" or Orson Spencer's open admiration for Israel's religious culture during the second temple period or John

Taylor's harsh assessment of Mosaic legislation or Orson Pratt's recourse to curses and imputation of guilt, all draw from the source and authority of the Bible as it was read and understood by the Saints. Thus considering how Mormons interpreted the Bible is the first step in understanding disputes which continued within Mormonism during the nineteenth century and which still have issue on the contemporary Mormon stage.

We have seen that the early Saints were not naive about the imperfections of Holy Writ, but Mormons in contrast to most orthodox Christians insisted nonetheless on a "literal" interpretation of scripture. What Mormons meant by this advocacy of "literal" interpretation and how such interpretative strategies affected their approach to religion and life thus is crucial to an investigation of Mormonism's view of Jewish people.

The Book of Mormon warned that "many plain and precious things" had been excised by gentile Christians after the scripture had "gone forth in purity from the Jews" (contrast this to the writings of Justin, Chrysostom, and Pratt), and Joseph Smith had qualified his trust in the Bible: "We believe the Bible to be the word of God as far as it is translated correctly." But Mormon authors writing in the half century between 1830 and 1880 were insulated from the disclosures of historical-critical scholarship of the Bible.[34] Their "literal" interpretation of canon did not equip the Saints' leaders to analyze critically the process of collection, composition, and redaction of scripture. Nor were they attuned to complex rhetorical, ecclesiastical, and theological intentions of biblical authors and editors.

For example, in spite of the traditional Christian reading of selected passages of the New Testament, there is no indication that it was Jesus' or Paul's intention to have their contextually specific criticism of fellow Jews translated by gentiles into a negation of Israel's covenant, law, and election. But this is exactly what occurred. Jesus' critique of his fellow Jewish sectarian contemporaries and Paul's running battle with critics of his gentile mission have been misunderstood by Christians as authoritative warrants for anti-Judaic theology and actions. Mormons were not immune to this interpretive mistake.

Orson Pratt's 1859 sermon illustrates this point. He could embrace without compunction the most skeptical conclusions of the "lower" or text/manuscript critics of biblical canon: "All, therefore, is uncertainty, not only in the Hebrew manuscripts, but also the Greek."[35] And yet it would scarcely occur to him or his colleagues to question the "literal" meaning of the text backed by a long-lived theological and exegetical tradition negating "old" Israel as a whole.

Mormon preachers and publicists insisted on biblical interpretation being governed by its "literal" reading. The term "literal" is used frequently by LDS authors throughout a wide range of sources, and from its use it would appear that they shared certain assumptions about its meaning. However, the concept of a "literal" reading for scripture is not self-evident to contemporary readers.[36]

The guiding principle in early LDS hermeneutics was the belief that biblical authors themselves intended their writing to be understood in a "literal" or *historic* sense. Adopting the terms of the two great patristic "schools," their reading was Antiochene rather than Alexandrian: Mormon authors stressed the "historical" over the "allegorical" sense of the text. This tendency falls under the medieval hermeneutical category of "literal" as opposed to allegorical, tropological, and anagogical options. Therefore they would have been more at home with Andrew of St. Victor's use of Jewish sources in the search for the historical sense of scripture and Aquinas's insistence that "The first signification whereby words signify things belongs to the first sense, the historical or literal and that the 'spiritual sense' of scripture is based on the literal and presupposes it."[37]

"Spiritualizers" or "allegorizers" would have it just the other way around. For them, according to one scholar, the "literal sense of scripture" was the "shadow which the body casts . . . [a] divinely authorized veil covering" that was the truly significant meaning.[38] Thus "Barnabas" held that the Jews of Jesus' time never penetrated the veil, that they were "beguiled by the literal sense of scripture" and thus rejected the spiritual message and kingdom taught by Jesus. Allegorizing allowed Justin in his polemic against the Jews to see Leah and Rachel as prefiguring the synagogue and the church. Augustine's interpretation of the parable of the good Samaritan is of a piece with this method, where he identifies the traveller as Adam, Jerusalem with the Heavenly City from which he fell, and the priest and Levite as the "ineffectual ministrations of the old covenant."[39]

The allegorical or spiritual method has been extremely influential and long lived in the Christian churches. This method, what early Mormons criticized as "spiritualizing," has also been employed by clergy as a principal tool for anti-Jewish theology as the brief references from "Barnabas," Justin, and Augustine suggest. Thus the Mormon attack on "spiritualizing" was entwined with its polemic against certain Christian views of Israel and with Mormonism's "correction" of Christian understanding of "Old" Testament passages dealing with the restoration of Israel. The interpretation of these passages was a matter of intense debate, for their "resolution," many believed, provided keys to reading the pattern imprinted on unfolding apocalyptic events. To whom did the term "Jew" refer? Which city did "Jerusalem" signify? What was actually meant by "restoration"? Deploying allegorical or spiritual principles of interpretation, Christians concluded frequently that Jerusalem was the "heavenly city" or the church of

Christ, that Israel pointed to the "New" Testament church or an apocalyptic one comprised of Jews converted en masse to a gentile church. To draw such conclusions, Mormons believed, meant concluding as well that the historical covenants and promises of God to a historical people—whether Jew or Mormon—were feckless and uncertain at best, malicious at worst.

The Mormon confrontation with Millerite adventism in the early 1840s provided a prime example of this concern for a historical reading of Israel in the latter days. According to Miller's exegesis, the "dispensation" of Israel's ancient covenant had ended with the rise of the Church of Christ. If Israel had been effectively displaced by the Church of Christ, then all of Israel's covenants, its promises, and all prophetic pronouncements concerning the end of its exile, its return, salvation, and restoration referred exclusively to Christians. Mormons were openly arrayed against such an approach to the scriptural record.

"I attended a Millerite meeting in the forenoon," reports Brigham Young on 6 August 1843 in his "Manuscript History": "Mr. Litz preached from Jeremiah, 24th chapter, concerning the good and bad figs. In speaking of the covenants made to Abraham, giving him the land of Canaan, Lits [sic] said is was not seeds, but seed, which was Christ, Hence the land belonged to Jesus, and not to the Jews. . . . the land has been taken away from the Jews, who shall have [it]? Not the Jews, the natural seed, but those who are baptized unto Christ, his spiritual children. The Kingdom . . . will take place when Christ comes with his church and body, and they will take possession of Jerusalem. The Jews, as a nation, will not go to Jerusalem, neither will they any more be His people, but the Jews will join other nations, and go against Jerusalem to battle and fight against the Lord and his Saints." Young concludes, "These were the arguments used by this Millerite to do away with *literal* fulfillment of the Bible concerning the return of the Jews and the rebuilding of Jerusalem." Much like his colleagues in other venues and other pages, Young denounces adventist understanding of the scripture as being "false and contrary to the restoration of the house of Israel, as predicted by all the Prophets."[40]

In the same year Mormon writer William Appleby attacked Miller's millennial calculations by asking, "Why believe that the world will come to an end this year . . . when the Jews are to be literally gathered back to Jerusalem."[41] Another Mormon missionary, Moses Martin, in his "A Treatise on the fulness of the everlasting Gospel . . . ," also insisted on the historical gathering and restoration of "Judah and Israel." Trying among other things in this "treatise" to prove that "God is unchangeable" and that his kingdom and laws are "immutable," Martin singled out as his most powerful argument the Lord's everlasting promises to the "literal seed of Abraham." In contrast to the Millerites, Martin wrote that "The seed of Abraham, together with all those who are grafted in, and numbered among the literal seed are to be gathered in the last days unto Zion and Jerusalem" and that "the literal seed of Abraham, not converted Gentiles" would be particularly favored in the latter days to come.[42]

Latter-day Saints contended with any who tried to usurp Israel's concrete scriptural promises and covenants as if these interlopers were modern Marcionites.[43] If Israel's covenant and worship had come to naught and its home in this world was acquired by an upstart church, despite all the promises and prophecies recorded in scripture, then the Saints' own community and worship and the "covenants" on which they were grounded would become similarly tenuous.[44] Devotion to a literal/historically interpreted scripture instilled in the Saints a trust in the integrity of God's promises and a respect for the example of Israel, its institutions, laws, and narratives.

On 5 January 1882 the *Deseret News* featured a lengthy editorial on the development and outbreak of anti-Jewish activity in Germany. The editorial, "Germany and the Jews," described the latest round of anti-Jewish activity as a "crusade against the Jews," which the paper viewed with "a feeling of indignation." The "Court Chaplain," Hans Stoeckler, was identified as the "principal figure in the present agitation," leading a wave of "prejudice," "jealousy," and "race antipathies" against the Jews' "remarkable growth into power through the force of their ability, thrift, and eminent business qualifications. "Reason" and "justice" are being cast aside by the "ignorance" of the masses and the "envy" of "the educated." The *News* concluded: "The truth is, that the 'times of the Gentiles' are nearly fulfilled. The day of Israel is dawning. Judah must come forth out of the dust and ashes and take a leading place in the affairs of the world."[45]

The phrase "the times of the Gentiles" focused on a commonly held tenet within the Mormon faith. Invoking this passage from Luke 21:24 was part of the stock-in-trade of Mormon preaching and prophesying.[46] "The meaning of this suggestive phrase is not clear," wrote biblical scholar A. B. Bruce,[47] and later commentators tend to agree that the passage is a subsequent "editorial elaboration."[48] However, Mormons understood that "times of the Gentiles" referred to a literal space of "time."[49] In this case Mormons believed the passage implied that a season had been accorded the gentiles, first to become "adopted seed of Abraham" or to enter the Church of Christ and second to exercise worldly, political supremacy over the nations, especially over the Jewish people.

This phrase constituted a repeating accent in the prosody of Mormon prophetic preaching about the "last days." From the outset of Smith's career, it was the belief of Mormons that the "times of the Gentiles" was coming to a close. In 1855 Apostle Parley Pratt discoursed: "Now there was a time allotted for the Gentile powers to reign, for their corruptions to bear rule . . . the times of their polity, of their nationality, their religion, and to prove them and to see what they would do with the power committed unto them." According to Pratt, that season, designated by Daniel as the "fourth monarchy," was in its final phase. He warned: "Now when that time arrives, ye nations look out. . . . [W]hen the times of the Gentiles are fulfilled there will be an uprooting of their governments and institutions, and of their civil, political, and religious polity. There will be a shaking of nations, a downfall of empires, an upturning of thrones and dominions."[50]

In the nineteenth century, abundant "signs" pointed to the imminent demise of the "fourth monarchy." The "restoration of the fulness of the gospel," the founding of the Latter-day Saint church, was one unmistakable sign. Natural convulsions, disasters, and the "wars and perplexities of the nations" all contributed to an accumulating weight of evidence pointing to the passing of the age. A public and unambiguous sign, according to many Saints, was the resurgence of Jewish aspiration for a return to Palestine and the restoration of a state. The return and restoration of the Jewish people would, Mormons confidently expected, confirm their reading of biblical prophecy,[51] vouchsafe the words and promises of God, add luster to the credentials of the Saints and their prophets, and inaugurate the last messianic/millennial dispensation.

The "prophetic," apocalyptic significance of Israel's restoration was an essential plank in many religious platforms in Great Britain and ante-bellum America. Latter-day Saints shared an assurance with other "prophetic" factions that Israel would be "gathered" and that their gathering was a condition for, a harbinger of, the Millennium. However, Saints and "prophetic" Christians diverged over the interpretation, Mormons foreseeing a "restored" Israel on the one hand and a separate "restored" church, or Zion, distinct from Israel, on the other.[52]

"[It] is a sight some of you will see," Parley Pratt prophesied in 1855. "This is the day of redemption . . . when Jerusalem and the Jews are about to be restored, and the full end of all Gentile polity is about to usher it." In other words, "Jerusalem is to be rebuilt, to be no more trodden down nor governed by them [the gentiles]." "The Jews," Pratt continued, "while wandering among the nations of the earth from age to age," while "the Gentile powers bear rule," are suffering through a period of "captivity." In words that would have resonated particularly within a Mormon audience, Pratt described the sign of the end of captivity as establishment of a Jewish "national polity: a national . . . form of government, a national priesthood, a national house of worship."[53]

Israel's fortunes were beginning to be reversed. The time of waiting "for the redemption of their nation and national polity, and for their triumph over their enemies . . . and for the establishment of the reign of righteousness on the earth" was, Pratt insisted, nigh at hand. "Do you believe this, ye young people, ye boys and girls," he demanded of the junior members of the congregation that autumn day, "Do ye believe this? All the prophetic sayings . . . have been fulfilled, down to this day . . . it is right before your eyes in its fulfillment."[54]

However, Parley Pratt's younger brother, Apostle Orson Pratt, proposed an interpretation of the last days which emphasizes the ultimate subordination of Judaism to Mormonism. In an important sermon delivered 26 March 1871, Orson Pratt confessed that fixing the precise time for the fall and rise of dispensations had always proved difficult: "chronology is so imperfect that many hundreds who have spent their lives . . . differ from each other in their conclusion. . . . We are utterly at a loss."[55] Nevertheless he was convinced that "you young men who sit here on these seats will live to see the times of the Gentiles fulfilled."[56] At that time these young Mormon men would "take up [a] mission to the scattered of Israel. . . . You will go in the Lord's power. . . . You will tell them [Israel] that their warfare is accomplished, that her iniquity is pardoned."[57]

Once again in ignorance or defiance of Orson Hyde's words and mission thirty years earlier, Orson Pratt signalled his belief that Israel or the Jewish people continued to labor under the burden of divine retribution for their sins. Moreover, according to Pratt, the ultimate destiny of the Jewish people was identity with the Saints through their conversion to the Church of Christ and its gospel message as taught to them by Mormon elders. "The everlasting gospel" dispensed from heaven was universal in its scope and was therefore to be taught indiscriminately to all nations: "Gentiles and Jews, all must hear it. . . . it is to be preached to all nations, kindreds, tongues and people. This of course includes Gentiles as well as Jews."[58]

Pratt predicted that a display of power "that will eclipse [that of] the Exodus" would attend this last great missionary endeavor: "They are not willing now and have not been willing for eighteen centuries past. . . . But when the day of his power comes they will be willing to hearken. . . ." The "set time for their deliverance and restoration will have come . . . in which the Gospel shall be proclaimed to them."[59] In describing the future of Mormon and Jewish peoples, Pratt would have considered mutual sovereignty to be out of the question. For him the destiny of these communities was convergence and virtual identity in the "last days."

But the tradition persisted within Mormonism that Israel would have autonomy after the "times of the Gentiles." Thus Erastus Snow, who was to become a prominent apostle and colonizer in Utah, asked a Mormon congregation in 1857: "How was it with Israel of old. . . . What think you . . . ye that are called Latter-day Saints, were they, as a people, more wicked than the rest of mankind, that God should have dealt with them thus? I answer, No. But of a truth they were the best people upon the face of the earth, and the only people that had the Priesthood of God among them. . . . [A]nd by his power, they were the only people God could make use of. They had faith sufficient that he could govern and control them . . . ; but upon them rested the responsibility [to preserve God's word among them]. . . ."[60] In an earlier sermon Snow had averred that "Israel must yet become a kingdom of priests, on their native land" and had cited Isaiah 1:26 to defend the restoration of autonomous Jewish cultic and political institutions.[61]

"The work of building up Zion," Brigham Young preached in 1862, "is in every sense a practical work; it is not a mere theory. . . . To possess an inheritance in Zion or Jerusalem only in theory—only in imagination—would be the same as having no inheritance at all."[62] A year later, Young asked a Mormon assembly: "Is the Lord going to convince the people . . . beautify [city and temple] and then place them there without any exertion on their part? No. He will not come here to build a Temple . . . or to set out fruit trees, make aprons of fig leaves or coats of skins, or work in brass and iron, for we already know how to do these things. . . . We have to build up Zion, if we do our duty."[63]

The work of building the foundations for the kingdom reposed on the Saints and on Israel if they were ever "to possess an inheritance in Zion or Jerusalem." Each community had its responsibilities and tasks. The labor and sacrifices of covenant communities would, the Saints hoped, then be capped by the advent of the Lord Jesus Christ who would reign personally on the earth for a thousand years from the messianic capitals of Jerusalem and Zion.

It was the task of the Saints, Brigham Young preached in May 1863, "to build up [the] *Zion* of our God, to gather the House of Israel, restore and bless the earth with our ability and make it as the Garden of Eden, store up treasures of knowledge and wisdom in our own understandings, purify our . . . hearts and prepare a people to meet the Lord when he comes."[64] Meanwhile "Jerusalem," Young opined, "is not to be redeemed by our going there and preaching to the inhabitants."[65] "We have a great desire for their [the Jewish people's] welfare," Young affirmed on another occasion, "and are looking for the time soon to come when they will gather to Jerusalem, build up their city and the land of Palestine. . . ."[66] Young, an avid disciple of Smith, varied from the tradition established by Joseph earlier in Nauvoo which construed Israel's restoration as temple-centered and independent from the church.

In an editorial in the church's *Deseret News* published in Salt Lake City after Young's death, the independence of Jerusalem was reiterated: "That Jerusalem will be rebuilt by the sons of Jacob, and that the [Davidic] kingdom will be established . . . is as definite a tenet of the 'Mormon' faith as the gathering of the Saints from 'the four quarters' of the earth to the Zion of God on this continent."[67] This "definite tenet" of "Mormon faith" fueled a keen and durable interest among the Latter-day Saints for news about Jewish affairs, movements, persecution, and immigration. An editorial in the *Deseret News* of 10 September 1879 entitled "A General Jewish Convention" is representative of this coverage. "The objects of this convention are not yet declared," the editor wrote. "But we hope some steps will be taken for the full emancipation of the Jews in all civilized nations, and that something will be done leading to the future occupation and redemption of the land of their forefathers. Prophecy points to this as one of the certain events of the latter times, and all things seem propitious for the speedy fulfillment of their sayings."[68]

The Pratts, Oliver Cowdery, Sidney Rigdon, and others who studied or at least were acquainted with theological traditions from Christian communities "outside" of and older than the community of the Saints inherited exegetical principles and prejudices from those sources. Cowdery and Orson Pratt in particular expected the triumph of the church's mission and doctrine. Due to their active and turbulent lives and times, their theologies never found expression in achieved and systematic multi-volumed works. But they believed that every knee would bow, every tongue confess, and Jew and gentile alike would be compelled by the logic of events and the gospel preached by the Saints to embrace the radiant body of the Church Triumphant. These hopes and expectations, shorn of their Mormon particularity, were of a piece with both the rapt theologies of revivalists and the dispassionate systems of the seminary professors who were their contemporaries.[69]

Those in Mormonism's second tradition which began with Joseph Smith and Orson Hyde were largely self-taught and grew up with only the most tenuous ties to organized Christian bodies. They expressed positive and independent ideas about the relation between Zion and Jerusalem. Ignorant of or underwhelmed by theologies and practices directed at the Jews by the Christian tradition, these other Saints, unlike Pratt and Cowdery, felt no obligation to respond to and had no reason to imitate this tradition. They felt compelled by events, by the word of scriptures and of living Jews, to search in the metaphors and language they possessed for an affirmation of the existence and integrity of the Israel of God, as well as that of the Saints.

Brigham Young, Joseph Smith's successor and disciple, was clearly in this second, "naive" tradition. He was a frequent critic of Orson Pratt.[70] Pratt's speculative erudition and frequent reference to what Young characterized as "gentile" schools of philosophy irked the self-educated church president. Young admonished the Saints: "With regard to doctrinal points, that which we do not understand should not be talked about in this stand; and the Elders of Israel should never contend about any point of doctrine that does not pertain to the present day's salvation."[71] The exemption to this rule was of course Young himself. Yet he also down-played his own calling as "prophet, seer, and revelator": "I am not going to interpret dreams; for I don't profess to be such a Prophet as were Joseph Smith and Daniel; but I am a Yankee guesser." Or: "I have never particularly desired any man to testify publicly that I am a Prophet; but, if I am not, one thing is certain, I have been very profitable to this people."[72] And his sermons generally dwelt more on issues of settlement, colonization and education, agriculture, home industry and care for the poor than on the "sons of perdition," foreordination, heaven, and the Millennium.[73]

On occasion he felt constrained to speculate on the nature of the great millennial age. "Many of our Elders," Young remarked, "labor under . . . erroneous expectations when reading over the sayings of the Apostles and Prophets in regard to the coming of the Son of Man." Young's corrections to "these erroneous expectations" were voiced on three separate occasions: 8 July 1855, 23 December 1866, and 16 August 1868.[74] In opposition to Pratt, Cowdery, and some of his own successors to the presidency of the church, Young foresaw a remarkably pluralistic future in the age to come.

In the 1855 discourse Young bluntly asked, "When the Kingdom of Heaven spreads over the whole earth, do you expect that all people composing the different nations will become Latter-day Saints?" The term "Kingdom of Heaven" on earth is later referred to as the "Kingdom of God" (1866) and "Zion" (1868), and becoming "Latter-day Saints" is restated as "joining the church" (1866). But the question remained the same. Young's answer was always negative: "If the Latter-day Saints think, when the Kingdom of God is established on the earth, that all the inhabitants of the earth will join the church . . . they are egregiously mistaken."[75]

Many Saints harbored hopes that their cause and their hardships would be vindicated unequivocally in the millennial age. Foes would be vanquished, the church would be crowned with laurels, rival religious traditions would wither away or collapse under the weight of millennial events, and the earth would once again be a paradise to humankind. Here finally beyond the horizon of the "times of the Gentiles," all the doctrines and opinions of the Saints would be verified. But Brigham Young in deference to his mentor and prophet, Joseph Smith, denied the Saints even this last sanctuary. And in his sermons he indicated to the Saints that the "truth" and integrity of their religion did not depend on their exclusive triumph in this age or in the age to come.

Young opposed those who maintained that all but the Saints would be swept from the earth's landscapes or that the earth's natural order would be miraculously transfigured "into a sea of glass, as John described it." "Will this be the millennium?" Young thundered, "No." Only a few fundamental changes would distinguish the millennial era from the present age. In the Millennium, Young opined, "there will be every sort of sect and party, and every individual following what he supposes to be the best in religion, and in everything else, similar to what it is now." The only essential differences between one age and the next would be that the nations would pay tribute "to the Most High, who created . . . and preserved" them. And finally "under the influence and power of the Kingdom of God, the Church of God will rest secure and dwell in safety."[76]

Young believed that even when "the veil of covering may be taken from before the nations, and all flesh see His glory together . . . at the same time [they will still be free to] declare they will not serve him." "Seeing the Lord does not make a man a Saint," Young concluded. Many of the Saints took the final confession of the nations—"every knee shall bend, and every tongue confess that Jesus is the Christ"—as a signal of the end of religious diversity and the final triumph of the mission of the Latter-day Saint church. But the ever-realistic Young believed that after bowing the knee and tripping the tongue in confession, people would yet "worship the sun, moon, a white dog, or anything else they please." "There may be more societies than 666 for aught I know," Young told his audience in 1868.[77]

Young learned from Joseph Smith that human free agency was an irreducible fact and birthright bestowed on all the children of God. Latter-day Saint theology and practice hinge to a significant degree on this agency and the related principle of accountability. Any social order be it mortal or celestial in which these principles were forfeited or suppressed was in principle repugnant to Young. He remembered the Saints' bitter experience of persecution and Smith's teachings on human agency and his vision of plural, temple-ordered societies. Thus Young felt compelled to oppose those within the church who projected a future, monolithic order dictated or enjoyed exclusively by the Saints.

It is not the case that Young considered all religious traditions of equal value or above criticism. He lived and died a staunch advocate of the Latter-day Saint cause and never failed to level withering blasts, solemn and satirical, at the follies of other religions when he deemed it fitting to do so. Yet for all his lack of ecumenical spirit, Brigham Young's ideas about the coexistence of plural religious societies display a wisdom that only now Latter-day Saints are beginning to appreciate. Contemporary members of the LDS church come from around the world. As the church thus inevitably confronts other religious traditions and communities, Young's opinions on the continued existence of a multitude of religions throughout the Millennium may yet enable the LDS church to reassess the integrity and staying power of the gentiles and the Jews.

Interreligious dialogue and sympathetic yet critical inquiry into other religious traditions were sanctioned by Young's unusual sermons on the Millennium and the "last things." After telling the congregation that "Jews and gentiles" will not "be obliged to belong to the Church of Jesus Christ of Latter-day Saints," Young went on to construe human, religious, and cosmic orders as eternally pluralistic. "Jesus said to his disciples, 'in my father's house are many mansions.' . . . There are mansions in sufficient numbers," Young then concluded, "to suit the different classes of mankind, and a variety *will always exist to all eternity* requiring a classification and an arrangement into societies and communities in the many mansions which are in the Lord's house, and this will be for ever and ever. . . ."[78] Young confessed that this may be "a strange doctrine to outsiders. But what do they know about the Bible, heaven, angels, or God?"[79] Contrary to fervent expectations of many, Young taught the Saints that membership in the church was not the inexorable, universal goal of humankind.

Mormon/Jewish encounter has been handicapped by the tradition of Cowdery, Pratt, and their ideological descendants. According to this tradition, the "seed" of the covenant with Judah will wither and lose its particular vintage when the millennial dawn erupts and will be grafted into the perennial, unfading growth of the Church of Christ. According to this reading, Jewish autonomy is provisional, Jewish religion and institutions ephemeral, and the restoration and gathering of Israel merely an instrumental means to an ultimate end—the vindication and triumph of the Church of Christ, a millennial body identical with and inclusive of the Kingdom of God. All of the good will, respect, support, kinship, and deference manifested by the church to the Jewish people is vitiated by this provisional grant. Young's eschatology is to be recommended in relations between Jews and Mormons and is crucial for the development of Mormon thought.

When Joseph Smith encountered Joshua Seixas, when Orson Hyde walked through the streets of Jerusalem the night before his "dedicatory prayer," and when Young encountered and analyzed the persisting distinctions between Jew and Mormon, Mormon and gentile, Mormon "theoretical" religion came face to face with an inherited, bewilderingly plural world.

Increasingly these men found that differences could not be defined or imagined away. Living Jews of the nineteenth century and their religion were not identical with those described in the pages of Chronicles, Leviticus, and Luke. Thus Smith began to report the concerns and thoughts of contemporary Jews unadorned with Mormon doctrine. Smith, Hyde, and Young began to perceive the Jewish and Mormon communities as essentially autonomous. But they also believed that "Saint" should cleave to Israel and that together they could labor for a just, equitable, and diverse world, a world vigorously at peace, a world coextensive with the domain of the Kingdom of God. "It is necessary," Young wrote, "to get a deed of it to make an inheritance practical, substantial and profitable. Then let us not rest contented with a mere theoretical religion."[80]

In the eyes of Joseph Smith and Brigham Young the promises and responsibilities of the covenant bestowed on Israel, as recorded in scripture and reiterated in the formative doctrine of the LDS church, argued forcefully for the independence, integrity, and continuity of the particular witness and reality of the Jewish people. After 1830, Latter-day Saints professed that another covenant community had been convoked from the nations to help lay the foundations of the coming messianic, millennial age. Thoughtful Mormons did not presume to denigrate or claim exclusive rights to Israel's covenant. Neither displacement of nor identity with the Jewish people characterize Mormon thought. Historically and emotionally, however, Mormon thought and practice have been grounded in the vision of two communities of covenant, who strive to approach a common value which limits, defines, and draws them both. That value is the Kingdom of God on earth. The dream of it, the pilgrimage toward and the work and sacrifice for it, may yet bring us into the house of our father, with its eternally pluralistic "arrangement into societies and communities" in the age to come.

NOTES

1. Bertram Korn in his introduction to S. N. Carvalho, *Incidents of Travel and Adventure in the Far West* (1854; reprt., Philadelphia: Jewish Publication Society, 1954), 136.
2. Ibid., 136.
3. Ibid., 139.
4. Ibid., 141, 142, 148.
5. Ibid., 143. As an admirer of Isaac Leeser, Carvalho would have been especially interested in this experiment in colonization of an arid region. Leeser's own views on Jewish settlement in Palestine were becoming increasingly "secular" and practical. See Maxine S. Seller, "Isaac Leeser's Views on the Restoration of a Jewish Palestine," *American Jewish Historical Quarterly*, 63 (Sept. 1968): 118-35. Leeser was the editor of *The Occident* and minister/hazzan of Mikveh Israel in Philadelphia.
6. Carvalho, *Incidents of Travel*, 142.
7. Ibid., 185.

8. Journal History, 28 July 1844, archives, Historical Department, Church of Jesus Christ of Latter-day Saints, Salt Lake City, Utah; hereafter cited as Journal History.

9. Ibid., 5-6 Apr. 1845.

10. *Times and Seasons,* 3 (15 Aug. 1842): 890.

11. Ibid., 3 (15 Oct. 1842): 952. The author of this assessment was probably the new editor, John Taylor.

12. Journal History, 8 Apr. 1853, 9.

13. Ibid., 14 Mar. 1869.

14. For a summary sketch of Wilford Woodruff, see Richard Van Wagoner and Steven Walker, *A Book of Mormons* (Salt Lake City: Signature Books, 1982), 395-401.

15. Examples of Woodruff's writings and sermons on the subject can be found in the following entries of the multi-volume *Journal of Discourses,* first published in Liverpool between 1 Nov. 1853 and 17 May 1886: 8:262, 263; 1:245; 13:161; 18:220-21, 225; 21:300-301, 343; 23:128 (hereafter JD); and in the Journal History entries for 27 Feb. 1857 and 30 June 1878.

16. JD 19:358-59, 361.

17. JD 23:128.

18. JD 11:245.

19. JD 18:221.

20. For a detailed bibliography, see Chad J. Flake, ed., *A Mormon Bibliography: 1830-1930* (Salt Lake City: University of Utah Press, 1978), 512-20; and Breck England, *The Life and Thought of Orson Pratt* (Salt Lake City: University of Utah, 1985), 339-41.

21. England, *Life of Orson Pratt,* 100.

22. JD 7:29.

23. Ibid., 27.

24. Ibid., 25.

25. For the entire address, see JD 14:58-70.

26. *Times and Seasons,* 2 (1 July 1841): 454.

27. Journal History, 18 Aug. 1844.

28. Ibid., 1 Nov. 1845.

29. Orson Spencer, *Letters Exhibiting the Most Prominent Doctrines of the Church of Jesus Christ of Latter-day Saints. . .* (1848; reprt., Salt Lake City: George Q. Cannon and Sons, Co., 1891), 104, 7, 105, 112. Spencer was a graduate of Union College and the Baptist Theological Seminary. He was a "pro-

fessor of languages" for the University of the City of Nauvoo and first chancellor of the University of Deseret founded in 1850 in Salt Lake City. Spencer died in 1855.

30. Ibid., 112.

31. Parley P. Pratt, *A Voice of Warning and Instruction to All People . . .*, (Salt Lake City: Deseret News Press, 1952) was described by Peter Crawley and Chad J. Flake as "the most important of all noncanonical Mormon books. . . . it was the first to emphasize the difference between Mormonism and traditional Christianity. More important, it erected a standard for all future Mormon pamphleteers. . . . Before the close of the century, *Voice of Warning* went through more than thirty editions in English and was translated into Danish, Dutch, French, German, Spanish, and Swedish." Item number 7 in Peter Crawley and Chad Flake, *A Mormon Fifty: An Exhibition in the Harold B. Lee Library in Conjunction with the Annual Conference of the Mormon History Association* (Provo, UT: Friends of the Brigham Young University Library, 1984).

32. Pratt, *A Voice of Warning*, 89, 197.

33. Ibid. 58, 48-49.

34. They were also on the far side of theological disputations raised because of discoveries in the natural sciences. For a discussion of the impact of Darwin on theology, see Ian G. Barbour, *Issues in Sciences and Religion* (New York: Harper & Row, 1971), 80-114.

35. JD 7:27.

36. For example, James Barr has pointed out both the ambiguity and misuse of this term by contemporary scholars of "fundamentalist" and "liberal" perspectives when promoting their presuppositions, methodologies, and conclusions—or attacking those of rivals. See James Barr, *Fundamentalism* (Philadelphia: Westminster Press, 1978), 40-89, 120-59.

37. Quoted in Robert Grant, *The Bible in the Church: A Short History of Interpretation* (New York: Macmillan Co., 1948), 105.

38. J. N. D. Kelly, *Early Christian Doctrines*, rev. ed. (San Francisco: Harper & Row, 1978), 8.

39. Ibid., 68.

40. Eldon J. Watson, ed., *Manuscript History of Brigham Young: 1841-1844* (Salt Lake City: Eldon Watson, 1968), 142-43.

41. William Appleby, *A Few Important questions for reverend Clergy to answer... (Philadelphia: Brown, Bicking & Guilbert, 1843), 8.*

42. Moses Martin, *A Treatise on the fulness of the everlasting Gospel...* (New York: J. W. Harrison, 1842), 7, 54.

43. Marcion, who died around 160 C.E., was an extremely influential early Christian "heretic." His work, *Antitheses*, proposed that the God of the Hebrew scriptures was a malign demiurge dedicated to law rather than love. Thus the God of Christianity and of the apostolic writings and the God of the Hebrew scriptures were not one and the same. Jesus came to reveal the "Supreme God of Love. . . . It was his purpose to overthrow the Demiurge." See *The Oxford Dictionary of the Christian Church*, ed. F. L. Cross, 2d ed. (London: Oxford University Press, 1974), 870-71. In a modern context "marcionite" would mean interpretations of Christianity and scripture, which "undervalue or ... misunderstand the place of the Old Testament in the elucidation of the Christian revelation." See Alan Richardson, "Marcionism," *The Westminster Dictionary of Christian Theology*, eds. Alan Richardson and John Bowden (Philadelphia: Westminster Press, 1983), 344-45.

44. Brigham Young in a sermon recorded in JD 12:242-43 noted that the delivery of Israel was a result of the faithfulness of God to his promises to the patriarchs and not the on-going state of Israel's righteousness and faith.

45. Journal History, 5 Jan. 1882.

46. "And they shall fall by the edge of the sword, and shall be led away captive into all nations: and Jerusalem shall be trodden down of the Gentiles, until the times of the Gentiles be fulfilled."

47. *The Expositor's Greek Testament*, ed. W. Robertson Nicoll, vol. 1 (Grant Rapids, MI: Wm. B. Eerdmans Publishing Co., 1983), 621.

48. S. Maclean Gilmore, "The Gospel According to St. Luke," in *The Interpreter's Bible . . . in Twelve Volumes*, vol. 8 (New York: Abingdon-Cokesville Press, 1952), 368.

49. Jeremiah Untermann and Paul J. Achtemeier, "Time," in *Harper's Bible Dictionary*, ed. Paul J. Achtemeier (San Francisco: Harper & Row, 1985), 1073.

50. JD 3:135.

51. See JD 13:161; 21:300-301.

52. The pursuit by Mormon readers of a "literal" reading of scripture did violence to the poetic devices of prophetic authors. The apposite titles of Zion and Jerusalem, twinned frequently together in Hebrew scriptures, pointed to a single territorial referent. Mormon exegetes split the single referent in two and contrived reference to more than one place. Zion and Jerusalem were two distinct capitals of the coming millennial age.

53. JD 3:134, 136, 137.

54. Ibid.

55. JD 16:324.

56. JD 14:64.

57. JD 14:65.

58. JD 14:61.

59. JD 14:65, 62.

60. JD 5:287-88, from a sermon delivered 4 October 1857. He went on to say that "They [the children of Israel] were set forth as examples of all who should live after. . . . The history of all religious generations and dispensations is similar, and shows this fact to us, that human nature is the same in every age, country . . . and among every people,—that men are subject to like weaknesses and have to be taught gradually."

61. *Times and Seasons,* 2 (2 Aug. 1841): 488-91; 2 (16 Aug. 1841): 504-507.

62. JD 9:284.

63. JD 10:172.

64. JD 10:22.

65. JD 2:141.

66. JD 11:279.

67. Journal History, 13 Aug. 1880.

68. Ibid., 10 Sept. 1879.

69. An excellent representative, non-LDS source is Charles Hodge, *Systematic Theology* vol. 3 (New York: Charles Scribner's Sons, 1872), especially "Part IV, Eschatology, chapter III, Second Advent," 791-92, 807-812.

70. See England, *Life of Orson Pratt,* 97, 141-42, 192, 202-11, 227-29, 264-66.

71. JD 7:47.

72. JD 5:77, 10:339.

73. See the "Index" to *Discourses of Brigham Young. . .*, comp. John A. Widstoe (Salt Lake City: Deseret Book, 1951).

74. JD 2:316-17, 11:275, 12:274.

75. JD 11:275.

76. JD 2:316-17.

77. Ibid.

78. JD 11:275.

79. JD 12:274.

80. JD 9:284.

Epilogue

It was "cloudy, breezy, [and] cool" in Jerusalem on Sunday morning, 2 March 1873. Two apostles of the Church of Jesus Christ of Latter-day Saints, George A. Smith and Lorenzo Snow, as well as a number of other Saints including Eliza R. Snow, Lorenzo Snow's sister, "rode to the Mount of Olives," pitched a tent, and assembled for a prayer meeting. With a "watchman outside" posted at the door, the small group robed themselves and "united in service in the order of the Holy Priesthood." After an opening prayer by Apostle Snow "in which the . . . dedicatory sentiments were contained," George A. Smith "dedicated" the land: "I was mouth, remembering the general interests of Zion, and dedicating this land, praying that it might become fertile . . . and the prophecies and promises unto Abraham and the prophets be fulfilled in the own due time of the Lord." Eliza R. Snow later recalled that "President Smith leading in humble, fervent supplication [then] dedicated the land of Palestine for the gathering of the Jews and the rebuilding of Jerusalem. . . . Other brethren led in turn, and we had a very interesting season."[1]

Thus thirty years after Orson Hyde's dedication of Palestine for the return of exiled Israel and the restoration of its national commonwealth, Mormons returned to the site on the Mount of Olives to confirm the work and vision of Joseph Smith and Orson Hyde. This confirmation by Brigham Young's apostolic envoys forged yet another link between his administration and that of his predecessor. What was confirmed was a view of covenant Israel which repudiated the traditionally anti-Jewish theology of mainstream Christian churches. This view was forged by figures in the LDS movement who attempted to rethink and refashion their encounter with Israel in terms affirming the integrity, autonomy, and witness of both groups.

This work of affirmation and critique ranged across a broad spectrum of LDS writing, rhetoric, and action. New works of scripture (as well as "translations" of the traditional canon) were produced reemphasizing the integrity and fidelity of God's promises to Israel. Gentile anti-Jewish bias was denounced. The righteous among the nations were enjoined to "cleave to the house of Jacob." Prayers of dedication and blessing were invoked in Mormon temples and in the hills of Judea calling for the end of Israel's forced exile, a gathering of its people to "lands of inheritance" in Palestine, and the renewal of its national commonwealth. Sermons, editorials, and tracts were penned affirming these notions and condemning Jewish missions and Christian theological intransigence. Voices of contemporary Jewry were sought out, and new media and terms for a Jewish/Mormon encounter explored. Israel's witness of its covenantal integrity "from Sinai to Shechem" through the nineteenth century and beyond to the eschaton was recognized.

Joseph Smith was the artisan of this theological and practical task. His preoccupation with the relationship between Israel and the Saints was crucial for the emergence of a "tradition" within the Mormon church affirming Israel's autonomy, covenant, and ongoing witness to the church.

However, this "tradition" was neither normative nor preeminent during the first decade. The dominant sentiments of the Saints during the 1830s were apocalyptic and primitivist. Thus many Saints shared two basic assumptions with their Christian contemporaries. First, they believed that the dramatic advent of Christ, an event which would reverse the world order, was imminent. Second, they believed that the only true refuge from "fallen" churches and the approaching cataclysm resided in a perfect church order and in practices structured on those of the primordial Christian community.

These concerns were articulated in the 1830s by such Mormon leaders as Sidney Rigdon, Oliver Cowdery, and Parley and Orson Pratt. These men figured among Smith's closest associates. Yet their preoccupations with the "New" Testament church and the approaching eschaton relegated Jewish people to an epiphenomenal category. Varying little from the views of non-LDS contemporaries, these Mormon elders either derided the "Mosaic economy" as one more instance of a fallen, bankrupt religious order or classed Jewish people as final eschatological witnesses whose eleventh-hour conversion en masse would herald the imminent triumph of Jesus Christ and his millennial kingdom. Thus their exclusive concern was to preach the "gathering" of a restored church to as many as would listen before the final curtain descended.

Circumstances of the 1830s increasingly placed Jews and Israel's covenantal heritage at the center of Joseph Smith's concerns and gave rise to his atypical theology. First, Joseph became increasingly estranged from Christian churches, creeds, and traditions. He sought throughout his life for myths, symbols, narratives, and institutions commensurate to his prophetic task as advocate for the "restoration of all things." Finding the heritage of the churches inadequate, he went far beyond the Christian primitivism of his colleagues when he turned to Israel's scripture and covenantal history for the compelling paradigms and institutions around which a new covenantal community could be constituted.

Second, the Parousia, Christ's advent and kingdom, was delayed. This delay contributed to Smith's estrangement from the apocalypticism rampant among the churches and espoused by his own colleagues. Instead he turned his attention to Israel's historical experience. Keith E. Norman has pointed out that several events delivered crushing blows to Mormon adventist expectations and led to reinterpretation of failed prophecies.[2] Smith responded to the disappointments of the late 1830s and early 1840s by concluding that the Saints could not rely on the Second Coming to deliver them from present conflicts and responsibilities. Instead the Saints were enjoined to act, to acquire the skills and knowledge which could prepare the way for the coming era of righteousness. Ten years after Smith's death, Jedidiah Grant, a counselor to Brigham Young, succinctly summarized Joseph's rearticulation of LDS millennial hope by telling a group of British immigrant Saints, "If you want a heaven, go and make it."[3]

As the emphasis shifted to making the Kingdom of God, Smith and those who followed him increasingly embraced those aspects of Israel's experience which abetted its enduring identity and vitality. Thus the categories and institutions of nation, people, temple, covenant, priesthood, gathering, restoration, and territoriality began to dominate in Joseph's writings, sermons, and activity. He worked at articulating an eschatology for the Saints which would prove more serviceable for their task of building Zion than would the vagaries of apocalyptic and the ever unattainable haven of a pristine church.

But Smith went beyond the theological abstraction of a people of the Old Testament. As a student of Hebrew under Joshua Seixas and as editor of the *Times and*

Seasons, he attempted to listen to the lively, full-bided Jewish community contemporary with that of the Saints. It is obvious from the work of Smith and Brigham Young that this encounter had a profound impact on the theology and institutions of the LDS church in the mid-1800s. And it is not surprising that the this-worldly emphasis of Joseph's and Brigham's eschatology contributed to the almost universal support with the LDS church for the nascent Zionist movement and for Israel's quest for statehood.

There persists in the LDS community to this day an elective affinity with Jewish people, an affinity forged by a comparable quest for a territorial patrimony, an autonomous state, and a unique culture. Latter-day Saints recognize the enduring debt owed to Israel's historical, covenantal heritage. Without it there could have been no "restoration of all things," no temples, no community, no abiding quest for Zion on this earth.

The views and acts of Smith, Hyde, and Young have been examined at some length. What follows are three brief sketches of Mormons who manifested the imprint of Mormonism's positive evaluation of covenant Israel.

In the spring of 1840, Heber C. Kimball (1810-68) returned to direct the LDS mission in the British Isles which he had opened three years before with Hyde. Born in Shelton, Vermont, Kimball had been a blacksmith and potter. He was a close friend to Brigham Young and was the third member of the original Quorum of the Twelve.[4] Kimball would be in the first company of Saints to enter the Great Salt Lake Valley, and he was chosen by Young to be second counselor in the First Presidency of the church.

The 16 August 1841 issue of the *Times and Seasons* published a letter by Kimball addressed to "The Editors of the *Times and Seasons*."[5] His letter recounts his observations of London, including his experience attending a sabbath service in "the Jewish Synagogue." "We visited the . . . Synagogue," he writes, "to see their order of worship, which was all performed in Hebrew." This was Kimball's first encounter with organized Jewish religious observance: "We stayed during the whole ceremony in their worship, and at the same time some were singing . . . in a sweet melodious manner, some reading, some praying and others in different attitudes of worship, all of which passed off with great solemnity and order."

Kimball then points out to Mormon readers that those entering the synagogue were requested to keep their hats on, "and no one [is] permitted to enter their place of worship" unless they comply with this rule. Kimball and his companions willingly obliged. But, he continues, "passing farther into their Synagogue, the beauty and splendor thereof caused us again to take them off." The worshippers again reminded the Mormon visitors about their hats, and Kimball confesses that they "might have appeared . . . a little *Clownish*."

However, Kimball's awkwardness did not compromise his response. "During their worship," he writes, "my mind was unusually solemn, and I looked upon those sons of illustrious sires with mingled emotions of sorrow for the unparalleled cruelties which have been inflicted upon their Nation, and joy that the day of their redemption was near." This last statement must be understood within the context both of Hyde's recent stopover with Kimball and others in Britain while on his way to Palestine and also Kimball's own closing observations. After having toured the synagogue and that "part of the city in which they reside," Kimball concludes, "They are the most spirited, ambitious, and perservering people I ever saw. They believe the gathering of Israel, in the last days, is near, and they are waiting for their restoration to the land of Palestine."

Kimball's response to the order of worship and to the worshippers in "the Jewish Synagogue" in London contrasts with that of Ezra Stiles, America's most prominent eighteenth-century Hebraist. Stiles was a Congregationalist minister, president of Yale University (1778-95), and in the pursuit of Hebrew frequently in contact with rabbis and lay Jewish leaders. Reflecting on a Jewish community in worship, Stiles wrote, "How melancholy to behold an Assembly of Worshippers of Jehovah, open and professed enemies to a crucified Jesus."[6] Stiles, scholar of the church and its traditions, could not acknowledge or allow what Kimball, the blacksmith, potter, and religious outsider, could not avoid. Ignorant of ecclesiastical histories and systematic theologies and informed instead by the positive LDS assessment of Israel's covenant and future, Kimball in contrast to Stiles could respond with respect and affirmation.

George A. Smith, as we have seen, participated in the "rededication" of Palestine in March 1873. By June he had returned to Utah. Summoned to address various congregations that summer and fall, Smith provided both a detailed account of his travels to Europe and the Levant and an analysis of the contemporary political and religious state of affairs in those areas. His remarks on Palestine are of particular interest.[7] Smith adopts a language which Saints from the water-scarce Great Basin would have doubtless understood: "the country [the region of Palestine] is dry and barren . . . though they have occasional rains." He was struck by its "barrenness, desolation, scanty population" and the "oppressed, poor and despised" condition of the native Jewish population.

For two decades the Saints themselves had labored much to their chagrin under a series of territorial administrations and courts imposed by and administered from Washington, D.C. Smith's remarks then would have sounded with particular resonance among fellow Saints when he observed that "in the land of their fathers . . . they [the Jews] are in bondage, under tutors, governors, and rulers, and have in reality no power of themselves." All of these observations caused George A. Smith, cousin to Joseph Smith, to engage in "some very serious reflections as to the causes which had operated to reduce the country to its present barren condition" and which led to the dispossession of the Jews with their "independent nation, blotted out."

Not surprisingly his response goes back to the Deuteronimical view of the dichotomies of righteousness/blessings, trespasses/curses, which were central to Mormonism's own theological identity. However, in the context of traditional Christian readings of Israel's "curse," Smith's analysis and his conclusions are something of a surprise.

Smith finds the cause of Palestine's desolation in three central factors. First, according to his reading of Malachi 3:8, Smith surmises that Israel "would not give him [the Lord] tithes[;] they robbed him of tithes and offerings." Second, "they lost this power [self-government and autonomy]—they fell into the hands of their enemies . . . because they married the daughters of aliens, worshipped strange gods, and [were] finally broken up . . . scattered to the four winds of heaven." Finally, "they have been subject to the most extreme abuse" at the hands of Christians. With sarcasm he refers to Ferdinand and Isabella as "a very pious couple," whose edits were responsible for the banishment, death, and conversion of "probably a half a million Jews." The Crusaders are depicted as hypocrites, who "while on their way to Jerusalem, plundered and killed thousands of the Hebrew race."

"Not withstanding all the oppression heaped upon them continuously from generation to generation," Smith concludes, "they still maintain their identity as the seed of Abraham. . . . [T]hey are a living record of the truth of the revelations of God." The day is "not far distant," he prophesies, "when Israel would gather, and those lands would begin to teem with people. . . ." And further: "The blessing of the Lord, which we invoked on the Mount of Olives, will rest upon his people. . . . [T]he time is not very far distant when God will fulfill his promises concerning Israel."

The lesson Smith draws from his observation is a "moral" and a political one "to us at home": not that the Jews were accursed for the crucifixion of Jesus Christ but that they fell "into the same snares" which tempt the Saints. The results of not heeding Israel's lesson, Smith warns, would be the dissolution of the compact binding the Saints as a people. "We profess to believe a great deal," he states, "but do our acts correspond with our belief?" If the Saints would faithfully gather out from among the gentiles and "Bring ye all the tithes into the storehouse," the Lord, according to Smith, "will rebuke the devourer. . . . [H]e shall not destroy the fruit of your ground. . . . And all nations shall call you blessed."

At the same meeting Brigham Young confirmed Smith's analysis. The aging Mormon prophet then turned his peoples' attention from the "Tithes and offerings" which they must render "that there may be meat in [the Lord's] house" and the Lord's Zion to the labor needed to produce offerings and tithes: "Hence we say, improve, be industrious, prudent, fruitful, make good farms, gardens and orchards, good public and private buildings, have the best schools. etc."[8] In his eyes these were essential components of building a kingdom of Saints.

Smith and Young concluded that Israel's exile was the result of religious and national accommodation and imitation of neighboring and occupying states whose cultures were inimical to Israel's covenant. Israel's "desolation" was not tied by either man to the death of Jesus of Nazareth. Rather they preached that Israel's exile was a cautionary tale to the Saints.

The 12 March 1880 issue of the *American Israelite* noted that some thirty Jewish families were "prospering" in the overwhelmingly Mormon territory of Utah.[9] Since 1857 when a Jew was reported as having been appointed chaplain to the Utah legislature along with Catholic and Mormon "clergy," the American Jewish press ran regular reports on the small Utah Jewish community.[10] These columns were often critical of Mormon religious practice, especially the practice of plural marriage, but they also noted the positive relations between the two groups. The *Occident* reported in 1866 that a site for a Jewish cemetery had been "donated by the Mormons"[11]; celebrations of the Jewish "New Year" often took place in "Mormon halls"[12]; and the Saints' *Millennial Star,* printed in England, republished a "Resolution" issued by the "Israelites of Salt Lake," which thanked "the Mormon Authorities formally and heartily for their kindness . . . in furnishing . . . spacious halls, free of cost, for celebrating their late religious anniversaries. The most tolerant and magnanimous religious sect we have ever known is the Mormons."[13]

Edward Tullidge's *Ben Israel or, From Under the Curse: A Jewish Play in Five Acts* was written in this social and religious environment of good will.[14] His choice of subject for a play and his characterization of its Jewish protagonists may well have benefitted from and in turn reflected both the congenial Jewish/Mormon relations in Utah settlements and the positive aspects of Mormon thought about the Jewish people.

Converted to Mormonism as a young man in England, Tullidge later settled in Utah. Initially he was an ardent enthusiast for Young's vision of a Mormon kingdom in the American rockies. A gifted journalist, Tullidge hoped, as described by one biographer, to be the "epic chronicler" of Young's "experiment in godly government."[15] Expansively the thirty-two-year-old Tullidge pointed out to the Mormon prophet that "as yet our people have no national drama . . . no national literature. . . . From the time I came into the Church, I fervently desired to see the Saints a great nation, and ranking in the first class of society . . . [and] to be numbered among the workers out of Zion's social and national greatness."[16]

However, Tullidge was to learn that elevating a physically and culturally isolated pioneer community into the social stratosphere was a daunting task. His plays and prose fiction suffered not only from the Saints' insularity in the Great Basin but also from his own modest creative literary capabilities. But one aspect of Tullidge's writing in *Ben Israel* rose above its author's handicaps. Louis Harap[17] and Ellen Schiff have noted how nineteenth-century American theater slavishly replicated the anti-Semitic conventions of the European stage. Jewish characters were invariably cast as Shylocks or as benighted outsiders "blinded by the wrongheaded vision of [their] people."[18] Tullidge's *Ben Israel* was marred by his devotion to certain dicta of British dramaturgy, but it manifested an independent vision in its depiction of Jewish characters.

The story of *Ben Israel* enacts the return to England during the reign of Charles II of a band of Jews headed by one David Ben Israel. The play turns on the efforts and intrigues of members of the court to thwart the return of the Jews to England, efforts which include false representation, arson, and murder. Tullidge turns the cultural habit of dramatic anti-Semitism on its head. With few exceptions the Christians are the "challengers of Truth" and the arrogant and duplicitous devotees of a "wrongheaded vision."

Tullidge's Jewish protagonists variously challenge and criticize their English enemies and detractors:

> Christian scoffer! Our race were princes when thy ancestors were robbers and barbarians!

> A Christian's covenant, and to a Jew! When was it kept . . . ?
>
> How apt these Christians are—ay wise men too—who are fortified by favored fortune—how apt to talk as if they were modern Solomons, risen to shame our great ancestor—with proverbs of the cunning of the Jews.
> Yet to the Christian gave they oracles! How hath he paid his debt of gratitude? Why, meanly taken advantage of their fall. . . .[19]

Christian enmity and meanness of spirit is contrasted with the prophetic vision which animates David Ben Israel. In a speech delivered to the British king, Ben Israel predicts:

> Thou shalt marvels see. There is a spirit in our sacred race
> Which, fan'd, shall send a blaze o'er all the earth.
> Our seers shall rise; our psalmists sing;
> Our Solomons give wisdom to the world,
> And every land shall bless, not curse, the Jew.[20]

But finally it is given to the young Jewess Rachel to speak the play's most dramatic and most militant lines:

> But Judah shall come *from under the curse*
> As gold from the refiner's fire. He shall
> *Redeem himself,* asking not Gentile grace.
> We've kissed the rod; but henceforth, if *ye* smite,
> Ye shall pay back for every blow,
> And crawl at Judah's feet to beg his helping hand.[21]

Certainly Tullidge's role-reversal of Christian and Jew serves mythic types rather than realism, but his play is of interest in the way it challenged routine prejudices of the day. Like Kimball and George A. Smith, Tullidge registered in print the impact of the visionary reevaluation of Mormon/Jewish encounter first ventured by Joseph Smith. They—and with them contemporary

Latter-day Saints—benefitted from an aspect of restoration which challenged traditional Christian ways of understanding the Jewish people.

Mormons continue to live with their fractured heritage—two traditions of thought and action concerning Jews and Judaism handed down by the church's first leaders. But the sobering light cast by recent history is compelling Latter-day Saints to excavate those traditions and repudiate the understanding of one tradition and critically appropriate the vision of another. Mormons can be instructed by the witness of the founder of their religious community and those disciples who sought to keep that vision alive for future generations of Latter-day Saints.

NOTES

1. George A. Smith, Journal, 1870-74, typescript copy, Special Collections, Marriott Library, University of Utah, Salt Lake City, 31, 331; George A. Smith et al., *Correspondence of Palestine Tourists: A Series of Lectures. . .* (Salt Lake City: Deseret News, 1875), 260.

2. Keith E. Norman, "How Long, O Lord: The Delay of the Parousia in Mormonism," *Sunstone* 8 (1983), 1-2: 48-58.

3. *Journal of Discourses,* 26 vols. (Liverpool: Latter-day Saints' Booksellers' Depot, 1853-86), 3:67 (hereafter JD).

4. Richard S. Van Wagoner and Steven C. Walker, *A Book of Mormons* (Salt Lake City: Signature Books, 1982), 137.

5. "Communications," *Times and Seasons* 2 (16 Aug. 1841):509.

6. See chapter four of this study.

7. Smith's remarks were made on 27 June 1873 and 6 October 1873. They are reported in JD 16:103-107, 220-21.

8. JD 16:66.

9. *American Israelite,* 12 Mar. 1880, 6. Cited in Hynda L. Rudd, *Mountain West Pioneer Jewry: An Historical and Genealogical Source Book (from Origins to 1885),* Western American Study Series (Los Angeles: Will Kramer Publisher, 1980), 37.

10. *Weekly Gleaner,* 16 Jan. 1857, 6. See Rudd, *Pioneer Jewry,* 31-37.

11. *Occident,* 23, 1866, 558-59. See Rudd, *Pioneer Jewry,* 34.

12. *Hebrew,* 27 Oct. 1865, 4; 10 Sept. 1869, 4. Cited in Rudd, *Pioneer Jewry,* 34.

13. *Latter-day Saints' Millennial Star* 33 (26 Dec. 1871): 823. See also *Israelite,* 1 Nov. 1867, 6.

14. Edward W. Tullidge, *Ben Israel or, From Under the Curse: A Jewish Play in Five Acts* (Salt Lake City: Star Publishing Co., 1887). Tullidge was born in 1829 and died in 1894.

15. Ronald W. Walker, "Edward Tullidge: Historian of the Mormon Commonwealth," *Journal of Mormon History* 3 (1976): 57.

16. From a letter to Brigham Young, 25 Nov. 1861. Cited in ibid., 58.

17. Louis Harap, *The Image of the Jews in American Literature* (Philadelphia: Jewish Publication Society, 1974), 257.

18. Ellen Schiff, "Skylocks Mishpocheh: Anti-Semitism on the American Stage," in *Anti-Semitism in American History,* ed. David A. Gerber (Urbana: University of Illinois Press, 1986), 79-99.

19. Tullidge, *Ben Israel,* 3, 7, 16.

20. Ibid., 53.

21. Ibid. Tullidge's emphasis.

Index